Religions
of
the East

**ENLARGED
EDITION**

Religions
of
the East

ENLARGED
EDITION

by
JOSEPH M. KITAGAWA

THE WESTMINSTER PRESS
Philadelphia

LIBRARY OF CONGRESS CATALOG CARD No. 60-7742

Published by The Westminster Press®
Philadelphia, Pennsylvania

PRINTED IN THE UNITED STATES OF AMERICA

7   8   9   10   11   12   13   14

To Evelyn

Without Whom . . .

Contents

◆ ◆

Foreword

◈　◈

There is a widespread notion in the West that the
"church" of Christianity is something unique, having no
equivalent in other religions. The term "church" as used
here does not refer to houses of worship — or to local con-
gregations — but to the total unity of all Christians in the
"holy community" or ecclesia of Christianity. According
to the celebrated Dutch historian of religions, G. van der
Leeuw, the church is "visible-invisible, at once humanly
organized and mystically animated, spiritual and cosmic."
Admittedly, each religion is unique, and as such Christianity can claim the uniqueness of its church. However,
van der Leeuw and others seem to imply more than this
when they hold that "a church exists solely in Christianity." But is this really so? Are there not counterparts of
the church — the "holy community" of Christianity —
in other religions? If so, what are the ethos and structure of
the "holy communities" of Eastern religions? Such is the
quest of this study.

Our approach to the study of major Eastern religions is
from the perspective of history of religions. That there
is no one single "right" approach in the study of religions
is well evidenced by the multiplicity of books available
today on the subject. An increasing number of philoso-

phers, historians, psychologists, and social scientists, as well as scholars of particular civilizations, are interested in various aspects of religions. In this situation, the discipline of *Religionswissenschaft* (variously known as the history of religions, science of religions, or comparative religions) maintains its own perspective and methodology. There are those who hold that each religion can be interpreted only by the adherents of that religion, and that a historian of religions who tries to deal with many religions from the outside, as it were, cannot do justice to the depth of individual religions. Nevertheless, our aim, ideally at least, is to try to study the ethos and structure of all religions in such a way that our perspective, method of inquiry, and interpretation are meaningful to the adherents and scholars of different religions. We hope that the concept of the "holy community" will provide a useful tool for this inquiry crossing religious and disciplinary lines. Thus, we will find in Eastern religions different but equally genuine "holy communities," which are analogous to the "church" of Christianity.

The task of the historian of religions is not an easy one. It is not difficult for him to study the doctrines, sacred books, rituals, and ecclesiastical institutions of various religions, and also the lives of their founders, prophets, and priests. But it is exceedingly difficult for him to maintain a balance between the study of historical facts and the systematic structuring and interpretation of these data. It is not a lack of information that hinders him in this task. On the contrary, thanks to the untiring labor of scholars of many disciplines, he knows a great deal about the geographical, historical, social, political, economic, and cultural backgrounds of various religions. He is made aware that religions are more than systems of doctrines and ecclesiastical institutions. Religions cannot be separated from peoples, some well known and many unknown, and yet religions are more than the sum totals of individuals. Religions imply communities, embracing within them those who have gone, those who are in them, and those who are yet to come. But the peoples cannot be understood solely in terms of their religions, just as religious communities cannot be understood solely in terms of their members, because religious communities have their own pace and law of growth, decline, and rejuvenation, apart from the cycles of individuals within them.

Moreover, every religious community, like a culture, " has fuzzy edges," to use Kroeber's phrase. The line of demarcation between the " holy community " and the " secular community " is always blurred. Furthermore, each religious community is grounded in its spiritual vision of the ideal human community. Indeed, each religious community is " visible-invisible, at once humanly organized and mystically animated." One task of the historian of religions is to grasp the inner nature of this living organism, and the unity that persists through successive events that occur both within and without the religious community. This requires not only an amassing of quantities of historical facts, but a selecting and depicting of important men and events, doctrines and scriptures, rituals and laws, and historical movements which contribute to and signify the unique quality, structure, and ethos of a given religious community.

Inevitably, such an endeavor will reflect something of the mind and person of the individual historian of religions. This does not belie the validity of the approach of the history of religions or the cohesiveness of the discipline. It simply means that a religio-scientific study such as ours —

no matter how impartial and objective we attempt to be — is necessarily conditioned by the religious and cultural backgrounds of the scholars in the field. Thus, it was but natural that the experience and background of the European pioneers of the history of religions influenced their understanding of all religions, both their own and others. This is equally true of American and Asian historians of religions.

In this connection, the author's position should be explicit. An Easterner coming to settle in the West faces a number of alternatives. He can consciously remain an Easterner and try to interpret Eastern religions from this perspective. Or he can identify himself with the West and study Eastern religions as a Westerner, at least in so far as his method and approach are concerned. Or again, he can choose to stand in a borderland, being conscious of what is happening on both sides but consciously refusing to be drawn into either side. This would have been regarded as an ideal state for a historian of religions in the last century, when detached objectivity was considered a supreme value in the study of religions. The writer has chosen still another alternative, and a more difficult one as he has been made to realize. He has tried to identify himself with the West without losing his identity with the East. To be sure, this is more a matter of aspiration than of achievement. Nevertheless, he has reason to be thankful for his dual background, and also for the fact that he can continue his teaching and research in America, with the cooperation and assistance of European and Asian colleagues.

The religions discussed in this book — Chinese religions, Hinduism, Buddhism, and Islam — were selected because of their historical and contemporary importance in the Eastern world. Other religions, which might be considered just as important or interesting in terms of other criteria, were omitted for the practical reason of space. For example, a chapter on Shinto could have been included, since it presents an interesting blending of an archaic " holy community " and a civilized man's " holy community," as well as a smooth transition from myth to history. References are made to Judaism and Christianity in the general discussion of religion and the religious community in Chapter 1, because both of these religions are familiar to Western readers. As the book is designed to give a general orientation to the history of religions (or the comparative study of religions) for college students and interested laymen, detailed bibliographical notes and references are not included. It is hoped, however, that the lines of inquiry suggested will interest more advanced students and scholars. A selected bibliography is included at the end as an aid for further reading.

A conscious attempt has been made to relate the structure and development of the " holy communities " of Eastern religions to general historical events and cultures. It is the experience of many who teach comparative religions that by and large students who wish to study Eastern religions have an inadequate knowledge of the history and culture of Asia. Furthermore, many students seem to feel that Eastern peoples, their religions and religious communities, are far away, not only in space but also in time. To them, Eastern religions seem as remote as ancient Egyptian or Sumerian religions. Thus the present volume tries to give special attention to the modern development of Eastern religions, especially with reference to the encounter of Eastern religious communities and modernity. In discussing the modern phase of Eastern religions, the author has tried to avoid the West-centered perspective which has characterized so many books dealing with this subject. Too often, simple categories such as the " resurgence of Eastern religions " or the " march of nationalism " are used to explain away the complex developments of Eastern religions in the modern period. That modernity was a by-product of Western civilization when it penetrated the East is granted. However, to treat the modern history of Eastern religions as a sort of appendage to the expansion of the West would be a gross distortion. To understand the dynamic character and continuity of Eastern religions in the present revolutionary age, by relating them to the historical and contemporary Eastern context as well as the total world-wide context, will prove to be a taxing and rewarding task for historians of religions both in the East and in the West.

In the midst of preparing this manuscript, the author was given the opportunity to spend a year (1958–1959) doing research in Asia. This gave him many opportunities to exchange ideas with learned scholars, religious leaders, and friends throughout Asia and the Near East, and resulted in the revision of many parts of the manuscript. While it is impossible to list the names of all the persons who helped, directly or indirectly, he cannot fail to mention Profs. Shoson Miyamoto, Hajime Nakamura, and Yoshinori Takeuchi in Japan; Luang Prinyayogavipulya of Bangkok; the Honorable U Nu and U Hpe Aung of Burma; Dr. E. W. Adikaram and Prof. W. Pachow of Ceylon; Profs. T. M. P. Mahadevan and T. R. V. Murti, Dr. S. Dutt, and Swami Ranganathananda of India; Prof. Ishaq Musa Hussaini of Cairo; and Prof. Nicola Ziadeh of Beirut. They are, of course, in no way responsible for any errors and imperfections in this work. It is the author's pleasant duty to thank the Rockefeller Foundation and the Federated Theological Faculty of the University of Chicago for making his field trip possible.

Grateful acknowledgment is made to Dean Jerald C. Brauer and Prof. Mircea Eliade for their encouragement throughout the preparation of this manuscript. Thanks are also due to Prof. Edmund Perry, who was good enough to use the first draft of several chapters as a text in his class at Northwestern University. The author will always be indebted to his former teacher and colleague, the late Joachim Wach, whose profound knowledge of religious communities will long remain a source of inspiration to all those who are engaged in the study of history of religions.

The tedious task of typing, proofreading, and completing the index was carried out efficiently by Mrs. Kathryn Atwater, assisted by the secretarial staff of the Divinity School of the University of Chicago. Above all, the author wants to acknowledge the innumerable kinds of assistance given by his wife, to whom the book is dedicated.

I am happy to learn that there has been demand for an enlarged edition of this book. Although no revision of the original text has been made, I have added a new chapter on Japanese religions for this edition.

JOSEPH M. KITAGAWA

University of Chicago

1 Introduction: " One World " and Religions

❖ ❖

Religion and Religions

There are few words in our culture that are so ambiguous and yet evoke such emotional reaction, positive or negative, as the word " religion." This term has been defined variously as power, belief in spiritual reality, piety, man's ultimate attitude toward the universe, experience of the Holy, and in numerous other ways. According to Webster, religion is defined as " the service and adoration of God or a god as expressed in . . . worship," "devotion or fidelity," or " an apprehension, awareness, or conviction of the existence of a supreme being, or more widely, of supernatural powers or influences controlling one's own, humanity's, or nature's destiny; also, such an apprehension, etc., accompanied by or arousing reverence, love, gratitude, the will to obey and serve, and the like; religious experience or insight." [1]

However religion is defined, one thing is clear. From the dawn of history man has been incurably " religious." In a real sense, the history of mankind has been closely intertwined with the history of religions. An amazing variety of religious systems and thoughts is unfolded in the history of religions. Religious men have often sought an explanation for the diversity of religions, which in many ways is com-

17

parable to the multiplicity of languages.

It is interesting to recall the ancient Hebrew account explaining how the descendants of Noah, originally speaking one language, developed so many different ones:

> Now the whole earth had one language and few words. And as men migrated in the east, they found a plain in the land of Shinar and settled there. And they said to one another, . . . " Come, let us build ourselves a city, and a tower with its top in the heavens, and let us make a name for ourselves, lest we be scattered abroad upon the face of the whole earth." And the Lord came down to see the city and the tower, which the sons of men had built. And the Lord said, " Behold, they are one people, and they have all one language; and this is only the beginning of what they will do; and nothing that they propose to do will now be impossible for them. Come, let us go down, and there confuse their language, that they may not understand one another's speech." So the Lord scattered them abroad from there over the face of all the earth, and they left off building the city. Therefore its name was called Babel, because there the Lord confused the language of all the earth; and from there the Lord scattered them abroad over the face of all the earth. (Gen. 11:1-9.)

Interesting though it is, the story of the Tower of Babel cannot explain the development of different linguistic forms any more than various theories of the unilineal origin of religion, which have been advanced by some scholars, can trace the development of diverse religions to one original religion. Other scholars are of the opinion that there was no one original religion of mankind, such as an original monotheism, and they insist on the plural origins of religions. This controversy will not likely be solved for a long time to come, and we can reasonably conclude with Tor Andrae that the origin of religions is a speculative question and not a historical one.

While we cannot solve the question of the origin of religions, we cannot evade the fact of the plurality of religions. Of course, interest in religions other than one's own is nothing new. The ancient Greeks were keenly interested in the religions of the Egyptians. The Romans, who were not particularly noted in spiritual matters, nevertheless produced important documents on Egyptian and Syrian religions. Early Christians, such as Clement of Alexandria and Augustine of Hippo, were well acquainted with other religions. During the Middle Ages, three monotheistic religions — Islam, Judaism, and Christianity — mutually influenced each other in the Mediterranean area, and friars visited far-off lands and wrote books on different religious customs. Men of letters during the Renaissance revived an interest in the religions and philosophies of antiquity. By the time of the Enlightenment, many were asking such questions as, " Is man by nature religious? " Significantly, during the Enlightenment period philosophers sought *religio naturalis,* a natural religion underlying the diverse religious phenomena. Many scholars of philosophy, folklore, ethnology, geography, and archaeology came to accept the rationalists' view of the inevitability of " progress " in world history, and postulated that there would come a time when one universal religion would be accepted by peoples of different cultural and religious backgrounds.

Prior to World War II, interest in the religions of the world was confined for the most part to scholars and religious thinkers. In the world of today, however, understanding other religions is a matter of urgent necessity. Shortly after World War II, a conference of Government officials and representatives of learned societies was called in Philadelphia to discuss the problems of Southeast Asia,

India, and its neighboring countries. After the conference, a Canadian participant remarked that although we talked so much about one world, we "simply do not know how to live as one world — and not for economic or technical reasons, but for spiritual." [2]

It is tragic but true that this "one world" in which we live today is a divided world. Politically the world is split into the free world, the communist world, and the uncommitted world of Asia and Africa. Furthermore, "many of the world's problems are not due just to Russia or communism. They would be with us in any event because we live in an era of revolution — the revolution of rising expectations. In Asia, the masses now count for something. Tomorrow, they will count for more. And, for better or for worse, the future belongs to those who understand the hopes and fears of masses in ferment." [3]

It must be added that today the world is divided not only along economic, political, and military lines, but also along cultural and religious lines. The one world, if it is to be a reality, must wrestle with the question of the diversity of religions. In this sense, the term "religion" cannot be identified exclusively with ideas, rites, or institutions; it must be conceived as the spiritual source of all human existence which provides ultimate meaning to all aspects of human life.

The term "religion," as we have seen, cannot easily be defined. Usually when we think of religion, we associate it with our own experience. To most of us, religion is what we and our groups, such as our family, church, or synagogue, accept religion to be. However, religion does not refer to any single area of our experience, be it feeling, thought, or deed, but refers to a whole gamut of elements of our total life. These are not scattered and independent elements, but can be seen as a mutually dependent whole-ness. Such is the peculiar " adhesiveness " of religion.

It must be granted that we use the term " religious " rather loosely. The fact that someone plays golf " reli-giously " does not have a religious connotation. But when one says that nazism, communism, or nationalism has "re-ligious " elements, he implies that such systems share some quality with religious systems per se. Although such semi-religious systems are becoming increasingly important in our time, our concern here is with the historic religious systems.

Even though we may question our own religion from time to time, we are inclined to feel that our own religion points to the truth, if not the absolute truth. As we look around, we come to the realization that other people have a similar attitude toward their own religion. Indeed, to a non-Buddhist, Buddhism is the religion of Buddhists; but to a Buddhist, Buddhism is the religion of the truth. Simi-lar assertions are made in regard to all other religions.

Those reared in the West are familiar with the divisions within Christianity. Usually, Christianity is divided into three main divisions, Eastern Orthodoxy, Roman Catholi-cism, and Protestantism. Upon closer examination we learn that each of the three major groups has numerous sub-groups. The Orthodox Church, or the Holy Eastern Ortho-dox Church, consists of a number of autonomous divisions governed by historic patriarchs. The Roman Catholic Church, which is by far the most centrally organized, has within itself many orders and societies as well as special groups such as the Uniats, all of which, to be sure, are under the supreme authority of the Roman pontiff. The term " Protestant " has been used loosely to include many autonomous groups such as Adventist, Baptist, Brethren,

Congregational, Disciples, Friends, Jehovah's Witness, Lutheran, Mennonite, Methodist, Moravian, Pentecostal, Presbyterian, Reformed, and Salvation Army. Whether such groups as Christian Science, Church of the New Jerusalem (Swedenborgian), Ethical Culture Movement, Latter-day Saints (Mormons), Unitarian, and Universalist can be included in the all-embracing classification of Protestantism is debatable. The Coptic Church, the Old Catholic Church, and the Anglican Communion are somewhere in between the Catholic and Protestant divisions.

While Judaism is divided religiously into Orthodox, Conservative, and Reformed groups, its cultural divisions are more complex. Other religions of the world, including Buddhism, Hinduism, Islam, Shinto, Zoroastrianism, Sikhism, Jainism, Taoism, and Bahaism, also have their own divisions and subdivisions. We add Confucianism to the list of world religions, although some scholars do not consider Confucianism a religion.

The multiplicity of religious groups is dramatically illustrated by the emergence of new religious groups in Japan. According to a survey in 1957, the following religious sects had been organized after World War II: (1) *Annai Kyo* (To-Tie-God-with-Man Teaching), (2) *Bussho Gonenkai* (Buddha-Protection-Pray Society), (3) *Daijyo Kyo* (Great-Vehicle Teaching), (4) *Daiei Kai* (Great-Wisdom Society), (5) *Dainichi Dairitsu Genri Kyodan* (Vairocana-Buddha-Establish-Principle Association), (6) *Enno Kyo* (Teaching-Application System), (7) *Gedatsu-Hon-Kansha Kai* (Emancipation-Repayment-Gratitude Society), (8) *Hino Oshie* (Teaching of Sun Goddess), (9) *Hommichi* (Proper Way), (10) *Ishin Kai* (Only-Gods Society), (11) *Kannagara Kyo* (Ancient Gods' Way System), (12) *Kodo Kyodan* (Filial-Way Association), (13) *Maruyama Kyo*

(Teaching of Maruyama), (14) *Myochi Kai* (Wonderful Wisdom Society), (15) *Myodokai Kyodan* (Wonderful Way Association), (16) *Nempyoshin Kyo* (Pray-Teaching-True System), (17) *Omoto* (Great Foundation), (18) *P. L. Kyodan* (Perfect-Liberty Association), (19) *Reiyu Kai Kyodan* (Soul-Friend Association), (20) *Rissho Kosei Kai* (Established-Righteousness Friendly-Intercourse-Becoming Society), (21) *Seicho no Iye* (House of Growth), (22) *Shishin Kai* (Thinking of Parents Society), (23) *Sekai Meshiya Kyo* (World Messianic Teaching), (24) *Shuyodan Hoseikai* (Spiritual-Training-Giving-Truth Society), (25) *Soka Gakkai* (Creative-Value-Study Society), (26) *Tenchi Kodo Zenrin Kai* (Heaven-Earth-Public-Way-Good-Neighbor Society), and (27) *Tensho Kotai Jingu Kyo* (Heaven-Shining-Great-Deity-Dwelling Teaching).[4]

Among the major religions of the world, there are some that are not mutually exclusive. For example, three teachings in China — Confucianism, Taoism, and Buddhism — have been traditionally regarded as inseparable. William Ernest Hocking appropriately calls this " plural belonging." " Plural belonging " is not confined to China, however. In Burma, Buddhism and *Nat* worship (an animistic religion) coexist. Slater observes how a Burmese boy learns that *Nats* appeared in many important events of the Buddha's history. Also, a Burmese boy pays homage to the *Nat* shrine on the day of his *shin-byu* (confirmation). When a Burmese dies, a Buddhist monk may be called to his bedside " because the good influence of the monk's pious presence keeps away evil spirits [*Nats*]." [5] Likewise, in Tibet, the homeland of Lama Buddhism, features and practices of the shamanistic Bon cult have been conspicuously preserved. In Japan, Shinto, the native cult, and Buddhism have developed a harmonious relationship. It is a well-known fact that many Hindus, believing that there are many roads to the truth, are willing to venerate Jesus and Buddha together with Hindu deities.

On the other hand, there are religions such as Judaism, Christianity, and Islam that demand singleness of allegiance from their adherents. Moses' war cry against "heathens" and Charlemagne's order of "baptism or death," are but two examples of this exclusive spirit. Although the beliefs and practices of conquered religions are not altogether dead in Judaism, Christianity, and Islam, nevertheless they have been submerged in the official religious and ecclesiastical teachings and institutions.

Religious Experience and Human Experience

Historians of religions have often been asked how far we can trace the development of religions. This is a difficult question. We can reasonably trace the development of religions to the so-called four major "cradles of civilization," namely, the ancient Egyptian civilization along the Nile, the Mesopotamian civilization around the Tigris and Euphrates, the Indian civilization in the Indus and the Ganges valleys, and the Chinese civilization between the Yellow and Yangtze Rivers. Archaeologists, however, remind us that traces of religions go farther back, dimly to be sure, to the Old Stone Age. Marett contends that we cannot really study the beginnings of the "major institutions of mankind," such as family, tribe, and state, government and law, morality and fine art, and above all, religion. He says that "in every case alike, when we work backward from the present, traces of them persist until they fade out together precisely at the point at which man himself fades out also." [6] Thus, religion has been one of the "primary institutions" of mankind from time immemorial.

Religion may also be viewed as one of the " primary experiences " of mankind, side by side with, or underlying, other kinds of human experience. There is a qualitative difference between religious experience and other kinds of human experience, however, which can be characterized in terms of Martin Buber's famous theory of two kinds of relationship: an " I-It relationship " and an " I-Thou relationship." [7] For example, in an " I-It relationship " one may know all about one's mother — her age, the color of her hair, and her tastes; in this way one knows her as " It " or a thing. But one also experiences another relationship with his mother. One comes to love her. In this way, he enters into love, or an " I-Thou relationship." Mother is no longer an " It " but a " Thou." Following this line of thought, we might say that in religion man experiences an intensive " I-Thou relationship," using the term religion in the broadest sense. Religious man does not live in a different world; he views the same world from a different perspective — the perspective of an " I-Thou relationship."

It has often been pointed out that prehistoric or primitive man did not live in a world of things but in a world of living beings. The distinction between " Thou " and " It " was slight to our ancient ancestors; to them, everything was a " Thou." Primitive man did not feel that he was the master of his surroundings. He depended on the assistance, guidance, and co-operation of " Thou's," whether " Thou " was a person or a piece of stone. Man in ancient times did not stand alone against the world of nature; he was a part of a fellowship of nature — a world of living beings. Understandably, the primitive mind did not differentiate too sharply between organic and inorganic nature. Everything had a potent power, which scholars call " mana." This mana was not fixed in anything, though it could reside in anything; it was viewed as a fluid potent force permeating every part of the cosmos.

As mankind began to make a distinction between " It " and " Thou," he differentiated between the mysterious power (mana) and nature itself. Gradually, this power came to be understood as spirit or soul, in a double sense — the cosmological soul of the world and the psychological soul of man. Mankind, throughout the world, has believed in some sort of spirit or soul existing behind the visible world of nature, and also in some kind of spirit living within each person. In many parts of the world, the cosmic soul has often been understood as the regulating principle of the universe. Inevitably, there arose the difficult question of how to interpret the antithesis " between the arbitrary rule of potencies in this world and the idea of a just order of the universe." [8]

Caught between arbitrary human experience and the idea of a just order of the universe, or between " ultimate frustration and ultimate meaning," to use Paul Tillich's phrase, man has found a number of " religious " solutions. Some religious solutions emphasize the affinity of man and the cosmic spirit. For example, Zoroastrianism and Christianity consider man as God's co-worker in a common fight against chaos and sin and in an effort to establish an order of truth, righteousness, and peace on earth. Also, Hinduism and the mystics of all religious traditions affirm the essential oneness of the human soul with the cosmic spirit. On the other hand, some religions emphasize the distance between man and the cosmic spirit. For example, ancient Greek myths tell how gods punished men " who did not realize the truth of the Delphian maxim . . . know yourself in your strictly human position. . . . Well-known portions of Babylonian literature testify to a similar anthropology: the gods are eternal and man is mortal." [9]

These religious views are more than mere theories. They are derived directly or indirectly from the " religious experience " of mankind. As we have already stated, religious experience does not exist in a vacuum; it exists side by side, or underlies, other kinds of human experience. For example, in Deuteronomy, we find the well-known account of Moses' human and religious experience. Moses led the Children of Israel from the land of Egypt and wandered forty years in the desert seeking the Promised Land. As they neared their goal, Moses was getting weak and realized his time had come. Thus, he prayed: " O Lord God, thou hast only begun to show thy servant thy greatness and thy mighty hand; for what god is there in heaven or on earth who can do such works and mighty acts as thine? Let me go over, I pray, and see the good land beyond the Jordan, that goodly hill country, and Lebanon." But God told him, " Go up to the top of Pisgah, and lift up your eyes westward and northward and southward and eastward, and behold it with your eyes; for you shall not go over this Jordan." (Deut. 3:23-27.) And Moses' lot is our own. The " promised land " we seek in this life is always beyond the " Jordan." We look for meaning in life, but we cannot quite reach it. But men have been known to " see in faith," as did Moses, the promised land stretching beyond the Jordan, even though they could not reach there. Thus, in a real sense, the starting point of religion is found in the gap between anticipation and achievement, between hope and reality, in human life.

Actually, human eyes cannot verify religious visions. We might even argue that what Moses saw was a mirage or hallucination. But in faith Moses saw, however dimly, the reality of the Promised Land. Religion implies that man does not accept the life that is given him. He seeks a richer, deeper, and wider life. He seeks something or some power that is superior to him, whether he tries to manipulate it as in magic, or to worship it as in religion.

Many accounts of religious experiences are not to be interpreted literally. One example, taken from Exodus, tells of Moses' encounter with God for the first time. According to this account, Moses was keeping the flock of his father-in-law and came to Horeb, the mountain of God. " And the angel of the Lord appeared to him in a flame of fire out of the midst of a bush; and he looked, and lo, the bush was burning, yet it was not consumed." As Moses was wondering what it was all about, God called him, " Moses, Moses! " And he said, " Here am I." The voice continued: " Do not come near; put off your shoes from your feet, for the place on which you are standing is holy ground. . . . I am the God of your father, the God of Abraham, the God of Isaac, and the God of Jacob." (Ex. 3:1-6.) Counterparts of Moses' " burning bush " are found in every religion. It has not been uncommon for religious man to believe in such encounters with the supreme power, and to him " this place on earth " becomes the holy ground. Jacob met the angel of God on the bank of a river, and Sakyamuni experienced the certainty of deliverance under a bodhi tree. Thus, every religion has its " burning bush " or its " bodhi tree." And the language of religion — myths and symbols — attempts to convey the inner experience of the " burning bush " or the " bodhi tree." There, man is confronted with an ultimate meaning, transcending power, and reality; Rudolf Otto has called this the experience of the Holy.[10]

Religious experience is one kind of human experience. However, it is qualitatively different from other human experience in the sense that it is decisive. It often causes a new life — a devaluation of all that preceded. Religious man is not satisfied with life as it is given; he seeks the fulfillment of life at the ultimate limit of life.

Holy Communities

It is the common experience of man that he is driven by two contradictory motivations. He seeks solitude in the midst of his fellow men, and he seeks fellowship in his solitude. These same contradictory traits are observable in accentuated form in religious experience. Man experiences the Holy in his utter solitude, and simultaneously seeks human fellowship or the experience of sharing. As in all human experience solitude and fellowship always converge, so in religion solitude seeks communion. In short, religion is by nature a fellowship and communion. Religious fellowship does not exist apart from human fellowship, because it is conditioned and colored by other kinds of human experience and fellowship. The relationship between religious fellowship and other human fellowships is intricate and complex. On the one hand, religion tends to intensify or even transform human fellowships. On the other hand, religion often creates its own " holy community " in the midst of, and yet apart from, other human communities. In some cases, religion sanctifies one form of the human community such as the family or tribe.

There are many similarities between the " holy community " and other human communities. For example, the religious community and the family are both characterized by conscious as well as unconscious factors of belonging together. In a family, the husband and wife perform different functions during the daytime, but in the evening they can sit together and share each other's experiences of the day. In the act of recollection, the husband's and wife's experiences become their common experience. Thus there is not only the fact that they share a common life, but " there is also for each of them their consciousness of the common life. They not merely do live a common life; they also know that they do. This knowledge — this common consciousness of the common life — is part of it and transforms it." [11]

Consciousness of a common life finds expression in various celebrations, such as anniversaries or holy days. Thus certain days of the year, and certain forms of celebration, come to have a special significance to the members of the community. In addition to this " conscious " element, there is also an " unconscious " factor in the fellowship, for to its members at least, the community is self-evident. The fact that they belong to the community is unconsciously taken for granted. Thus, in any community, the " conscious " and " unconscious " elements are intricately intertwined.

Archaeologists and anthropologists have studied many precivilized communities. In comparing precivilized society with present-day primitive society, Redfield found some common characteristics such as isolation, smallness, homogeneity, persistence in a common effort to make a way of living under relatively stable circumstances. Furthermore, in both cases society " exists not so much in the exchange of useful functions as in common understanding as to the ends given. The ends are not stated as matters of doctrine, but are implied by the many acts which make up the living that goes on in society." [12] In other words, " the primitive and precivilized communities are held together essentially by common understandings as to the ultimate nature and purpose of life." [13] Thus primitive and precivilized men know only one community, which is both the human community and the holy community. In it the sacred and the secular are interpenetrating, and the individual's biological cycle finds its corresponding social and religious cycles.

In civilized societies the social and religious communities tend to separate. Some religions create their own holy communities, for example, the Samgha in Buddhism and the church in Christianity. Other religions, however, instead of creating a new holy community, have utilized one unit of the social structure. For example, the family system provides the framework of the Confucian holy community, and the caste system the framework of the Hindu holy community. Each holy community has a dual character, the " invisible body and the visible church," to use a Lutheran phrase. Thus, while each holy community may be viewed as a human community, its *raison d'être* is based on the religious notion that it is the reflection or expression, however imperfect, of the cosmological order. So each religion's interpretation of the cosmos, man, and society is reflected in the structure of its holy community. The holy community defines normative principles not only for the spiritual life of the individual but also for the interpersonal and intergroup relations of society.

Let us visualize for a moment the world view of precivilized society. Archaic man considered the earthly society a counterpart of heavenly society. According to Mircea Eliade, precivilized man viewed the " symbols of the Center," that is, cities, temples, and houses, as the connecting link between the celestial and earthly societies. Thus to archaic man, rituals and cults had transcendental meaning because they were imitations or repetitions of their heavenly counterparts.[14] To him, the earthly cities were replicas of the heavenly city, and the human community was the holy community in the sense that it was the extension of the celestial community.

Chinese religions never articulated a doctrine of the holy community, but they implicitly accepted the family system as a reflection of the cosmic structure. Therefore, if the term " holy community " is to be applied to Chinese religions, it should be focused around the family system. Historically, there have developed in China specific " religious " societies, but at no time did they supersede the family as the primary collective unit of religious life. While there is an element of conscious selectivity involved in the family, it has been held by the Chinese as a form of existence in its own right over and above all other human, social institutions. As such, the Chinese family, according to Confucianism, is a biological, social, and religious unit, and its head is *de facto* a priest. Traditionally, even the state has been understood as an extension of the family.

Hinduism, the all-embracing religious, social, and cultural system of India, accepts the caste system as a divinely sanctioned cosmological order of stratification. Traditionally, a Hindu has no place outside his preordained caste, because social solidarity is based on a rigid hierarchical system. In the course of history, various attempts have been made to loosen the caste system, but it has remained to this day as the basic framework of both the social and the religious communities.

The ancient Hebrew holy community was a " covenanted " community, which implied a special agreement between the Hebrews and their God. According to Genesis, their God told Abraham: " Go from your country and your kindred and your father's house to the land that I will show you. And I will make of you a great nation " (Gen. 12:1-2). While Judaism was convinced of the universal implications of its faith, the Hebrew " covenanted " community had a biological basis. While Gentiles might be used for God's purpose, ultimately the Jewish holy community was to be the bearer of the divine enterprise on earth.

The Christian holy community considers itself an extension of the Hebrew "covenanted" community, which was spiritualized so as to embrace all those "who were born, not of blood nor of the will of the flesh nor of the will of man, but of God" (John 1:13). The Christian ecclesia (church) in its initial period was regarded as existing in the world but not of the world. After the period of Constantine, however, Christianity developed into the religion of the Roman Empire, and took on political and social responsibilities. Today, Christianity exists throughout the world, crossing national, social, cultural, and ethnic lines. Despite denominational and other divisions within Christianity, all Christian groups subscribe to the doctrine of the church as the normative principle of their ecclesiology.

Islam, a spiritual heir of Judaism and Christianity, started as an Arabic religion, but quickly developed into a world faith. From its inception, Islam had to face the problems of administering the state, for the Islamic holy community (known as the Ummah) was ideally a theocratic state, even though this ideal has never been achieved. The lofty concept of the unity of all Muslims in a single holy community has always been threatened by sectarian and national divisions. This problem has been accentuated in the present century with the elimination of the caliphate, the visible symbol of the Ummah, and with the rise of many Muslim nation-states. Nevertheless, from the religious point of view, the cross-cultural and cross-national Muslim holy community plays a significant role in the religio-political life of the Muslims.

Buddhism presents a sharp contrast to Islam in this respect. Buddha founded, not a religious-political order as did Muhammad but a religious community for the monastics and laity. In the main, the core of the Buddhist holy Community (Samgha) has been the monastic orders, and even today the term Samgha refers generally to the Buddhist monasteries. Nevertheless, the laity also played an important role in the Buddhist tradition. Thus all Buddhists, whether or not they are in the cloisters, constitute the Samgha universal, as it were, which unites all Buddhists, crossing national and cultural lines.

Holy Communities and " Modernity "

While all holy communities have, implicitly or explicitly, normative principles about the role of man and society, they have been frustrated in their attempts to implement these principles in history. Ancient Hindus had the lofty ideal of a universal empire of enduring peace under a just and virtuous monarch (cakravartin), but such an empire was never realized. Confucius' dream of the grand commonwealth based not on might but on morality has not been realized either. An ancient Hebrew psalmist, too, prayed for the emergence of a theocracy under the reign of a divine king:

> Give the king thy justice, O God,
> and thy righteousness to the royal son!
> May he judge thy people with righteousness,
> and thy poor with justice!
> Let the mountains bear prosperity for the people,
> and the hills, in righteousness!
> May he defend the cause of the poor of the people,
> give deliverance to the needy,
> and crush the oppressor!
>
> May he live while the sun endures,
> and as long as the moon, throughout all generations!

May he be like rain that falls on the mown grass,
  like showers that water the earth!
In his days may righteousness flourish,
  and peace abound, till the moon be no more!

(Ps. 72:1-7.)

By definition, the holy community participates in two societies, spiritual and empirical. It also recognizes two histories, the history of salvation and empirical history. However, even in a strict theocratic state, religious motivation and sociopolitical motivation do not coincide altogether. While, in the main, both the holy community and the political state have been compelled to recognize the inevitability of coexistence and co-operation, they have never worked out an ideal solution for the relationship between " church " and " state," or between " religion " and " culture." For example, a spokesman of the Hebrew state church, in his admonition to the prophet Amos, suggested one solution by defining the boundary between the universal judgment of God and the prerogatives of a king: " O seer, go, flee away to the land of Judah, and eat bread there, and prophesy there; but never again prophesy at Bethel, for it is the king's sanctuary, and it is a temple of the kingdom " (Amos 7:12-13). But such a " division of labor " between the church and state has never been accepted by religious man. So, even at the height of King David's popularity, Nathan, the prophet, would point the finger at the king, accusing his sin: " You are the man " (II Sam. 12:7).

In the struggle between the state and religion, the political state makes every effort to " domesticate " the holy community, although religion does not relinquish its claim to higher truth. H. Richard Niebuhr depicts five historic types of relation between Christianity and culture:

(1) Christ Against Culture, (2) the Christ of Culture, (3) Christ Above Culture, (4) Christ and Culture in Paradox, and (5) Christ the Transformer of Culture.[15] Similar options have been known, to a greater or lesser extent, in other religious contexts as well.

The tension between the religious community and the political state has become accentuated in the modern period. In the West, since the emergence of the modern nation-states in the early eighteenth century, governments have become increasingly powerful in defining norms of behavior and values for their citizens. Modern nations, following Rousseau's famous principle, tend to educate citizens to become patriots by inclination, by passion, and by necessity, and they create in time of crisis an atmosphere in which, as George Bernard Shaw pointed out, Temples of Peace are transformed into Temples of War. Hocking astutely states, " In our contemporary world, the secular state tends to regard itself as the more reliable interpreter of human nature . . . and as a sufficient interpreter." [16] In analyzing the premise of the secular state, Hocking finds in modern history two types of experiment: " the explicit experiment of laïque political constitutions in the present century, expressly rejecting religion as a factor in political life; and the unintentional experiment of far longer and wider range — the experiment we call ' modernity,' " which " in begetting a secular science and secular arts, has also incidentally promoted a secular interpretation of state and law." [17] While the secular state attempts to deal with crime, education, the family, the economy, recreation, and law, it is Hocking's prophetic judgment that the experiment of " modernity," in creating the ideal of the secular state, has resulted " in a radical impotence in the very field of the state's own functions, an impotence only now and slowly but irresistibly becoming evident." [18]

One of the important by-products of the Western influence on the East is the introduction of " modernity " and the concept of the modern nation-state, which has greatly changed the traditional equilibrium between the holy community and the political community in the East. Although historically the political community had played an important role in the East, loyalty had been defined more in terms of the family, caste, guild, or tribal-territorial community. Today, however, the nation-state in the East has become the chief instrument of self-conscious social change, posing as the object of the citizen's supreme loyalty. Self-conscious nationalism played an important role in the emancipation of Eastern peoples from European colonial rule, and in this process nationalism allied itself with the resurgence of Eastern religions. Without implying a simple causation theory — that the resurgence of religion caused emotional nationalism or vice versa — it must be observed that nationalism and the resurgence of Eastern religions complemented each other. For example, Burmese nationalism and Buddhism have been closely identified in the minds of the Burmese people.

Now that many former colonial peoples have gained political independence, the problem of the relation between the political state and the holy community has become a crucial issue in the East. Faced with seemingly insurmountable economic and social problems, the new nation-states are compelled to engage in vast social planning, leaning heavily toward the idea of a social welfare state. In this situation, as Hocking points out, the religious community " instead of tending to wither away, becomes increasingly necessary to the vitality of the state, its function being to maintain that integrity of motivation which the state requires and cannot of itself elicit or command." [19] Thus the leaders of the new nation-states in the East are inclined to regard the holy community as a department of the state, albeit an important one.

Today the holy communities of Confucianism, Hinduism, Islam, and Buddhism are confronted by a series of complex problems. Historically, these religions either had developed their own ecclesiastical structures, which were congenial to Eastern social environment, or they had relied on some elements within traditional Eastern societies. Modern technology, urbanization, and industrialization are changing the texture and the character of Eastern social structures, and the traditional religious communities are faced with the task of relating themselves to the modern situation. While the new nation-states are genuinely interested in maintaining their traditional religious values, they nevertheless impose the supremacy of the secular law, thus undercutting the historic claims of the holy communities. This raises the possibility that the holy communities of Eastern religions may be " domesticated " and become subservient to the political order.

There is no denying that the resurgence of Eastern religions has been strongly influenced by nationalism in the twentieth century. However, nationalism alone cannot account for the modern developments in Islam, Buddhism, Hinduism, Confucianism, and Shinto. Eastern religions have had to cope with ideological and practical issues raised by "modernity," and they are making every effort to understand themselves as well as to interpret themselves to outsiders. New leaders of the holy communities in the East are trying to make their adherents " religiously " conscious of the nature of their religions. While Eastern religions traditionally have been allied with national or regional cultures in the East, the spokesmen of these religions are aware that " the religious community is by definition universal in extent as in norms of will: it speaks not primarily to the man-within-the-nation but to the man-within-the-world." [20] On the other hand, they know only too well that their holy communities are heavily burdened with the weight of tradition. The question is whether or not modern Islam, Hinduism, Buddhism, and Confucianism will develop into genuine world religions.

Within this framework, we shall undertake to examine and analyze, as sympathetically and accurately as we can, the character and development of the " holy communities " of Chinese religions, Hinduism, Buddhism, and Islam.

2 Chinese Religions and the Family System

◈ ◈

THE MIDDLE KINGDOM

The " Good Earth "

The rise of Mao Tse-tung after World War II marked a decisive turning point in the modern history of China and, to a significant degree, of the rest of the world. For centuries China had regarded itself as the center of the world or the " Middle Kingdom," and considered other nations inferior to it. During the last century, however, beginning with the infamous Opium War, foreign powers took advantage of the declining Manchu dynasty and imposed humiliating treaties on China. After the revolution in 1911, China's relations with Western nations improved somewhat, and many Western ideas began to influence the youth of China. During the Japanese invasion of China in the 1930's, as well as during World War II in the 1940's, China depended heavily on the West for assistance. Thus, China's sudden switch of alliance from the Western nations to the communist bloc after the war shocked and bewildered many Westerners.

Sardar Panikkar, who served as Indian ambassador to China both before and after the emergence of Red China, recalls the confusion of the Western diplomats in Nanking in 1948 and 1949. He notes particularly the attitude of the then American ambassador, J. Leighton Stuart, who had previously spent forty years as a missionary educator in China and had boundless faith in the Chinese character. Knowing the Chinese student's traditional attitude toward his teacher, Stuart expected that "his own position as teacher of many of the young communist leaders would help to shape their policy in favor of the West." [1] In this respect, Stuart and many others like him were greatly disappointed. The events that followed the formation of the communist regime under Mao Tse-tung made it plain that China would lean toward the communist bloc, with little regard for recent "Western teachers."

Today many outsiders wonder if the time-honored Chinese culture is destined to be exterminated by communism, or if it will have the tenacity to survive and eventually transform communism as it had tamed the Mongols and Manchus in the past. Whatever happens in China is bound to influence the course of history for many years to come. Standing as we are at the threshold of a new era in world history, it is meaningful for us to reflect on the religious and cultural heritage of the Chinese.

To understand China is not an easy task, for China gives different impressions to those who look at it from different perspectives. [2] All students of China, however, agree that China has been an agrarian nation from time immemorial. Those who have read Pearl Buck's *The Good Earth* will never forget the figure of the farmer Wang Lung, who worked tirelessly throughout his life against all kinds of difficulties and misfortunes and finally became a landowner. Toward the end of his life Wang Lung often visited the family cemetery, especially the little spot which he had selected as his resting place. " Spring passed and summer passed into harvest and in the hot autumn sun before winter comes Wang Lung sat where his father had sat against the wall. And he thought no more about anything now except his food and his drink and his land. . . . And he was content, holding it thus, and he thought of it fitfully and of his good coffin that was there; and the kind earth waited without haste until he came to it." [3] Indeed, the story of the " good earth " is the story of China. Dynasties have come and gone, but millions and millions of Wang Lungs have lived close to the soil throughout the ages, preserving an amazing continuity of their ancestral beliefs and ways of life.

Specifically the term China refers to the eighteen provinces known as " China proper," but in a loose sense it also includes outlying dependencies, such as Manchuria (now known simply as the Northeast), Mongolia, Tibet, and Sinkiang (Chinese Turkestan). China proper, covering roughly 1,500,000 square miles, is nourished by the Yellow River in the north, the Yangtze River in the middle, and the West River in the south. Its inhabitants are often divided into five " races," referring to Han (the dominant group), Mongol, Manchu, Tibetan, and Muslim; the last, however, is a religious and not an ethnic group. Also, there are many other ethnic minority groups, such as Chuang, Uigur, Hui, Miao, and Puyi. According to the 1953 census, roughly 583,000,000 people were estimated to be living in Red China, and we are told that the figure had increased to about 648,000,000 in 1958. (In addition, nearly 7,600,-000 people lived on the island of Formosa in 1951, and well over 10,000,000 persons of Chinese descent lived abroad.)

At the risk of oversimplification, we may cite three factors that have bound together the vast populace of China into a cohesive social and cultural group over two millenniums. The first is a common written language. Historically, China's neighbors were influenced by Chinese culture through the Chinese written language, even though they could not speak Chinese. Internally, however, emphasis on the written language, which required many years of formal training, divided the Chinese people rather sharply into two classes, a minority of educated gentry and the illiterate masses.

The second factor is the family and kinship system. Traditional Chinese society rested upon the principle of " Family-ism," which, in turn, was based on the Confucian concept of filial piety. The nation-state in the modern sense never existed in China until recently. Instead, the state was regarded as a super family — a projection of the patriarchal family — in which the relationships among members of different social strata were governed by Confucian moral principles. The cosmos too was apprehended through the family principle. In short, the family in China has been a " metaphysical " focus as well as a " sociological " unit. The third unifying factor is the religious outlook implicit in all the religious and semireligious schools and systems of China. The core of Chinese religious conviction is the belief that the world of man and the world of nature are inseparable and interdependent, and that beyond and within the mysterious and seemingly incomprehensible operation of the universe in its relation to human destiny lies an Eternal Order (Tao). Various beliefs, ceremonies, and practices of the religious schools are motivated by the main " religious " concern of maintaining harmony between man and the universe, as well as between man and society. Lin Yutang once stated that China's contribution to philosophy is a distrust of systematic philosophy, and we might say, paraphrasing him, that China's contribution to religion is a distrust of organized, institutionalized forms of religion. " How to realize Tao " — more than " What is Tao? " — is the religious problem that has concerned lofty philosophers and superstitious masses alike.

Of course, there are other factors that have bound the Chinese people together, but their written language, their family and kinship system, and their religious outlook are most significant from our point of view.

From Legend to History

China, located in the North Temperate Zone, provided favorable conditions for human habitation. However, it is very difficult to determine whether the ancestors of the Chinese people came from other parts of the Old World. In the 1920's, archaeologists discovered a late Paleolithic (Old Stone Age) creature, Sinanthropus Pekinensis, so named because it was unearthed about thirty miles southwest of Peking. Significant though this discovery was, there is not enough other archaeological evidence to connect the period of this " Chinese man of Peking " — roughly dated about 400,000 years ago — and the Neolithic period (New Stone Age) . " Then suddenly, at the very end of the Neolithic, at a time only four thousand years distant from our own, the hitherto seemingly empty land [in the North China Plain] becomes teeming with busy life. Hundreds, not to say thousands of villages occupy the terraces overlooking the valley bottoms. Many of these villages were surprisingly large and must have harbored a considerable population. Their inhabitants were hunters and stock raisers but at the same time agriculturalists." [4] This Neolithic culture in northern China was noted for its painted pottery, and was followed by a more sophisticated culture, characterized by black pottery, which foreshadowed the emergence of the historic Chinese civilization of the Bronze Age.

There are numerous legends regarding the origin of the Chinese people and of the world. For example, the name of P'an Ku is usually given as the first man who separated the heaven and the earth. He is also said to be the first ruler, succeeded by a dozen Celestial Sovereigns, eleven Terrestrial Sovereigns, and nine Human Sovereigns. According to legend, the last of the Human Sovereigns, Yü, founded the so-called Hsia dynasty in 2205 B.C., which lasted until 1765 B.C. However, most historians are skeptical of the historicity of the Hsia dynasty and hold that the first historic dynasty was the Shang, but here again they are not altogether certain about the chronology of this dynasty, which has been given variously as 1765–1122 B.C., 1550–1050 B.C., and 1523–1050 B.C.

The earliest archaeological evidences of the Chinese Bronze culture were unearthed near An-yang, the ancient Shang site, and they are dated around 1300 B.C. The Shang people made use of bronze utensils, chariots, horses, and domestic animals, and they had an elaborate system of divination as well as the forerunner of the Chinese script. According to Bishop, " the Shang priest-kings, of primitive type, worshiped the spirits of their ancestors and also various divinities, of whom the chief was Shang Ti, ' the Ruler Above.' In war, they and their followers used spears, dagger-axes, and helmets of bronze, as well as compound bows and two-horsed chariots. . . . [The Shang] political organization took the form of city-states, of which the one ruled by the Shangs themselves claimed the allegiance and tribute from the rest." [5] Among many archaeological finds, the most interesting for our purpose are ritual bronzes, which were used for religious purposes, and oracle bones, made

of ox bone or tortoise shell and used for divination. Inscriptions on the oracle bones not only provide us with
keys to deciphering the earliest forms of the Chinese script
but also give us clues to ancient Chinese religious beliefs
and practices.[6]

The records of the oracle bones tell us that as early as
the second half of the thirteenth century B.C. the Shangs
had troubles with the Chou, the people in the Western
frontier. Sometime around 1020 B.C., the Shangs were
finally defeated by the Chou forces. The long dynastic era
of the Chou (ca. 1027–255 B.C.) served as the formative
period of ancient Chinese civilization. In this connection,
although many scholars characterize the Chou society as
" feudalistic," Wittfogel stresses the single-centered bureaucratic nature of the Chou social order despite its deceptive
similarities to feudalistic societies. Wittfogel also calls Chou
society a " hydraulic " society, dominated by farming based
on large-scale waterworks, as distinguished from " hydro-
agriculture " (small-scale irrigation farming) and rainfall
farming.[7] At any rate, the Chou political order was more
effective than the tribute-collecting system of the Shang,
and it provided the basis for the longest dynastic period in
Chinese history.

The Chou dynastic era may be divided into three main
periods. The first, roughly from the eleventh to eighth
centuries B.C., is known as the Western Chou period. The
most famous among the early Chou rulers was Chou Kung
(" the Duke of Chou ") , under whose administration Chou
influence was firmly established in the eastern district,
which was the traditional center of the Shang people and
culture. He established many territorial states in order to
consolidate the internal unity of the kingdom as well as to
ward off barbarian invasions from outside, and appointed

members of the royal family as princes of these territorial states. The unity of the kingdom was maintained only as long as there was a strong central authority, and this began to decline after the tenth century B.C.

The middle Chou period (ca. 771–474 B.C.) is called the Ch'un Ch'iu (Spring and Autumn), or the Eastern Chou period. During this period, a western tribe called the Jungs penetrated China and forced the Chou rulers to move eastward, deep into north central China. Although the prestige of the Chou monarchy suffered, the threat of invasion from outside and the necessity of maintaining a balance of power among competing territorial states kept the ceremonial and religious authority of the Chou king alive.

From the fifth to the middle of the third century B.C., commonly known as the Late Chou or the Chan Kuo (Contending States) period, there was a complete decline of central authority. The king's position was purely nominal, and the territorial states became autonomous for all practical purposes. Five strong states competed for power — Ch'i in the northeast, Chin in the north, Ch'in in the west, Sung in the plain, and Chu in the south. The Ch'in gradually gained strength and defeated the other states one by one. In 221 B.C., China was unified by the Ch'in.

The founder of the Ch'in empire assumed the title Shih Huang Ti, or the " First Emperor." He endeavored to create a united China, with a standardized written language, a strict domestic morality, and a cult of emperor worship. The empire was divided into forty provinces, which were subdivided into prefectures and towns, and the whole nation was governed by an elaborate bureaucracy which was set up under the autocratic emperor. The First Emperor undertook many public works, such as creating canals and building the colossal Great Wall. He attempted to regulate the conduct of his subjects by law, and depended heavily on the " Legalists," who instigated the burning of unorthodox books. After his death in 210 B.C., his empire declined quickly. His successor was assassinated in 207 B.C., and after a decade of political unrest the Middle Kingdom was unified again by the Han dynasty.

CHINA'S RELIGIOUS HERITAGE

" Universism "

There is a rather widespread notion in the West that the Chinese people are humanistic rather than religious and that Chinese philosophy has been free from religious influence. Hu Shih reminds us, however, that the Chinese people are capable of highly religious emotions and that Chinese philosophy has been greatly influenced by " Siniticism " and Buddhism. He coined the word " Siniticism " in referring to the native religion of the Chinese people. " It dates back to time immemorial and includes all such later phases of its development as Mohism, Confucianism (as a state religion) , and all the various stages of the Taoist religion." [8]

Historically, what Hu Shih calls " Siniticism " can be traced to the Shang Ti (" Ruler Above ") cult of the ruling families, as well as the fertility cult of the peasants during the Shang period (second millennium B.C.) . Both the ruling class and peasants regarded the dead as an integral part of their social group, and they depended on the shamans for spiritual mediation between the living and the dead. While veneration of ancestors and belief in divination were two outstanding features of the Shang peoples' religion, it is equally important to note that " the daily routine of

cultivation of the soil, social intercourse, intergroup relations, and political life was regarded as religious and was
performed with deep insight and fervor." [9]

The Chou people who defeated the Shangs around
1020 B.C. believed in spirits (*shen*) and ghosts (*kwei*), as
well as in an omnipotent and omniscient T'ien or Hao-t'ien
(August Heaven) and his consort Ti (Earth). The Chou
notion of T'ien was superimposed on the Shang notion of
Shang Ti, and in the course of time the Chou people developed a rich pantheon of spirits, ghosts, and deities of
conquered tribal groups, forming a court, as it were, under
the supreme deity, Hao-t'ien Shang Ti (Heavenly Lord).
T'ien-tao (the Way of Heaven), an art of divination based
on two forces called Yin and Yang (female and male, negative and positive), developed during the latter part of the
Chou period. This school of diviners was known as the
Yin-Yang School, and compiled *The Book of Change*
(Manual of Divination). Just as Heaven (T'ien) was believed to have a heavenly court, the Chou king (T'ien-tzu,
Son of Heaven) was surrounded by princes of the territorial states and his ministers of agriculture, defense, public works, religious rites, justice, and the imperial household. The Chou society — in effect, a super family — was
welded together by a sense of filial piety on every level
from the peasant to the king. The two guiding principles
of the state were *li* (rites, ceremonies, proper conduct)
and *hsing* (penalties), applicable to reciprocal relations
between superiors and inferiors.

Similarly, according to the ancient Chinese, the world of
man and the world of nature constitute a seamless whole,
governed by reciprocal relationships. Two characteristics
of Chinese religious life have been its ceremonial and
ethical emphases. Furthermore, in contrast to religious de-

velopment in the West, Chinese religion never made a distinction between the sacred and the secular. The only significant distinction was between the " ceremonial " and " informal " aspects. Here we must not hastily equate religion with the " ceremonial," as many people have been inclined to do. Rather, the religious ethos of the Chinese must be found in the midst of their ordinary everyday life more than in their ceremonial activities, though the latter should not be ignored. The meaning of life was sought in the whole of life, and not confined to any section of it called specifically " religious." In Lin Yutang's words, the Chinese " are in love with life, with its kings and beggars, robbers and monks, funerals and weddings and childbirths and sicknesses and glowing sunsets and feasting days and wine-shop fracas." [10]

However, this life, which the Chinese love so dearly, was understood in its cosmological setting, and not as something independent of nature. Even though ancient Chinese religion did not articulate metaphysical theories about the indivisibility of nature and man, a metaphysical structure based on the inseparability of man and nature was taken for granted. For lack of better terminology we use de Groot's expression, " Universism," to describe the implicit metaphysical structure of the Chinese. According to this cosmic-human, monistic world view, the world was not created; the world *is*. The world has no beginning or end, and time is a chain of ever-repeating seasons. In this sense, " creation " is a constant re-creation of nature, and man is an integral part of nature. Bodde points out that early Chinese had vague ideas about a celestial realm and a nether region, but there was no belief in divine retribution after death. " Each human being was supposed to have two souls: the *p'o,* or anima, produced at the time of conception, and the *hun,* or animus, which was joined to the *p'o* at the moment of birth. After death the *hun* ascended to heaven; the *p'o* remained in the tomb with the corpse for three years, after which it descended to the Yellow Springs." [11] The birth and death of man, as well as changes and processes in the world of nature, are not accidental; they are manifestations of the cosmic Tao (Eternal Order). Tao is the path which the universe follows, and all beings evolve from it. Tao manifests itself in the dual principles of Yin and Yang (female and male, or negative and positive). Out of the alternate actions between Yin and Yang develop the five primary elements (fire, water, earth, wood, and metal). Although Yin and Yang are diametrically opposed in character, they are equally essential for the existence of the universe.[12]

Throughout the long history of China, all sages and all schools of religion and philosophy have been exponents of Tao. However, no Chinese thinkers have ever attempted to prove the existence of Tao by way of induction or generalization based on empirical analysis of the phenomenal world. They all accepted Tao as the highest category of apprehension of the world and life and also as the underlying principle, which realizes itself in the ordered life of man and the harmonious relations of man to the universe. How to keep this harmony intact and how to actualize Tao in everyday life have been the fundamental "religious concerns" of the Chinese. Differences among various religious and philosophical schools were found in their approaches to the realization of Tao. Ironically, however, the genuine "religious concerns" of various schools in China, like religious movements in other parts of the world, were often submerged by sociopolitical and ecclesiastical developments.

Confucianism

The term Confucianism refers to *Ju Chia* or the School of Literati. According to Confucius: " A *Ju* is like one who has jewels in his keeping waiting for sale; he cultivates his knowledge morning and night to prepare himself for requests for advice; he cherishes integrity and honesty of character against the time when he is appointed; he endeavors to order his personal conduct against the time when he shall be in office. Such is his independence! " [13] Teachers of this school were scholars of ancient classics and transmitters of ancient cultural legacies.

In a narrower sense, however, Confucianism refers more strictly to the teaching of Confucius and the scholars of his school. It has been said that in this narrow sense Confucianism is half the man and half the teaching. It is difficult to say whether it is a religion, an ethical system, or a political philosophy. Having no creed, priesthood, or ecclesiastical organization, Confucianism nevertheless has elements that can be considered religious, or at least can serve as a basis for religion. Actually, Confucius did not claim to be either a religious leader or a philosopher. Confucius or Master Kung (ca. 551–479 B.C.) was born in the state of Lu, son of Kung Shu-Liang Ho, probably a minor military officer. Confucius married at the age of eighteen or nineteen, and although we know nothing about his wife, we know that they had one son and at least one daughter. Later tradition made generous allusion to his noble lineage, traced back to the royal family of the ancient Shang dynasty. But all we know for certain is that he managed to acquire an education despite the fact that his family was poor. Confucius lived in the Ch'un Ch'iu (Spring and Autumn) period, when the Chou kings were nothing more than puppets in the hands of powerful territorial rulers engaged in constant power struggles. In this situation of sociopolitical and cultural chaos, Confucius acquired a sense of mission. "He became convinced," says Creel, "that it was his mission to save the world, and he undertook to do so in the only way that appeared possible, by trying to win a commanding place in the administration." [14] He held, for a short time at least, a position of considerable political influence, and worked hard but was not understood or appreciated by the prince. Deeply disappointed as a political reformer, Confucius left the state of Lu and traveled for twelve or thirteen years. Everywhere he was received with respect but was not given an opportunity to put his teaching into practice, so he returned to his native state and engaged in study and teaching. Despite many hardships, he never lost his sense of mission. Himself an ardent student, he proved to be a devoted teacher, though a strict one. His curriculum was multidimensional, including poetry, history, ceremonies, grammar, rhetoric, and, above all, orientation for a gentleman civil servant. By temperament Confucius was a traditionalist, with a nostalgic view of the ancient sage-kings; yet he interpreted ancient tradition with a new spirit. He was an interesting combination of an agnostic and "at the same time the teacher of a new religion, based, not upon any worship of gods or god, but upon the central idea of filial piety," which according to Hu Shih was not a revival of the old ancestral worship, "but a new interpretation which amounted to a new creation." [15] He was concerned equally with the individual and society. Regarding the individual, his central notion was *jen,* variously translated as goodness, love, true manhood, human-heartedness, benevolence, or that which a man *is* to be a man. By inference he taught the inherent goodness of human nature, but his followers were split on this issue, even though they all acknowledged the educability of man. Confucius advocated moral perfection for the individual, and he gave detailed recommendations and requirements for a superior man. In his view, a superior man is dignified but not proud, while an inferior man is proud but not dignified.

Regarding society, his central notion was *li* (rites, ceremonies, proper conduct). The ultimate goal was *chung yung,* the Golden Mean or Central Harmony. To this end, Confucius tried to make politics subordinate to morals, and he tried to " rectify " names, by making every name stand for concrete obligations and duties. In his view, society must be based on the harmonious operation of five relationships — between father and son, between ruler and subject, between husband and wife, between elder and younger brothers, and between friend and friend.

The tradition of Confucius was maintained by his followers. Notable among them were Mencius (d. 289 B.C.?) and Hsün Tzu (d. 235 B.C.?). Mencius held that human nature was fundamentally good, while Hsün Tzu took the opposite view and advocated moral discipline and rules of social conduct. According to Mencius, man has intuitive marks of goodness which will develop in response to proper environment and education. Like Confucius before him, Mencius was also interested in political order and sought an opportunity to put his teaching into practice; and, following Confucius, he held that the ruler's character conditions the character of the government. However, he was a more systematic thinker than Confucius. He advocated economic planning. He was unpopular among the princes, not only because he was their severe critic, but also because he justified rebellion if a ruler should fail to perform his duties. Mencius' teachings were compiled in a book bearing his name; this book later attained a canonical status under the influence of Neo-Confucianism.

Taoism

Although Taoism appears to be quite different from Confucianism, both were rooted in the cosmic-human, monistic world view of Chinese antiquity. In their application, however, they seem to be poles apart. In contrast to Confucianism, which advocated " I-Thou relationships " (in the sense Martin Buber uses the term) among human beings, Taoist tradition emphasized an " I-Thou relationship " between man and nature. We can go so far as to say that Confucianism developed an art of sociopolitical engineering, and Taoism an art of cosmic engineering.

The term Taoism refers both to *Tao Chia* and *Tao Chiao*. According to Fung Yu-lan: " *Tao Chia* denotes a philosophy, while *Tao Chiao* a religion. The teaching of Taoism as a philosophy and that of Taoism as a religion are not only different, they are even contradictory. Taoism as a philosophy teaches the doctrine of following nature, while Taoism as a religion that of working against it." [16] The philosophical tradition of Taoism was articulated by Yang Chu, Lao Tzu, and Chuang Tzu. The legendary account of Lao Tzu as the keeper of the archives of the Chou court, and a senior contemporary of Confucius, has been discredited by many modern scholars, although it is possible that there was a man of the same or similar name at the time of Confucius. At least *Tao Te Ching*, the scripture ascribed to Lao Tzu, was a work of much later date than Confucius.

Yang Chu (ca. 440–366 B.C.) was neither a hedonist nor an egoist, as he was accused by orthodox Confucianists. He was a naturalist in the Taoist sense of the term. About Lao Tzu we know practically nothing, except as the legendary author of *Tao Te Ching*. This work is a remarkable anthology dealing with many subjects, such as " the importance of keeping the original simplicity of human nature, the danger of overgovernment and interference with the simple life of the people, the doctrine of *wu-wei* or . . . 'noninterference' . . . the lessons of humility." [17] The opening sentence of *Tao Te Ching* has been translated differently by three scholars: " The Tao that can be told of is not the Absolute Tao; the Names that can be given are not Absolute Names " (Lin Yutang).[18] " The Way that can be told is not an Unvarying Way; the names that can be named are not unvarying names " (Arthur Waley).[19] " There are ways but the Way is uncharted; there are names but not nature in words " (R. B. Blakney).[20] All seem to imply that the Tao (Eternal Order) taught in *Tao Te Ching* is a natural process, in the Chinese sense of " original." In the Taoist tradition, Tao is the supreme, rejecting the anthropomorphic notion of T'ien or Shang Ti; Tao does nothing and yet achieves everything. Chuang Tzu (d. 295 B.C.?), a noted literalist, held that Tao produced all things, is the ground of all things and is in all things. What he advocated was man's unity with the universe, which is the unity of all things. Lin Yutang calls Chuang Tzu the " Chinese Nietzsche." Different though they were in many ways, these Taoist sages all stood for the preservation of natural life, avoiding injury. According to Fung Yu-lan, Yang Chu's method for doing it was " to escape " from society, while Lao Tzu taught that one must understand the laws underlying the change of things and live in conformity with them. Chuang Tzu taught another kind of escape, that is,

" to see life and death, self and others, from a higher point of view." [21]

In the course of time, Taoism came to be greatly influenced by the Yin-Yang system and occultism. Later, after the second century A.D., Taoism developed into a superstitious popular religion.

Other Schools

Among the other classical traditions developed during the Chou period, Mohism and Legalism were important.

The founder of Mohism, Mo Ti or Mo Tzu, who lived in the fifth and fourth centuries B.C., was a great religious leader, reformer, and the first articulate opponent of Confucius. In Hu Shih's opinion, Mo Ti is the only Chinese who founded a religion. At any rate, his followers organized a semireligious society. Mo Ti's teaching has been characterized variously as universalism, socialism, and utilitarianism. The doctrine of universal love (*chien-ai*) and the Will of Heaven are two cardinal teachings of Mo Ti. He traveled long distances under great hardships, appealing to various rulers to adopt his principles. He was convinced that the promotion of human happiness was the *raison d'être* of government, and with this objective in mind he advocated frugal living and curtailment of unnecessarily expensive funeral rites and customs, and the use of peaceful means to settle interstate problems. He was critical of Confucian atheism and determinism, and considered fatalism the greatest of heresies. He was an authoritarian by temperament, but defended his views not by dogmatic utterances but by the art of polemics. " He invented the logic of threefold argument which required all reasoning to be tested by three criteria: first, it must have the authority of the ancient sages; second, it must agree with the common experience of the ordinary people; and lastly, it must pass the test of practical utility." [22] Mohism was severely persecuted by the Legalists during the Ch'in period, and after the victory of Confucianism during the Han dynasty Mohism lost its influence altogether.

With the rise of the Ch'in empire, the religious situation changed. The Ch'in adopted the Chinese culture for the most part, but retained their own animistic and polytheistic tribal beliefs. The First Emperor, in addition to fostering emperor worship, introduced many tribal deities, notably the five gods representing not only the five elements (metal, wood, water, fire, and earth) but also five directions (east, west, north, south, and center). Notoriously superstitious, the First Emperor came under the influence of alchemy — hoping to transform base metals into gold — and the cult of longevity. He died in 210 B.C. while in the midst of a feverish search for a miracle drug for immortality. However, during his reign he sought a guiding ideology for the new empire. Rejecting Confucianism because of its ethical emphasis and its nostalgia for the golden past, Taoism because of its mystical emphasis and avoidance of political involvement, and Mohism because of its religious idealism and uncompromising attitude toward government, the First Emperor favored the school of Legalism, which accepted the new situation and faced new problems realistically. The unification of China was accomplished largely with the help of the Legalists.

Legalism (*Fa Chia*) was a school of political administration, and not a religious or philosophical system, although it had some philosophical assumptions. The importance of this school was due solely to the role it played during the Ch'in period, although its thoughts later were incorporated into the Confucian tradition. Undoubtedly, the Legalists were able and realistic statesmen. For example, Shang Yang, known as Lord Shang (d. 338), is credited with the abolishment of the traditional landholding system and the institution of a systematic jurisprudence. It was another Legalist, Li Ssu, who as imperial adviser helped unify the whole nation. To him, "there was to be only one empire, one language, and one system of thought and belief." [23] But the Ch'in empire, which the Legalists played such a decisive role in creating, crumbled shortly after the death of the First Emperor, and the Middle Kingdom was again unified under the Han dynasty.

THE DEVELOPMENT OF CHINESE RELIGIONS

Han Confucianism and Taoism

The development of Chinese religions cannot be understood without reference to the historical setting. The short-lived Ch'in dynasty prepared the way for the longer Han dynastic period; the Han period was divided into the Western or Earlier Han (206 B.C.–A.D. 8) and the Eastern or Later Han (A.D. 25–220) dynasties; in between, Wang Mang established the Hsin dynasty. During the Han period, Confucianism became the state religion of China, and popular Taoism emerged as an institutionalized religion. Also, in the early part of the Eastern Han dynasty, Buddhism was introduced to China. The Han period was followed by nearly four centuries of political unrest until the rise of the Sui dynasty in A.D. 589, and the Sui was followed by the T'ang dynasty (A.D. 618–907), which is known as "the Buddhist Age" in China.

Under the Western Han dynasty, Confucianism asserted itself as the guiding religious and political ideology. As early as 195 B.C., a state cult of Confucius was established.

The fifth Han monarch, Wu Ti (ruled 140–87 B.C.) declared the *Shih Ching* (The Book of Poetry), the *Shu
Ching* (The Book of History), the *I Ching* (The Book of
Change), the *Ch'un Ch'iu* (The Spring and Autumn Annals), and the *Li Chi* (The Book of Rites) to be Confucian
classics. The *Yo Ching* (The Manual of Music), previously
included in the so-called six classics, had disappeared by
the time of Wu Ti. Under Wu Ti, the Confucian classics
were made the basis of civil service examinations, and a
Confucian College, consisting of five faculties corresponding to the Five Classics, was inaugurated. He also employed
Confucian scholars to devise court ceremonials. However,
in the opinion of Granet, Wu Ti really wanted to be " the
high priest of a syncretistic worship, full of splendid ceremonials." [24] Being personally very superstitious, he gathered together many alchemists and sorcerers, and he offered
sacrifices to various divinities, especially to Heaven and the
Sovereign Earth. Even Confucianists accepted the new
heavenly ruler, T'ai-i (the Great One). Important state
decisions were greatly influenced by alchemists and occult-
ists who held high government positions. Forty years of
magic, alchemy, witchcraft, and occultism inevitably resulted in the wholesale persecution of witchcraft in 99 B.C.,
which resulted in the death of two prime ministers, one
empress, one crown prince, and tens of thousands of inno-
cent people.[25]

Reflecting the eclectic spirit of the age, Confucianism
was deeply influenced by the theory of divination and nu-
merology, the Yin-Yang system, Taoism, popular super-
stitions, and Legalism. This syncretistic Confucianism developed into a national religion. " It had triumphed," says
Creel, " but at the cost of such transformation that one
wonders whether it can still properly be called Confucian-

ism." [26] The Yin-Yang metaphysical theory was blended with Confucian political and social ethics by Tung Chung-shu (177–104 B.C.), who formulated the theory of correspondence between Heaven and man. According to this theory, the cosmic harmony which is based on Yin and Yang is manifested in a sociopolitical harmony which is based on Confucian principles concerning the five relationships (father-son, ruler-subject, husband-wife, elder-younger brothers, and friend-friend). Hu Shih points out that the " science of Catastrophes and Anomalies," a residue of the ancient Chinese belief in retribution, became the central doctrine of Han Confucianism. According to this " science," natural catastrophes and disasters were regarded as warnings from Heaven or retribution for actions of the state. Not only were the ancient classics reinterpreted in accordance with this belief, but new texts or complementary books to the classics were also invented. " The authority of this class of apocryphal literature became so exalted, that throughout the first two centuries of the Christian era many important state policies . . . were decided upon strange confirmations from these forged books." [27]

Between the Western and Eastern Han dynasties, the throne was usurped by Wang Mang, a relative of the royal family. Not only was he an able administrator and socioeconomic reformer, but he was also devoted to Confucian classics. He paid honors to Confucius and repaired Confucian temples. However, Wang Mang, like many Confucianists of the Han period, was superstitious and believed in omens. During his short reign, known as the Hsin (new) dynasty, he made many sweeping changes, such as nationalizing and equalizing the distribution of land and abolishing slavery. He idealized the Chou period and studied the *Annals of Lu,* edited by Confucius, as a guide for his political administration. His policies were too novel and antagonized many vested interests. A coalition of powerful families dethroned him and Wang Mang was killed at the hands of a rebel.

The empire was unified in A.D. 25 by the Eastern Han dynasty, which also venerated Confucius. A ceremonial of sacrifice in honor of Confucius was inaugurated in A.D. 59. An able but little understood Confucian thinker of this period was Wang Ch'ung (A.D. 27–97), author of *Lung Heng* (Critical Essays). He was critical of the superstitious beliefs that had crept into Confucianism, and he opposed the Yin-Yang doctrine of correspondence between Heaven and man. However, he felt congenial to Taoistic thought. "The Way of Heaven is that of spontaneity, which consists of nonactivity. . . . The school of Huang [the legendary Yellow Emperor] and Lao [Lao Tzu], in its discussion on the Way of Heaven, had found the truth." [28] In so stating, Wang Ch'ung unconsciously prepared the way for the revival of Taoist naturalism that became a vogue among the intellectuals after his time. In turn, the Taoism of this period which Fung Yu-lan calls "Neo-Taoism," considered Confucius greater than Lao Tzu, although Neo-Taoists reinterpreted the Confucian classics from Taoist perspectives. Neo-Taoism was also stimulated by Buddhism, which was spreading widely during the first three centuries of the Christian era. Huan Ti (ruled A.D. 147–167) built an altar to Lao Tzu and worshiped him with Buddha, and in the third century a temple was built in the alleged birthplace of Lao Tzu.

Meanwhile, there also developed a popular Taoist movement known as "Five-Bushel-Rice Taoism," so called because every believer was taxed five bushels of rice. Dubs suggests that the leader of this movement, Chang Ling or

Chang Tao-ling, who lived sometime during the second century A.D. in Szechuan, was a follower of Zoroastrianism (Mazdaism), as evidenced by the fire temple, a mark of Persian religion, which he built. Chang had organizational ability and developed a hierarchical priesthood. He was also ingenious in matching the Zoroastrian god, Ahura Mazda, with Chinese Tao, and Persian angels with Chinese folk deities.[29] This strange cult became rather widespread, and the Taoist organization helped maintain law and order in certain parts of China. In A.D. 184 the " Five-Bushel-Rice Taoists " rebelled against the government, and established a semitheocratic state in the territory between Shensi and Szechuan for more than thirty years. Latourette goes so far as to say that " the downfall of the Han was due to a Taoist revolt against the Confucianism dominant in the bureaucracy." [30] This cult continued to grow during the third and fourth centuries in the Yangtze delta. " In 415, in Lo-yang, the Taoist practitioner K'uo Ch'ien-chih (chien-jzh) amalgamated the Religion of Five *Tou* of Grain [Five-Bushel-Rice Taoism] with Taoism and gave himself the title previously held by Chang Ling and his successors — Heaven's Apostle, T'ien-shih (tien-shzh) ." [31] The amalgamation was successfully accomplished, and the Taoist religion thus created has survived till our day as one of the three major religious systems in China.

Buddhism

Buddhism made its appearance in the Middle Kingdom in the latter part of the first century A.D., during the reign of Ming Ti (ruled A.D. 58–75) . Initially, Buddhism found an ally in Taoism. In fact, a legend was invented to the effect that Lao Tzu had traveled to India and was the teacher of Gautama Buddha. At any rate, due to some external similarities between Buddhism and Taoism, the new faith found an opening wedge into Chinese society. Considering the fact that Buddhism was introduced to China through Central Asia, it is understandable that it found adherents in the border areas. At this time many of the Central Asian tribes were highly mobile between the eastern frontier of the Roman Empire and the western frontier of China.[32] Many of the Central Asian tribes who migrated into the northwestern frontiers of China had been influenced by Buddhism, and they began to infiltrate into Chinese life after the decline of the Eastern Han dynasty (A.D. 220). It is reported that by the end of the fourth century, nine tenths of the inhabitants of northwestern China were Buddhists. Even today the memory of early Chinese Buddhism is preserved in the famous Man-hewn Caves in northern Shansi. The countless Buddhist images carved in these sandstone cliffs were the works of the Toba Tartars, who migrated from the Lake Baikal region to northern China and established the Northern Wei dynasty (A.D. 385–532).[33]

The arrival of Kumārajīva in the fourth century marked a new page in the history of Chinese Buddhism. Not only was he a capable translator of Buddhist texts into Chinese, but he also was instrumental in fostering many able Chinese Buddhist thinkers, including Seng-chao (d. 414) and Tao-sheng (d. 434). The rise of the Sui dynasty (A.D. 589–618) helped the cause of Buddhist expansion. Its founder, Wen Ti (ruled 581–604), was an ambitious and shrewd monarch. Motivated no doubt by his personal faith but also by political considerations, Wen Ti attempted to " use Buddhism as an ideological means of unifying the races, cultures, and diverse areas of his vast empire." [34]

Fung Yu-lan makes a distinction between *Fo Hsüeh*

(Buddhist philosophy) and *Fo Chiao* (Buddhist religion) . Admittedly it is difficult to reconcile the lofty metaphysical system, logical method, and theory of knowledge of Buddhism with the morbid features of some Buddhist practices, for example, the monks' public self-mortification recorded in the Buddhist biographies.[35] Chinese Buddhism, however, managed to maintain some basic unifying factors that were Buddhist and Chinese at the same time. The chief characteristic of Chinese Buddhism is its strong emphasis on man, which "contributed to the shift in outlook from otherworldliness to this-worldliness, in objective from individual salvation to universal salvation, in philosophy from extreme doctrines to synthesis, in methods of freedom from religious discipline and philosophical understanding to pietism and practical insight, and in authority from the clergy to the layman himself." [36] This emphasis on man is clearly discernible both in the Pure Land School and in the Meditation School (Ch'an or Zen) of Chinese Buddhism.

The T'ang period (618–907) has been often characterized as "the Buddhist Age in China," with a certain amount of justification. It was also marked by the introduction of other religions as well. For example, Muslims were active both in the Canton area and in the north; and Persians, Manichaeans, and Nestorian Christians were all tolerated and protected by the government. Confucianism continued to be a guiding principle of the state, and Taoism was also accepted by the T'ang monarchs, who claimed to be Lao Tzu's descendants. However, by far the most important was Buddhism, which not only prospered as a religion but also influenced the art and culture of T'ang China a great deal. During the reign of Hsüan-tsung (ruled 712–756) , the T'ang reached its zenith. China's influence extended to Central Asia, and Ch'ang-an, the capital of China, which boasted a population of two million inhabitants, was called the largest and most elegant city of the world. It was also the center of learning, with Hanlin Yüan (the Academy of Literature) established by the royal patronage. Tsukamoto tells us that in the eighth century there were ninety-one Buddhist monasteries and nunneries in the city of Ch'ang-an alone, and for the whole country the number of Buddhist temples was estimated as 5,358.[37] " This was the time when with ample funds at their command the great monasteries, containing thousands of monks in any one of them, were able to build up impressive rituals of various kinds." [38]

Among all the Buddhist schools, the Esoteric School became the most influential during the eighth and ninth centuries. This school was introduced in China by Subhakarasinha (d. 735), Vajrabodhi (d. 723), and Amoghavajra (d. 774). Amoghavajra, known by his Chinese name, Pukhun, was held in high esteem in court as spiritual counselor to three successive emperors, and he is credited for some of the popular Chinese Buddhist rituals, such as the memorial service for the dead and the Feast of the Wandering Souls.

The rapid growth of Buddhism created many problems too. Scholars of Confucianism were critical of the excessive wealth and power of Buddhist institutions. In 819 Buddha's bones were officially received at the Chinese capital, and this occasion prompted a noted Confucianist, Han Yü (768–824), to present a strongly worded protest to the emperor. In 845, under the Taoist emperor Wu-tsung, a severe persecution of Buddhists took place, in which 4,600 monasteries and 40,000 other edifices were destroyed and more than 260,000 priests and nuns were forced back into lay life. Although this persecution was a serious blow to Buddhism, it gradually recovered in subsequent decades. Ironically, this persecution aimed at Buddhism gave a death blow to Manichaeism, Zoroastrianism, and Nestorian Christianity in China.

Neo-Confucianism

The greater part of the Middle Kingdom was unified in A.D. 960 by the Sung dynasty (960–1279). However, the northernmost part of China was ruled by the Khitan tribe, who established the Liao dynasty (907–1124) ; this marked the beginning of a series of barbarian dynasties. The periodic eruption of the northern tribes throughout Chinese history has been attributed variously to population pressure, economic needs, and climatic change in the steppes. Whatever the reasons, the northern tribes began to penetrate China proper after the tenth century A.D. They were no longer just troublemakers in the border areas; they were determined to rule the Middle Kingdom itself. In the twelfth century the Liao was replaced by the Chin (Gold) kingdom of the Juchen tribe, while south China was under the rule of the Southern Sung dynasty (1127–1279). In the thirteenth century, the Chin was defeated by the Mongols, who established the Yüan dynasty (1279–1368) in China. Although the Ming dynasty (1368–1644) restored " Chinese rule," the Ming was followed by the Manchu rule of the Ch'ing dynasty (1644–1911). It was during this millennium (960–1911), which saw many non-Chinese monarchs on the throne, that the Confucian tradition reasserted itself as the leading cultural force in China.

The Sung period (960–1279) was an important era in the cultural history of China. Not only did various kinds of art and culture prosper, but, aided by block printing, books became accessible to a wider reading circle. Also, as a by-product of the encroachment of the northern tribes, Chinese culture penetrated southern China, as evidenced by the fact that many intellectual leaders from this period onward came from south of the Yangtze River. In the main, the Sung monarchs depended on Confucianism as the socio-political ideology, without, however, rejecting Buddhism and Taoism. The founder of the Sung dynasty sponsored the first printed edition of the Chinese Tripitaka (Buddhist scriptures), and the second emperor erected a huge stupa in the capital. In the twelfth century, Emperor Hui-tsung came under Taoist influence. " By imperial decree the Buddha and his Arhats [Arahats] were enrolled in the Taoist pantheon; temples and monasteries were allowed to exist only on condition of describing themselves as Tao-ist." [39] The Southern Sung dynasty (1127–1279) did not favor Buddhism either; it was " the only great dynasty which did not revise the Tripitaka." [40] Lack of royal patron-age, however, did not eliminate the influence of Buddhism, especially among the educated. Both Wang An-shih in the eleventh century and Chu Hsi in the twelfth century de-plored the fact that the intelligentsia of their times turned toward Buddhism and Taoism, neglecting Confucianism.[41] Most creative among the Buddhist schools was the Medi-tation School, Ch'an (or Zen). The total effect of Ch'an, which was both Buddhist and Chinese in ethos, was " to abandon the entire Buddhist organization, creed, and lit-erature and to reduce Buddhism to concern with man him-self." [42] Also, the Ch'an master was pragmatic enough " to test his spiritual attainment in life activity and express it in art and poetry." [43] It was this school of Buddhism that greatly stimulated Neo-Confucianism.

Fung Yu-lan points out that the foundation of Neo-

Confucianism was laid through the efforts of Han Yü and Li Ao in the T'ang dynasty.[44] Ch'u Chai, however, feels that the term "Neo-Confucianism" was a misnomer: "The Neo-Confucianists were no doubt the offspring of Confucius, but in their early years they were believers in Taoism and Buddhism, and only afterward went back to Confucius."[45] In fact, Neo-Confucianism was a complex cultural and semireligious movement. It was a cultural nationalism asserting itself during a time when China was politically at a low ebb. It was a "secular" movement, a reaction against the decades of preoccupation with Buddhism and Taoism. It was a "further development of Ch'annism," in the sense that moral activities were evaluated from a supermoral perspective, which was provided by Ch'an (Buddhism).[46] It was also a reaction against Ch'an's subjective philosophy which denied the existence of objective reason, for Neo-Confucianists "postulated the basic concept of Li (reason), which has universal validity, and which the human mind is capable of seeking and verifying."[47] In short, "Neo-Confucianism was a kind of summing up or revision of the ethics, morals, and beliefs of the past, and as such was in keeping with the spirit of the times."[48]

Neo-Confucianism developed in three stages: (1) the Reason School in the Sung period (960–1279), (2) the Mind School in the Ming period (1368–1644), and (3) the Empirical School in the Ch'ing period (1644–1911). The objectives of Neo-Confucianism were succinctly stated by Ch'eng I: "For moral cultivation, we must practice reverence; for intellectual improvement, we must extend our knowledge to the utmost."[49] It was not only an intellectual movement, but also a moral and semireligious, or a secular religious, movement. The Neo-Confucianists raised

the Four Books — the *Ta Hsüeh* (The Great Learning),
Chung Yung (Golden Mean or Central Harmony), *Lun
Yü* (The Analects), and *Meng Tzu* (The Works of Mencius) — to canonical status, which had been previously
reserved for the Five Classics (The Books of Poetry, History, Change, and Rites, and The Spring and Autumn
Annals). In contrast to early Confucianism, which was
primarily concerned with human relations and the social
duties of man, Neo-Confucianism developed a metaphysical system and emphasized the importance of a higher understanding of the universe, through which moral values
can be transformed into supermoral values.

Chu Hsi (1130–1200) was considered the spokesman of
the Reason School in the Sung period. In his youth he
studied Buddhism, but later he became its severe critic.
According to him, there is Li (principles or laws) for everything, and the Li is the highest ideal, prototype, and standard of things. Not only did he hold Li as the metaphysical
principle of government, but he also presupposed the presence of Li even before the formation of heaven and earth.
To him, the ultimate standard of the universe as a whole
is *T'ai Chi* (the Supreme Ultimate) : " Everything has an
ultimate, which is the ultimate Li. That which unites and
embraces the Li of heaven, earth, and all things is the Supreme Ultimate." [50] Thus, according to the Reason School
of Neo-Confucianism, only by bringing out the Supreme
Ultimate that is within us, through " the extension of
knowledge " and " the attentiveness of mind," can we attain
complete and sudden enlightenment.

The religious and cultural situation in China changed
in the thirteenth century with the rise of the Mongols.
Little need be said about Jenghiz Khan (d. 1227), who
swept out of the steppes and conquered most of the known

world. The ancestral religion of the Mongols was shamanistic and animistic, and they worshiped the spirit of light or the sky. Jenghiz (which means " the spirit of light ") Khan believed in the Everlasting Sky's intervention in his own destiny.[51] But, once the Mongols had established the Yüan dynasty (1279–1368) under Kublai Khan (d. 1294), they proved to be tolerant of all religions. John of Montecorvino and other Roman Catholic missionaries were welcomed, and a number of Nestorian Christians were found among Mongol army officers, government officials, and members of the court. In Baghdad, a monk of Chinese background was elevated in 1281 to the position of patriarch of the entire Nestorian Church, and a Nestorian monk was made Kublai's envoy and sent to Frankish courts in 1287. Kublai, despite his personal dislike of Taoism, conferred the title of Heavenly Father on the head of the Taoist cult, and Kublai's successors restored the civil service examination based on Confucian classics and bestowed honors on Confucius, Mencius, and Yen Hui. Nevertheless, the Mongol period was not conducive to the development of Neo-Confucianism. After his Tibetan campaign, Kublai became a convert to Tibetan Buddhism (Lamaism). "Hitherto, whatever may have been the religious proclivities of individual emperors, the empire had been a Confucian institution." [52] But, having no such preconceived notions, the Mongol rulers appointed Lamaist ecclesiastics as imperial preceptors, the highest religious post in the realm, and regarded Confucianism merely as one of many religions in China.

Following the " alien " rule of the Mongols, the Ming dynasty (1368–1644) made a conscious effort to restore the pre-Mongol type of " Confucian state," a centralized bureaucratic civil government, with Confucianism as the official faith of the nation and Confucian classics as the basis of the civil examination system. This atmosphere gave a new impetus to the Confucian tradition. While the school of Chu Hsi remained strong during this period, Wang Yang-ming (1472–1529) systematized the so-called Mind School of Neo-Confucianism. He had a varied career as a judge, army general, and high government official, besides being a scholar. Once he offended an influential eunuch and was sent to a remote mountain region, and having no intellectual companion he concentrated on meditation. One night he suddenly came to understand what was meant by " investigating things for the purpose of extending knowledge to the utmost." He came to realize: " My nature is, of course, sufficient. I was wrong in looking for principles in things and affairs." [53] Thus, rejecting Chu Hsi's view of the Li (reason) as eternal and independent of human consciousness, Wang equated the Li with the mind and interpreted the individual mind as the manifestation of the universal Mind. In his own words: " The mind of man is Heaven. There is nothing that is not included in the mind of man. All of us are this single Heaven, but because of the obscurings caused by selfishness, the original state of Heaven is not made manifest." [54] In so stating, Wang, despite his severe criticism of Buddhism, revealed the Buddhist influence on his thinking, for as Fung Yu-lan points out, " before the introduction of Buddhism there was in Chinese philosophy only the mind, but not THE MIND." [55]

It was also during this period that Roman Catholic missionaries engaged in evangelical and educational works in China. Notable among them was Matthew Ricci, who held a unique position in China (1583–1610) as a missionary, teacher of science, and an accomplished scholar of Confucian classics. Ricci was deeply impressed by Confucius and stated, " Of all the pagan sects known to Europe, I know of no people who fell into fewer errors in the early ages of their antiquity than did the Chinese." [56] With rare sensitivity, this " missionary-mandarin " came to feel that Neo-Confucianism deviated from the teachings of Confucius and Mencius and that it was tinged with Buddhism: " The doctrine most commonly held among the literati at present seems to me to have been taken from the sect of idols "; and so he added that " this philosophy we endeavor to refute, not only from reason but also from the testimony of their own ancient philosophers to whom they are indebted for all the philosophy they have." [57]

The declining Ming dynasty was easily taken over by the rising Manchu Tartars who established the Ch'ing dynasty (1644–1911). Although the Manchus continued to worship their own tribal deities privately, they accepted Chinese culture and Confucianism more than any other " barbarians " who had ruled China. Some of the early Manchu monarchs were tempted by Catholicism, but the controversy as to whether or not Chinese ancestral rites could be tolerated in the Roman Church alienated them from Christianity.[58] During the Manchu period, both the Reason School and the Mind School of Neo-Confucianism continued to grow. But there were some Confucianists who rejected the Neo-Confucianism of the Sung and Ming periods and advocated a restoration of " Han Confucianism " on the ground that the Confucianism of the Han period (206 B.C.–A.D. 220) was not contaminated by Buddhism. The Manchu period produced some independent thinkers such as Yen Yüan (d. 1704) and Li Kung (d. 1748). Probably the most creative thinker of this period was Tai Cheng (d. 1777), who has been characterized as an empiricist. According to him: " Since desire is part of our nature, it has its rightful place, just as the vital force has its rightful place beside reason. As a matter of fact, reason can only be discovered in daily events and experience, or in short, in the vital force itself." [59] In general, however, the traditions of Chu Hsi and Wang Yang-ming were so strong that thinkers like Yen, Li, and Tai were not understood by their contemporaries.

Triumph of the Confucian Tradition

" Family-ism "

Usually Chinese religions have been characterized by animistic polytheism, ancestor worship, ceremonial emphasis, and humanistic and ethical tendencies. As our brief survey tells us, the Chinese from the second millennium before Christ have taken for granted the existence of spirits and ghosts. Also, the ancient Chinese worshiped Shang Ti (" Ruler Above ") or T'ien (Heaven), and the " Mandate from Heaven " has been the central doctrine of the philosophical systems as well as popular beliefs. While the term " worship " may be somewhat misleading, it nevertheless indicates the Chinese attitude of reverence toward Heaven, ancestral spirits, and the spirits of the sages. Traditionally, the emperor considered it his duty as the Son of Heaven and the representative of the people to pay homage to Heaven. State officials and individuals were encouraged to venerate various sages, especially Confucius, and shrines and temples were established in honor of the Wise Teachers. At home, ancestral spirits were venerated as though they were alive, and the continuity of the family through the male line is as important to the Chinese as the transmigration of souls is to the Hindus. While the Chinese have not lacked an aptitude for metaphysics and mysticism, their primary tendencies have been rationalistic, humanistic, this-worldly. At the same time their passion for this-worldly values, such as wealth, health, and longevity, has resulted in the development of numerous kinds of divination, astrology, dream interpretation, fortunetelling, and witchcraft, especially among the uneducated people. The strong element of superstition in folk religion " is based on the belief that the Great Ultimate (*T'ai Chi*), Yin Yang or the negative and positive cosmic forces, the Five Elements (*wu hsing*), and the Eight Trigrams (*pa kua*) could be so co-ordinated and controlled as to bring about good fortune." [60]

Underlying these confusing and contradictory tendencies in Chinese religions is the cosmic-human, monistic world view which we have called " Universism." According to this view, the universe is supported and governed by Tao (Eternal Order). Earlier, we quoted several different translations of the opening passage of *Tao Te Ching: "Tao k'o tao fei ch'ang Tao."* Soothill's literal translation helps us to realize how elusive this word " Tao " is. " [The] Tao [that] can be tao'd (or ' expressed ') is not [the] eternal Tao." [61] Although Taoism claimed this word to designate its system, all other schools of philosophy, religion, and ethics have also been concerned with the theory and practice of Tao. Using Martin Buber's category of " I-Thou relationship " we may characterize the differences among the three major religions of China as follows: Taoism emphasizes an " I-Thou relationship " between man and nature; Confucianism, an " I-Thou relationship " between man and man; and Buddhism, an " I-Thou relationship " between being and nonbeing. Notwithstanding these theoretical differences, " the great mass of the people have no prejudices and make no embarrassing distinctions; they belong to none of the three religions, or, more correctly, they belong to all three." [62] Hocking considers it " as one of the peculiar points of Chinese psychology that a good householder can be Confucian in his daily habits and yet call on Taoist or Buddhist priests to conduct a funeral." [63] In a more whimsical mood, Lin Yutang states that " every Chinese is a Confucian when he is successful and a Taoist when he is a failure." [64]

While it is in keeping with the eclectic tendency of the Chinese to regard *San Chiao* (the three religions, Confucianism, Buddhism, and Taoism) as three facets of the same truth, the most important among them is Confucianism. In this situation, we must interpret the term " Confucianism," not in a narrow sense referring to the teachings of Confucius and other teachers of his school, but as a historic expression of the tradition of Literati (*Ju*), which has been the main thread of Chinese culture. Seen in its total historic setting, the teachings of the sages, which undoubtedly provided the core of the tradition of Literati, have during the past two thousand years undergone transformations, conditioned by the sociocultural and historic factors and influenced by other religions and systems of thought. " Confucianism thus regarded is a convenient term for that complex of moral and cultural forces which has made the Chinese what they are today. One can best understand it by attempting to abstract the distinctive qualities of Chinese life as it has actually been flowing on down to the present, its hopes and fears, its incentives to noble conduct and its inhibitions, its ethical dynamic and its religious implications." [65]

But in what sense is Confucianism, even in the broadest sense of the term, religious? This is a difficult question, mostly because our understanding of the term " religion " is based on the conceptualizations of Western religions. But our task is not to look for religion in the Western sense in a Chinese setting, but rather to try to grasp the " religious " characteristics of Chinese life. Wing-tsit Chan rightly reminds us that if religion is interpreted as an organized system, then Confucianism cannot be classified as a religion. In this connection, it is interesting to note that " the last of the great Confucianists, K'ang Yu-wei (1858– 1927), believing that the Western powers became strong because they had organized religions, made repeated attempts to establish Confucianism as a formal and official cult. But he met with no success." [66]

But the fact that Confucianism is not organized à la Christianity or Islam does not make it any less religious, just as the lack of belief in personal deities does not make Buddhism nonreligious. In fact, Confucianism never developed its own specifically ecclesiastical organization precisely because it regarded the empirical sociopolitical order *in toto* as the framework of its holy community. This is what was implied by the earlier statement that the Chinese did not make a distinction between the sacred and the secular. Tao is to be realized in the midst of everyday life or in and through the empirical sociopolitical realm. In China, religion did not create its own holy community apart from human fellowships; it sanctified these human fellowships.

Of the various human fellowships, the family and the nation provided the two focuses for Chinese religion. In a sense, Winston King and others are right in characterizing the religious element of Chinese culture as a state cult.[67] However, throughout the long history of China, the state was regarded as the projection of the family, which alone commanded supreme respect and maintained the strongest grip on the loyalties of individuals. For example, out of the five reciprocal relationships — between ruler and subject, father and son, elder and younger brothers, husband and wife, and friend and friend — three are family relationships. Moreover, " in the *Erh Ya,* which is the oldest dictionary of the Chinese language, dating from before the Christian era, there are more than one hundred terms for various family relationships, most of which have no equivalent in the English language." [68] This does not mean that the Chinese neglected other human relationships. On the contrary, the Chinese had a keen sense of being involved in a series of relationships, including, in addition to the family relationship, one's relationship to the village community, to one's guild, and to the universe, all of which constitute a set of concentric circles. The central core of these circles is the family relationship. The Confucian tradition was the theoretical expression and the rational justification of the Chinese family-centered world view, which may be characterized as the religion of " Family-ism."

The importance of the family cult in China is hard to exaggerate. It explains why Confucianism and Taoism did not develop any system comparable to the parish in Christianity, and why Buddhism in China became to all intents and purposes a family religion. In a traditional Chinese house one finds a family shrine in the main hall. In the central portion of the shrine are placed the ancestral tablets, going back five generations including the last deceased head of the family. On both sides of the shrine are inscribed names of various deities and guardian spirits of Confucian, Taoist, and Buddhist origins. In other parts of the house one also finds an assortment of tablets of guardian spirits, such as the gate god, the kitchen god, and gods of bed-

chambers. Candles, incense-sticks, wine, and food are offered
before the shrines of these gods on the new and full moons
and other festival occasions. Some of the important festivals
include the New Year's Day, the Dragon Boat Festival (the
fifth day of the fifth month) , and the Mid-Autumn Festival
(the fifteenth day of the eighth month) , and the day of the
winter solstice. More important are the religious observ-
ances centering around " transitional rites " (*rites de passage*) , such as birth, naming, marriage, sickness and recovery, death and burial, and memorial days of ancestors.
" Whenever anything of significance happens to the family
. . . the dead ancestors are informed, for they are still
concerned and interested though unseen." [69]

On such special occasions as funerals and memorial days,
Taoist or Buddhist priests are called in to perform services.
If sickness requires the attention of some deities known
for their healing powers, either the sick or his representatives may visit the temples and give offerings. Otherwise,
religious observance is pretty much a family affair. If the
head of the family is pious, he serves the family shrines
himself; if not, his wife is entrusted with this task. Should
the family be engaged in a trade that involves a number
of apprentices living in the household, the youngest appren-
tice must serve the needs of the patron deity of the trade.
Joyous occasions bring relatives and friends to the family,
and they exchange gifts and enjoy merrymaking with the
members of the family. Sad occasions also bring relatives
and friends, and they also observe mourning, depending
on their relationship to the family.

Of course, similar examples of the family cult may be
cited in other parts of the world. In all religions throughout the world, the family plays a significant role, because
" regardless of other social arrangements the individual

family is an omnipresent social unit." [70] This is especially true where the enlarged family is found, for example, in India, Israel, many parts of Africa, and among the Slavic peoples. The old Roman *familia,* which included not only a householding unit but members of the *gens,* or the larger unit, and servants, also had its cult. Such family and kinship cults have tended to disappear with the disintegration of the enlarged family, with changes in sociopolitical and economic conditions, or under the influence of powerful religions. In China, however, the family cult maintained its vitality to the twentieth century because the Chinese family was not only a biological, economic, kinship, and social unit, but also a prototype of the human community. Chinese " Family-ism " implies more than the centrality of the family cult in the lives of the Chinese people; " Family-ism "·determines the values and norms of behavior of the people in all spheres of life.

National Family

The influence of " Family-ism " has produced among the Chinese what Lin Yutang calls " the family mind " at the expense of the social mind. " The family system and the village system, which is the family raised to a higher exponent, account for all there is to explain in the Chinese social life. Face, favor, privilege, gratitude, courtesy, official corruption, hospitality, justice, and finally the whole government — all spring from the family and village system." [71] In this respect, Confucianism has left lasting marks on the Chinese sociopolitical order.

Undoubtedly, Confucius' personal experience influenced his political theory. Living in a time of social and political unrest, due largely to the decline of the Chou monarchy, Confucius hoped to see the emergence of a new central authority which would unify Chinese society. He did not believe in government by the people because he considered the masses ignorant. Rather, he was convinced that only the virtuous and capable should rule the nation for the people. " If those in the higher rank of society be devoted to ritual, then none of the common people can dare not to venerate them. If they be lovers of justice, then none of the common people can dare not to obey them. If they be worthy of confidence, then none of the common people can dare to prevaricate." [72] In essence, what Confucius had in mind was government by moral example. " Not negative punishment but positive example; not tirades about what people should not do but education as to what they should do. Not a police state dominated by fear but a co-operative commonwealth in which there is mutual understanding and good will between the rulers and the ruled." [73] To this end, he advocated the principles of *jen* (human-hearted-ness) , *li* (rites, ceremonies, proper conduct) , *chun* (loyalty to one's nature) , *shu* (practical application of the principles) , and *chung yung* (the Central Harmony) .

There is no question that Confucius considered filial piety (*hsiao*) the supreme virtue and the basis of general morality. Theoretically at least, filial piety implied respect for all parents, and the same principle can be extended to one's relations to all elders and superiors as well as to the spirits of ancestors. According to this scheme, good for man means good for man as a member of the family. If the individual is properly brought up within his family and if he is a filial son, there is every reason to believe that he will turn out to be a good citizen. Furthermore, if a person is a filial son, he cannot be a criminal. This hierarchical ethics, however, presupposed reciprocity in the sense that parents and superiors were expected to be just, thoughtful, and tender ·

in their relations to children and inferiors.

Underlying the principle of the five relationships was a metaphysico-social structure based on the concepts of *ming* (name) and *fen* (duty). The term *ming* refers to one's position and status in society and universe, and one's status defines his duties to others. The best way to realize Tao is not so much to gain speculative knowledge about the will of Heaven as to know one's position in relation to others and to live accordingly. For example, one may not be in a position to take an active part in the administration of the country, but the sage taught, " Be filial, only be filial and friendly with your brothers, and you will be helping in the administration of the country." [74] It follows, then, that the best way to serve the spirits of the dead is to begin by serving men who are alive. Thus, the principle of filial piety can be extended to the whole gamut of ethics: " My way has one string which threads it all together." [75] However, the concepts of *ming* (name) and *fen* (duty) do not rest on a stereotyped formalism or the mechanical observance of rules and regulations. " The possession of high station without generosity, the conduct of ritual without reverence, the discharge of mourning duties without grief, these are the things I cannot bear to see." [76] Indeed, the way of Confucius was not an easy one. It required constant effort to train one's mind and discipline one's heart and will, and Confucius was convinced that such moral training, which involves the discipline of one's whole personality, must begin at home.

From the third century B.C. to the twentieth century, China was ruled by a succession of imperial dynasties. Empires in China were based on a curious combination of an enlarged family system and a centralized bureaucratic state. Administratively, the empire was divided into provinces,

prefectures, towns, and villages, but the unit of social organization was the enlarged family. The family provided
the basis for social cohesion, and family authority bul-
warked state authority. In one sense, the state was a " national family," with the emperor fulfilling the role of
father. Just as in the individual family, so also in the " national family " the guiding ethical principles were the Confucian concepts of filial piety and paternal love. It must be
remembered in this connection that the family was the connecting link between ancestors and descendants. Ancestors
were to be honored, and descendants must be procreated
in order to maintain the family organism and also to continue to honor ancestors.[77] The head of the family was the
pivotal point between these two lines, and as such he was
held responsible for the welfare of both the living and deceased members of the family. He was not only the head
of the family but also the " priest " of the religion of
" Family-ism," although he could delegate the priestly function either to his wife or to his elder son. Similarly, the
emperor as the pivotal point of the " national family " was
concerned with the welfare of the people as well as the
spiritual welfare of the national ancestors and Heaven.
In short, the emperor was both the father image and the
supreme priest.

On the other hand, the nation was also a centralized
bureaucratic state, with the Confucian principles of *li*
(ceremonials) and *hsing* (penalties). In this respect, too,
Confucianism provided the guiding principles for the solidarity of the nation. At the top of the government was the
emperor (the Son of Heaven) who was given a mandate
(from Heaven) to rule as long as he could keep law and
order. He was held responsible for mismanagement of the
government, and also for natural disasters such as flood and

pestilence, which were regarded either as warnings to him from Heaven or signs that his mandate was coming to an end. In this situation, it is readily understandable that astrology and astronomy played an important role in Chinese government. Under the emperor was an enormous bureaucracy made up of Confucian scholars recruited from the gentry, and beneath the gentry was the peasant base of society. " The peasantry was subdivided into several strata along occupational lines: the farmer at the top, and in descending order, the gardener, woodsman, artisan, merchant, weaver, servant, and unskilled laborer. At the very bottom were the outcasts: the jobless, bandits, smugglers, convicts, slaves, actors, ragpickers, barbers, and prostitutes." [78]

Although the monarch had ultimate authority in all legislative, executive, and judicial matters, the power of the bureaucracy was considerable. For example, except under a few despotic emperors, the promulgation of laws was not solely the act of the throne. " Laws were developed by Confucianist scholars in agreement with the moral system, and promulgated by the ruler. In promulgating a law and in deciding law cases, the ruler was bound by the moral system." [79] In this situation, the bureaucrats who interpreted the moral law and who transmitted the Confucian moral principles enjoyed prestige and power. These bureaucrats were chosen from the gentry on the basis of an examination on the Confucian classics, and as a result new personnel were regularly brought into the ruling class. " The system gave the officeholders and the bureaucratic gentry an ideological training that was matched only by the training of the Brahmin in traditional India." [80] This bureaucratic system was initiated by the Legalists in the third century B.C. From time to time offices were coveted by some Taoists and Buddhists, but the Confucianists who began to monopolize the bureaucracy under the Han dynasty managed to maintain their supremacy until the twentieth century despite the ups and downs of the ruling dynasties. Even some of the monarchs who had little sympathy with Confucianism knew " the latent power of Confucianism, the endemic Confucianism of orderly family and community relationships which could bring harmony to society, and Confucian political theory, which provided the most complete body of sanctions available for one who would govern a unified Chinese empire." [81]

In retrospect it is apparent that Confucianism triumphed both as the articulate expression of " Family-ism," which was the religion of the national family and the individual family, and also as the guiding ideology of the bureaucratic state. The gradual ascendancy of Confucianism may be symbolized by the honors conferred on Confucius posthumously. He was made " Duke " in A.D. 1, " the Foremost Teacher " in 637, " King " in 739, and " the Perfect Sage " in 1013. Finally, in 1906, the same sacrifice was offered to him as to Shang Ti.[82] The triumph of the Confucian tradition was decisive. The veneration of Confucius achieved the status of a state cult. Confucianism became the backbone of bureaucratic government. The family system was regarded as the cornerstone of the social and political life of the people. Even the " barbarians " who ruled China found Confucianism indispensable. While Confucianism did not develop its own " holy community " as such, the Confucian-inspired " Family-ism " developed what might be termed an " immanental theocracy," grounded securely in the family system.

CRISIS OF "FAMILY-ISM"

From Empire to Republic

The emergence of a republic in modern China will be discussed with reference to three factors: (1) an inherent weakness of "Family-ism," (2) the deterioration of Manchu rule, and (3) the impact of the West. Although we discuss them separately, in reality these three factors were closely interrelated and intertwined.

As noted earlier, the family relationship is the central core of the Chinese family-oriented world view, which we have called the religion of "Family-ism." This Confucian tradition taught that filial piety could be translated automatically into guiding principles for all social and political problems.

"If there is righteousness in the heart, there will be beauty in the character; if there is beauty in the character, there will be harmony in the home; if there is harmony in the home, there will be order in society; and when there is order in society, there will be peace in the world " (*The Great Learning*). This idealistic — or even romantic — political philosophy never took adequate account of the inevitable conflict between family loyalty and national loyalty. The result was the development of a "family mind" at the expense of the social mind. " It is only fair to mention that Confucius never intended family consciousness to take the place of social or national consciousness and develop into a form of magnified selfishness — consequences which, with all his practical wisdom, he had not foreseen." [83] Confucian moral ideals applied to politics without provision of adequate institutional checks fostered a political system that was vulnerable to nepotism and corruption. Also, Confucianists " sometimes fell into the common error of assuming that their morality can be realized automatically, through the preaching of lofty doctrines, without regard for the practical difficulties that lie in the way of realization of these doctrines." [84] The Confucian philosophy of moral harmony never articulated a philosophy of law or social control, and despite an impressive bureaucracy that carried on the functions of the central government, in reality the most effective form of social control was maintained by communal " village " governments. The central government " à la Confucius with its tremendous moralizing has always been one of the most corrupt the world has ever seen." [85]

Together with its moralism, Confucianism had an element of determinism, which created a sense of apathy among people in regard to political justice. Hu Shih traces the Confucian determinism to an ancient belief in divination, and suggests that it is a logical outcome of a naturalistic conception of the universe. " A man who believes in determinism will abide by his lot, and will not worry about the pleasure or displeasure of the gods." [86] Confucius himself held that if the truth prevails, it is fate; if it fails, it is also fate. In addition, the lack of a specifically religious and ecclesiastical organization deprived the people of an effective spokesman for social justice. The rulers were suspicious of religious societies which might become too powerful as a social force. Consequently, many of the spontaneous religious movements developed " secret societies," which never had opportunities to exercise moral restraining power on the government.

Ironically, Confucianism, in trying to model the nation after the image of the family, created a huge bureaucratic state with a rigid system of social status. While the teachings of the ancient sages no doubt served as a corrective to the despotic tendencies of the rulers, Confucianism after many centuries of being the official ideology of the bureaucracy tended to uphold the *status quo*. In viewing the state as a projection of the patriarchal family, Confucianism was compelled to rationalize the worst features of the patriarchal system, namely, authoritarianism and the irrational prerogatives of the elders over the inferiors. Consequently, Confucianism, with all its humanitarian and democratic elements, was exploited by the ruling dynasties, especially by the Manchus, as " a broad foundation upon which they might base their theocratic, paternal, and autocratic powers." [87]

In all fairness to the Manchu rule (1644–1911) we must recognize that they were the most " Sinized " of all the so-called barbarians who ruled China. Under the Manchu rule, externally at least, China appeared to be the epitome of a Confucian state. The Manchu rulers kept the pre-Manchu system of administration, such as the grand secretariat which was the highest advisory body to the throne. They regarded the Confucian bureaucracy as the backbone of the central government, and the family system as the unit of social cohesion. The Manchu monarch considered himself the Son of Heaven, and offered sacrifices to Heaven. The state cult of Confucius was promoted, and it was a Manchu emperor who conferred the supreme posthumous honor to Confucius by offering the same sacrifice to him as to Shang Ti.

However, there was another side to the Manchu regime. Privately, the Manchu rulers continued to worship their own tribal deities; they retained the " banners " or their own military machine and placed Manchu forces in key places in addition to regular Chinese regiments. The Manchu tribal nobility stood above ruling Chinese gentry. Each of the six governmental departments had a Manchu minister in addition to a Chinese minister. Intermarriages between the Manchu and the Chinese were discouraged. The monarch was a despot, and his power was not encroached upon by the ministers; he might or might not accept the recommendations of the grand secretariat. High officials were removed, accused, investigated, put into jail, or ordered to strangle themselves at the will of the throne. Notwithstanding the Confucian principles promoted by the regime, the masses were made to " tremble and obey " their superiors, especially the Manchus. " The happy and prosperous state, as pictured by the Manchus," says Eckel, " was one built on filial respect and blind obedience of the people. This training must begin with the children and be carried into every department of home and state." [88]

The effectiveness of the combination of Manchu despotic rule and traditional Confucian " Family-ism " is evident in the fact that the Manchu rulers expanded their domain to Mongolia, Tibet, Formosa, and Sinkiang. During the reign of Ch'ien Lung (ruled 1736–1796), Manchu rule reached its zenith, with Korea, Annam, Burma, and Ryukyu added to the Chinese empire as vassals. However, political corruption, economic distress, and the advance of the Western powers brought about the deterioration of the Manchu regime in the nineteenth century.

In 1861 the Hsien Feng emperor died, and Yehonala or Tz'u Hsi, the concubine of the deceased emperor, controlled the affairs of state as empress dowager during the reigns of T'ung Chih (ruled 1861–1875) and Kuang Hsü (ruled 1875–1908). She was reactionary, scheming, ruthless, and violently antiforeign. China under her iron rule faced internal as well as external crises. Among its vassal states,

Burma was taken by Britain, Indo-China was occupied by France, while Sinkiang and Outer Mongolia were exploited by Russia. After the Sino-Japanese War (1894–1895), Formosa was ceded to Japan, and various other concessions were made in favor of Russia, Germany, France, and Britain. Shortly after Sun Yat-sen's unsuccessful rebellion (1895) in Canton, reformers persuaded the Kuang Hsü emperor to reorganize the government. But their plot to eliminate the empress dowager backfired, with the result that the reformers were executed. After the antiforeign and anti-Christian Boxer Rebellion in 1900, Tz'u Hsi reluctantly agreed to accept a constitutional monarchy, to reorganize the government structure, and to revise various laws. In 1907, the establishment of a National Assembly at a future date was announced, and in 1908 a tentative constitution was proposed. The reform program faced a crisis in 1908 with the death of both the emperor and the empress dowager, leaving young and helpless Pu Yi on the dragon throne. In the midst of the confusion, the National Assembly was convened in 1910, and although a constitution of nineteen articles was promulgated by the throne in the following year, it was overshadowed by anti-Manchu and prorepublican movements. In 1911, Pu Yi, the last Manchu monarch, abdicated and China became a republic.

The decline of the Manchu rule in China coincided with the rise of European colonial imperialism, which had both economic and political interests. This was not the first time China had encountered Western powers. In comparing the first Western encounter with China in the sixteenth century and the second encounter in the nineteenth century, Toynbee observes that in the first round the Chinese remained the master of the situation, while in the second round it could not compete with the technological challenge of the

West. In his opinion, the West presented itself as a " strange religion " in the sixteenth century, and as such the West was welcomed at first but was rebuffed in the end, whereas in the second encounter the West presented itself primarily as a " strange technology," and through it the Western way of life was destined to influence Chinese society and culture.[89]

The contrast between the West and China during the nineteenth century can hardly be exaggerated. China was an agrarian nation, a self-contained country with the age-old Confucian culture grounded in the family system and ruled by the autocratic Manchu regime, while the West, having undergone the industrial revolution, was advancing in science, technology, and commerce. Also, many Western nations had constitutional governments which guaranteed the liberty and dignity of their citizens. Understandably, China tried to resist the influence of Western civilization which was so diametrically opposed to its own. But the combined effect of the advance of the West and the decline of the Manchu rule brought about a series of far-reaching social revolutions, including the revolution led by Sun Yat-sen in 1911 which overthrew the Manchu rule.

Crisis of " Family-ism "

The revolutionary movement in twentieth-century China had many undercurrents. First was an anti-Manchu element, which wanted to restore the rule of China to the Chinese. Second was a trend in favor of a republican form of government and against authoritarian, imperial rule. Third was an iconoclastic spirit which, under the influence of Western science and democracy, vigorously attacked the state cult, as well as Confucian-inspired moral and cultural values. Fourth was a tendency to reject not only the traditional culture and institutions but also the basic world view of the Chinese, epitomized by " Family-ism."

The Chinese resentment against the autocratic Manchu rule helped the revolutionary movement to overthrow the Manchu regime, but it was more difficult to introduce a republican form of government into China. The father of the revolution was Sun Yat-sen, a physician by training, educated in Hawaii and Hongkong, and influenced by Western civilization and Christianity. His major slogan was " modernization without Westernization " of China. Another important figure was Yüan Shih-k'ai, a Chinese trained in the art of practical politics during the latter days of the intrigue-ridden Manchu regime. When the Manchu government crumbled, he was in control of the army and the finances of China. It was he who became the provisional president of the new republic, with which he had little sympathy or understanding. Under him, the new government became a military dictatorship. Yüan not only dissolved Sun Yat-sen's Kuomintang (the National People's Party) but also suspended the National Assembly. Yüan died in 1916 without realizing his dream of founding a new dynasty. After his death, northern China was ruled for a decade by a number of competing war lords. In the south, Sun's effort to reorganize his Kuomintang was not successful. Ousted by his own party, and not understood by the Western powers to whom he appealed for help, Sun's only support came from Chinese living abroad and from the U.S.S.R. With the assistance of Russian advisers, Sun reorganized the Kuomintang, which held its first congress in Canton in 1924. His efforts to reach an agreement with the northern war lords failed and he died in 1925, leaving behind him a Kuomintang that was steadily gaining strength.

The guiding principles of the Kuomintang were stated

in Sun Yat-sen's *San Min Chu I* (The Three Principles of the People), and included the sovereignty of the people, national independence, and a sufficient livelihood for all. Sun was convinced of the necessity of a unified nation-state, based on the principle of equality of all ethnic groups before the law. He advocated popular sovereignty, while recognizing the need of rule by experts. He felt that China, a great agrarian nation, could prosper by taking full advantage of modern civilization. Sun's concepts of nationalism and democracy were totally unknown in the China of his time, and realizing that these concepts must be grafted onto the continuum of Chinese tradition, Sun interpreted nationalism as the goal of the ancient Confucian utopia, and democracy as the will of Heaven. He made frequent references to the Chinese virtue of filial devotion and the Chinese love of harmony and peace. It was Sun's genuine belief that the Confucian tradition must be reinterpreted but preserved and synthesized with Western science and democratic political ideology.

Far more radical than Sun Yat-sen's moderate approach was that of the New Tide or New Culture Movement, which advocated Western science and democracy and rejected the traditional Chinese cultural values. This movement began in 1916 but was most influential between 1920 and 1923. Among the leaders of this movement were such notables as Ts'ai Yüan-p'ei and Hu Shih. Many Western ideas were introduced by this movement, and the prolonged visits to China of Bertrand Russell and John Dewey, among others, stimulated this trend. The New Tide Movement advocated the use of *pai hua* (plain speech) rather than the classical Mandarin, and engaged in a rationalistic re-examination and reformulation of Chinese philosophy. Some members of this cultural movement, dissatisfied with its nonpolitical character, joined the Chinese Communist Party which was formed in 1920.

There was some controversy over the place of the cult of Confucius in modern China. Those intellectuals who wished to preserve the cult as a religious and cultural legacy formed the Confucian Society, and in 1913 petitioned the Parliament of the Republic to adopt Confucianism as a state religion. The death of Yüan Shih-k'ai, who was in favor of this movement, was a serious blow to this society, which faded away quickly afterward. The effective opposition to the Confucian Society came, strangely enough, from some of the able Confucian scholars.[90] Notable among them were Ch'en Tu-hsiu (d. 1942) and Hu Shih, who led the movement to undercut Confucianism as a cultural force. In Ch'en's words, " The Confucian doctrine of filial piety, obedience, subordination of women, Confucian mores, and Confucian elaborate funerals are all unsuitable to the contemporary world." [91] After a decade of attacks, the downfall of Confucianism seemed inevitable. Students were fascinated by modern science and Western philosophy, totally neglecting the Confucian classics. While ancestor worship still continued, especially in the rural areas, Chan observes that " in modern homes there is not even provision for an ancestral shrine." [92]

The rise of Chiang Kai-shek as a political power in 1928 marked the return of a pro-Confucian trend. Chiang had resigned from public office in 1927 after a split with the Communists, but the following year he resumed his position as commander in chief. Almost immediately, he started advocating the importance of the Four Books (*The Great Learning, Golden Mean, The Analects,* and *The Works of Mencius*). In 1934 Confucius' birthday was declared a national holiday, and the New Life Movement was inaugu-

rated. Although this movement was not a Confucian movement, its four principles were the Confucian concepts of *li*
(socio-moral rules of propriety), *yi* (righteousness), *lien*
(discrimination or honesty), and *ch'ih* (conscientiousness
or integrity). Chiang found no conflict between Christianity and Confucianism. In 1937, he wrote in his Good Friday message to the Eastern Asia Conference of The Methodist Church, " The greatness and love of Christ burst
upon me with a new inspiration, increasing my strength
to struggle against evil, to overcome temptation, and to
uphold righteousness." [93] To him, righteousness meant
Confucian morality, and Confucian morality was the cornerstone of his romantic nationalism. The Confucian way
" has supreme value because it is Chinese, the source of
our great past, the promise of *our* great future. . . . The
task of revolution is ' to revive our Chinese culture, to
restore our people's ancient virtues, to proclaim our Chinese national soul.' " [94] Thus, the Kuomintang under
Chiang's leadership engaged in a vigorous indoctrination
program, which promoted Confucian ceremonies and virtues and a " read the classics " movement. " To counter the
left-wing pamphlets and the learned Marxist treatises which
offered new solutions for the country's ills, special popular
editions of traditional works were released in the most disturbed areas, and books in conflict with the doctrine of the
rites (*li-chiao*) were banned." [95]

The efforts of Chiang Kai-shek to lead China with a
modified Confucian ideology ended with the collapse of
the Kuomintang regime in mainland China. There are
many reasons why the Kuomintang failed and the Communist Party came into power in China. We cannot help feeling that one important reason was that the Confucian
concepts of loyalty and filial piety — adopted as the guiding

ideology of the Kuomintang regime — were inadequate to nurture the social revolution started by Sun Yat-sen. Paraphrasing Northrop, we might say that the Kuomintang failed " not because it was corrupt but because it was moral in the [Confucian] meaning of the word moral." [96] Caught in this situation, some of the Chinese intelligentsia who were neither Marxists nor communists drifted toward communism because of the lack of practical alternative to the Kuomintang regime.

Unlike Eastern Europe, where the communists seized power with the help of the Russian Army, in China the communists depended neither on the Red Army nor on the proletariat, but primarily on peasant armies, to defeat the Kuomintang forces and take over political control of the nation. Although the Chinese communists have acknowledged the leadership of the U.S.S.R. as a senior partner, if they choose they can follow a policy " which is determined not by the interests of the Soviet Union . . . but by the traditional interests of China." [97] For example, Mao Tse-tung has tried to blend Marxism and the Chinese social revolution. Mao and other theoreticians of the Peking Government have been making generous use of Confucian ethical concepts, for, as Nivison observes, " the Communist need to induce acceptance of authority and uniformity of thought is likely to be a permanent one, and it would seem . . . that Confucian ethics, whatever its virtues, can be made to serve this need persuasively." [98]

The use of Confucianism for ideological propaganda is not a new trick of the communist regime. It was used in the past by various ruling dynasties and also by the Kuomintang. Each of them superimposed its own ideology and program on the traditional Confucian sociopolitical structure. However, the communist regime, despite frequent references to Confucian concepts, is trying to reshape the total culture and society of China after a model that is diametrically opposed to the ideal of Confucianism. Whereas in the Confucian tradition the family was the ultimate unit of human fellowship, in the communist scheme the family is swallowed into " people's communes." It is not the family but the state that commands the supreme loyalty of the individual. The Peking Government is attempting to destroy the foundation of the family system by incorporating peasants into " communes," which is a novel system unknown even in other communist nations. By this means, it is reported that in the year beginning October, 1957, irrigation was extended to an additional 80 million acres, and 66 million acres of the barren mountainsides were reforested. " While emphasis is upon integration of all functions in the commune, there are repeated admonitions from Peking to keep the Party distinct so it can retain its ' objectivity.' Actually, one of the chief purposes of the communes is enhanced Party control of peasants. This is accomplished by bringing so many more of the peasants' activities under supervision of Communists working through the commune management and ' seeding ' Communists in at lower levels." [89]

The revolutionary movement begun in 1911 has come a long way. The Manchu rulers were overthrown, and with them imperial rule. A new China emerged, largely through the initiative of Sun Yat-sen, who tried to blend the old and the new, and China with the West. Subsequent developments in China, especially since the rise of Mao Tse-tung, have gone far beyond the goals of Sun Yat-sen. The Peking Government is attempting to eliminate the family-oriented loyalties that have in the past superceded the national loyalty. It may tolerate religious institutions so long as they do not interfere with the policies and practices of the Government. But the communist regime is determined to destroy the underlying religion of " Family-ism," which has determined the values and the norms of behavior of the Chinese from time immemorial.

The communist Government, according to Panikkar, " has released great energies, given the Chinese people a new hope, and a new vision of things. It has brought forth great enthusiasm and an irresistible desire to move forward, but the means employed to achieve these very desirable ends are in many cases of a kind which revolts the free mind. Compared to the state the individual has lost all value, and this is the strange thing in China which adds a tinge of sorrow even when one appreciates and admires what the revolution has done for China." [100]

3 Hinduism and the Caste System

◈ ◈

INDIA

A Land of Contrasts

India has often been described as a land of contrasts. Europe has known something of India since the invasion of Alexander the Great in the fourth century B.C. In the thirteenth century, Marco Polo visited India, and in the fifteenth century Vasco da Gama discovered an ocean route to India. Although this ocean route involved a trip around the continent of Africa, a number of Europeans visited India for a variety of reasons. With the appearance of the first Latin edition of the Upanishads early in the nineteenth century, European intellectuals had a glimpse of the spiritual teachings of ancient India. The writings of Rudyard Kipling and others introduced many aspects of Indian life to the English-speaking world. In our own time, the poet Tagore, the mystic Srī Aurobindo, and the saintly reformer Gāndhi have come to be known throughout the world. Visitors to India are impressed by the sharp contrasts they find there — the modern metropolis of New Delhi and muddy villages, the unbelievable poverty of the masses and the extreme wealth of a few, widespread illiteracy and an educated elite.

99

The Indian subcontinent covers an area of 1,581,410 square miles, extending from the Himalayas on the north to the tropical oceans on the south; to its east lie Burma and the Bay of Bengal, and to its west the Arabian Sea and Afghanistan. Its inhabitants constitute roughly one fifth of the world's population. In August, 1947, with the end of British rule, the Indian subcontinent was split into two major political units, Pakistan and India. The pre-Partition (1941) census reported a total of about 389 million persons on the Indian subcontinent. The total population of the Republic of India was over 356 million, according to the 1951 census (excluding Jammu and Kashmir and some tribal areas of Assam), and a population increase of some 42 million was reported for the 1941–1951 decade. The average density of population is 312 per square mile, as compared with densities of 23 in the Soviet Union, 50 in the United States, and 579 in Japan.[1]

There are three major language families represented on the Indian subcontinent: Indo-Aryan, Dravidian, and Tibeto-Burman. Indo-Aryan languages are spoken in the north. The old Indo-Aryan language was introduced during the second millennium B.C., and its classical form, Sanskrit, is the sacred language of Hinduism. The middle Indo-Aryan languages include Pali, the sacred language of Theravāda (Southern) Buddhism. The new Indo-Aryan languages include Hindi (spoken by 42 per cent of the population), Marathi, Bengali, and Gujarati. Urdu, which developed during the Mogul or Mughal dynasty (1526–1857) as a combination of a Western Hindi dialect and Persian characters, is currently one of the official languages of Pakistan. Dravidian languages are spoken in south India; among them are Telugu, Tamil, Kanarese, and Malayalam. Tibeto-Burman languages are spoken along the Himalayan ranges and in the Assam district. The constitution of India recognizes fourteen languages: Assamese, Bengali, Gujarati, Hindi, Kanarese, Kashmiri, Malayalam, Marathi, Oriya, Punjabi, Sanskrit, Tamil, Telugu, and Urdu. Hindi has been declared the official language of the Republic and will replace English by 1965.[2]

The size of the various religious groups on the Indian subcontinent in 1941, according to the pre-Partition census, was as follows: 255 million Hindus, 92 million Muslims, 25 million Tribal religious adherents, 6 million Christians, 6 million Sikhs, 1.5 million Jains, 232 thousand Buddhists, 114 thousand Parsis, and 434 thousand others. After the Partition of 1947, approximately five to six million non-Muslims fled from Pakistan to India, and about six million Muslims left India to resettle in Pakistan. No additional large-scale emigration of Muslims from India to Pakistan or of non-Muslims from Pakistan to India is expected unless the political climate changes greatly in one or both states. In the Republic of India, Hindus claim 85 per cent of the population, while Muslims claim nearly 10 per cent, Christians 2.3 per cent, and Sikhs a little short of 2 per cent.

Although our primary concern is Hinduism, we cannot altogether exclude reference to Islam and Pakistan. After all, the subcontinent of India was under Muslim rule from the sixteenth century to the middle of the nineteenth century, and today India is keenly conscious of the existence of the two sections of Pakistan. We follow the historic usage of the designation of India to include the entire subcontinent, although the same term is used to refer only to the Republic of India since 1947.

Its Religious Heritage

Today, it is commonplace to speak of the resurgence of Hinduism. A social and cultural revolution is taking place in all parts of India. The rajas and maharajas have ceded their territories to the Republic, and the new constitution has outlawed the discrimination against untouchables. However, " it would be wrong to mistake modification in traditional religious and cultural forms for the weakening of Hinduism itself." [3] The leaders of new India are trying to establish their own brand of democracy, " based on their own past and the character of their own people, and growing and taking form according to their own needs." [4] In the words of Nehru, " We are citizens of no mean country and we are proud of the land of our birth, of our people, our culture and traditions." [5]

Thanks to the tireless efforts of archaeologists, we are beginning to know something about the prehistoric past of India, for example, about the Bronze Age communities of western India, and the towns that developed later in the Indus Valley. Some urban trade centers, notably Amri, Harappa, and Jhangar, are believed to have developed between 2500 and 1900 B.C.

Scholars agree that the historical period of India starts with the invasion of Aryan tribes from the northwest somewhere between 1500 and 1200 B.C. Various theories have been advanced concerning the origin of the Aryans and their migration to India. Although there is no one definitive theory on the Indo-Aryan problem, it is reasonable to believe that " by about 2000 B.C. there was at least a loose confederacy of tribes, stretching from south Russia to Turkestan, who shared certain elements of culture, including a dependence on the higher centers of civilization for their metal-working techniques, and who spoke closely related dialects within the Indo-European framework." [6] Probably there never was a clear-cut transition from pre-Aryan culture; in all likelihood both existed side by side for some time and there was gradual fusion of the two. It is believed that while the pre-Aryan people in India had a relatively advanced civilization, the invading Aryans had better organizational skills, both politically and militarily. In the main, the Aryans were primarily pastoral and agricultural people, and their society was patriarchal and hierarchical. Between the tenth and sixth centuries B.C., the Aryans consolidated their power in northern India. This period is usually known as the Vedic period, because during this time the Vedas (denoting " Wisdom "), the sacred scriptures of the Indo-Aryans, were formulated.

The language of the elite was Sanskrit, and the Indo-Aryan civilization is often called the Sanskrit civilization. The priest-teacher class was called Brāhmin or Brāhman, and the Indo-Aryan religion was known as Brahmanism; Brahmanism was the early form of Hinduism. In Brahmanism the Ultimate Reality of the universe is Brahman, and Brahma is the name of the first member of the Brahman trinity. These similar terms often cause confusion. At any rate, the Aryan invasion of India was accompanied by the " Sanskritization " (Indo-Aryan cultural propagation) and " Brahmanization " (Indo-Aryan religious penetration) of India. It also resulted in the gradual stratification of Indian society according to Indo-Aryan hierarchical principles (the " caste " system) .

The term " Hinduism " (or its earlier form, " Brahmanism ") defies any simple definition. It has an amazing capacity to include within it various contradictory and conflicting beliefs and practices. Pantheism, polytheism, the-ism, and atheism have been accepted and tolerated in the Household of Hinduism. In a sense, Hinduism is nothing more than a generic term for a family of diverse religious tendencies, from magical, superstitious animism to lofty, abstract philosophical systems, all of which accept the authority of the Vedas (sacred scriptures) and the religiously sanctioned system of social stratification.

The sacred literature of Hinduism is divided into two categories: the " Sruti " or " revealed " literature, and the " Smriti " or auxiliary literature. The four Vedas (Rig Veda, Yajur Veda, Sāma Veda, and Atharva Veda) constitute the " revealed " (" Sruti," or " that which was heard ") literature, and they provide the basis of religious authority in Hindu orthodoxy. Each Veda contains " hymns " (Mantras) , " treatises on sacrificial rites " (Brahmanas) , " Forest Books " (Āranyakas) , and Upanishads (literally, " to sit down near someone ") ; the Upanishads are actually the last portion of the Forest Books. Other writings dealing with religious practices and social customs, based on the Vedas, are classified as auxiliary (" Smriti," or " that which is remembered ") literature. This category includes, for example, Dharma Sāstras (manuals of moral conduct and social law) and Purānas (sacred legends about deities and heroes) .

Hinduism has never insisted on the acceptance of any one interpretation of its doctrines. Uniformity of beliefs has never been a criterion of orthodoxy in Hinduism. What unites all Hindus is the acceptance of the " givenness " of the metaphysico-social principle expressed in the social and cosmic hierarchy. From this standpoint, the society, which is in essence the superindividual, consists of numerous castes and subcastes, while the life of an individual is divided into four main stages. Underlying this metaphysico-social principle is the beginningless and endless divine cosmic law (*sanatana dharma*). "That which supports, that which holds together the peoples, that is *dharma*." [7]

The development of Hinduism has been characterized by two diametrically opposed movements. First was a movement toward unity. All the local pre-Aryan civilizations were absorbed into the great Sanskrit civilization, all the local tribal deities were transformed into Brahman deities, and different tribes and professional groups were incorporated into the caste structure. This process, variously known as " Sanskritization," " Brahmanization," or " Hinduization," took place not only in India but also in its neighboring areas, which may be regarded as India's religio-cultural " satellites." Second was a movement toward diversity. The fusion of the invading Sanskrit civilization with local pre-Aryan civilizations produced numerous hybrid civilizations at the local level; in this process the Brahmanic deities took on numerous manifestations or incarnations, and the castes were subdivided into subcastes. These contradictory tendencies — unity and diversity, or absorption and differentiation — make it difficult to characterize Hinduism in simple terms. Every belief or practice considered basic by some Hindus has been rejected by other Hindus. And yet, despite bewildering inconsistencies and conflicting tendencies, Hinduism has remained intact throughout the ages.

HINDUISM IN HISTORY

Ancient Period

The early period of Hinduism, known as the Vedic period, is usually divided into three parts, the age of the Mantras, the age of the Brahmanas, and the age of the

Upanishads. During the age of the Mantras (hymns), the concept of the cosmic order (*rita*) was accepted as the supreme law over gods and men. In this connection, the many gods mentioned in the Rig Veda have been characterized as polytheism by some and " henotheism " or " kathenotheism " (a successive belief in single supreme gods) by others. During the age of the Brahmanas (treatises on sacrificial rites), rituals were emphasized, and the conservative outlook of the priests influenced religion and society. About this time, society became divided into four hierarchical " castes ": priests, warriors, commoners, and serfs. During the age of the Upanishads a contemplative trend developed partly as a reaction against the overemphasis on sacrificial rituals of the previous age. Although the stories and discussions in the Upanishads are not systematic treatises on philosophy, these records of the mystics' experience of Ultimate Reality have stimulated philosophical thinking throughout the history of India. The Upanishads also provided the Hindu religion such key concepts as Brahman (Ultimate Reality), *ātman* (the Self), *moksha* (deliverance from the chain of finite existence), *samsāra* (world of phenomenal existence), *karma* (moral law of causation), and *jnāna* (saving knowledge). Probably many of the upanishadic thinkers came from non-Brāhman castes, and this factor may account for the de-emphasis on caste distinctions in the Upanishads. True to the mystical tradition, the Upanishads stress mystical intuition rather than human reason.

Between the sixth and third centuries B.C., the Aryan expansion followed the Ganges Valley, blending diverse cultural elements, while in the south a pre-Aryan, Dravidian civilization continued to exist. This period was marked by the rise of two important religious systems,

Jainism and Buddhism, both of which rejected the authority of the Vedas, and as such they are regarded as " heretical " schools by orthodox Hindus. The origin of Jainism is not clear, although Mahāvira (599–527 B.C.) is regarded as the systematizer or the " last guide " of this religion. Jainism has remained solely in India to this day. Buddhism was founded by Gautama or Sakyamuni, a younger contemporary of Mahāvira. Sakyamuni was born in or about 500 B.C. His religion was destined eventually to develop outside India.

Our knowledge of the political and cultural history of India during this period is not at all adequate. However, we know for certain that King Darius I of Persia occupied the northwestern part of India shortly before 500 B.C., and that Alexander the Great invaded the Punjab in 326 B.C. We also know that Chandragupta established the Maurya dynasty around 322 B.C., and that his grandson Asoka ruled the country between 274 and 232 B.C. It was Asoka who became the great propagator of Buddhism.

In 185 B.C. the Maurya dynasty came to a tragic end, and northern India was invaded successively by the Greeks, Sakas, Parthians, and Kushans. One of the famous Greek kings of this period was Milinda or Menander (ca. 150 B.C.) . In the first century A.D., northern India came under the rule of the Kushans, a leading Iranian tribe, whom the Chinese called Yüeh-chi. The most important Kushan king was Kanishka, who lived in the second century A.D. He patronized the missionary activities of Buddhism in his vast empire, which stretched beyond the borders of India to Central Asia. Early in the third century, the Kushans declined, caught between the rising Sasanian empire in the west and the Guptas in India.

During the time from the fall of the Maurya empire (185

B.C.) to the fall of the Kushans (A.D. ca. 300), a new religious spirit permeated India. In the Buddhist fold, various Mahāyāna schools developed and influenced the subsequent expansion of Buddhism in the Far East. From the point of Hinduism, this era is referred to as the Epic Period, for to this period belong the great epics, the Rāmāyana and the Mahābhārata. The Bhagavad Gītā, which is a part of the Mahābhārata, has been a source of inspiration to many Hindu philosophers and religious teachers. These epics deal not only with religious questions but with the entire domain of human life in all its aspects. Many of the Dharma Sāstras (manuals of moral conduct and social law) were also compiled. This period witnessed the rise of the three great sects of Hinduism: Saivism which worships the god Siva, Vaishnavism or Vishnuism which worships the god Vishnu or one of his incarnations, and Sāktism which worships the Divine Mother. This period was also marked by the Hinduization of Southeast Asia, including Sumatra, Java, and Borneo, as well as Malaya and Indo-China. Within India, Hinduism harmonized its Aryan tradition with Dravidian elements. The authority of the Vedas, the caste system and the four stages of life, and the beliefs in the law of moral causation (karma) and rebirth, as well as the three approaches (ritual, devotional, and knowledge) to gods, were widely acknowledged. On the practical side, pilgrimages to holy places and image worship became popular among the pious masses.

Middle Period

In the year A.D. 318, Chandragupta I inaugurated the Gupta empire which ruled most of northern India. The Guptas never seriously attempted to incorporate southern India into the empire. Under the Gupta rulers the Hinduization of Southeast Asia continued, and Indian navigators traveled farther into Egypt, Arabia, and the Roman Empire. In the fifth century, the Ephthalites, better known as the White Huns, began to invade northwest India. The White Huns eventually destroyed the cultural and religious life that had developed under the Guptas. Although Harsha (606–647) re-established Hindu supremacy for a short period of time, after his death northern India was split into a number of small principalities.

Under the Guptas Hinduism experienced its golden age. We owe much to the record of a Chinese pilgrim, Fa Hien or Fa-hsien, who made an extensive trip to Central Asia and all parts of India at the turn of the fifth century. During the Gupta period, a number of systematic treatises on doctrinal matters (Sūtras) and pious legends about deities and heroes (Purānas) were written. Inevitably the differences between the religious life of the masses and that of the elite, which had always existed in Hinduism, became accentuated. The masses venerated popular deities and found consolation in the esoteric beliefs and practices of the Tantras (spiritual disciplines related to the worship of the female energy or Divine Mother, Sakti). Intellectuals, on the other hand, indulged in speculation of the six orthodox schools — the Nyāya (logical realism), the Vaisesika (realistic pluralism), the Sāmkhya (evolutionary dualism), the Yoga (disciplined meditation), the Mīmāmsā (investigations of the Vedas), and the Vedānta (the "end of the Vedas").[8]

Indian history between the eighth and fourteenth centuries was marked by internal rivalry and external threats. The Gurjara-Pratihara dynasty, which established itself in northern India in the eighth century, was under the constant threat of Muslim invaders, who had occupied Sind in 712. Toward the end of the tenth century, the Gur-

jaras' supremacy declined, and northern India was split
into rival powers, thus providing the Muslims with a
golden opportunity to seize political control. The Punjab
fell to Mahmūd of Ghazni (998–1030), but internal rivalry
among various Muslim powers and the threat of Mongol
raids prevented the Muslims from invading south India.
Only under the sultanate of Muhammad ibn Tughlak
(1325–1351) did the Muslim rule extend from Madura to
Kashmir.

In northern India, Hinduism suffered under the Muslim
rulers. For example, it is reported that Mahmūd of Ghazni,
a zealous servant of the Prophet, destroyed, in one of his
campaigns, the Hindu temple of Somnath and massacred
over 50,000 supporters of the temple. One of Mahmūd's
Muslim contemporaries, al-Biruni, had this to say about the
caste system of Hinduism: " We Muslims, of course, stand
entirely on the other side of the question, considering all
men equal, except in piety; and this is the greatest obstacle
which prevents any approach or understanding between
Hindus and Muslims." [9]

In contrast to northern India, where Hinduism declined
under Muslim rule, Hinduism in south India manifested
an amazing spiritual vitality. Sankara or Samkara (788–
820?), a south Indian Brāhman who advocated nondualism
(Advaita Vedānta), was by far the most important philosopher in the history of Hinduism. Equally significant was
the bhakti (devotional) movement in south India, led by
the Vaishnavite Alvars (twelve poets) and Saivite Nayanars
(sixty-three poets). There is much truth in D. S. Sarma's
statement that " the Alvars and Nayanars sang Buddhism
and Jainism out of southern India." [10]

Scholars have advanced various theories to explain the
decline of Buddhism in India. At least three factors must

be mentioned in this connection: (1) Internally, Buddhism came under the spell of Hindu Sāktism and Tantrism and lost its own religious identity; (2) philosophically, Buddhism was attacked by Kumarila, Sankara, and others; and (3) devotionally, it lost ground to the Vaishnavite and Saivite *bhakti* movements.

The spiritual vigor of south India also produced Rāmānuja, the eleventh-century advocate of qualified monism (*Visishtadvaita*), and Madhva, the thirteenth-century spokesman of dualism (*dvaita*). Equally significant was the Saiva Siddhanta, a unique philosophical system of the Tamil mind, which "allies itself with other systems of Hindu thought, while, at the same time, it claims to set itself apart from them as *the* acme of religious truth." [11]

Hinduism Under Mughal Rule

India was consolidated in 1526 under the Muslim Mughal dynasty founded by Baber, or Zahir ud-Din Muhammad, a descendant of both Tīmūr Lang (Tamerlane) and Jenghiz Khan. The greatest of the Mughal rulers was Akbar (ruled 1556–1605), under whom the empire stretched from Ahmednagar in the Deccan to Kabul and Kashmir in the north. " His greatest achievement as a ruler was to weld this collection of different states, different races, different religions, into a whole. It was accomplished by elaborate organizations — Akbar had an extraordinary genius for detail — still more by the settled policy which persuaded his subjects of the justice of their ruler." [12] He abolished the *jizya* (the poll tax on non-Muslims) and proclaimed universal tolerance. At the expense of a conflict with the Muslim doctors, he invited Hindus, Jains, Zoroastrians, and Christians to his Hall of Worship for religious discussions. He went so far as to create a new synthetic religion, *Din-i-Ilahi* (the Divine Faith), although it disappeared quickly after his death.[13] The later Mughal rulers suffered increasing loss of political power. In the meantime, Western Europeans began to invade the undefended Indian coasts, and during the eighteenth century the French and English competed for commercial and military interests in India, ignoring the dying Mughal dynasty.

The *bhakti* (devotional) movement was started in northern India in the fifteenth century. The northern *bhakti* movement was primarily Vaishnavite, which was subdivided into the worshipers of Rāma and of Krishna, the two incarnations of the Lord Vishnu. Rāmānanda (d. 1467), an advocate of Rāma worship, was known for his rejection of caste discrimination, because he recognized the equality of all men — whatever their caste, color, or creed — in the eyes of God. A disciple of Rāmānanda, a Muslim weaver named Kabīr (1440–1518), also taught all men to worship the one God, transcending caste and separate religions. Kabīr later was venerated as a saint by the Hindus. His followers are called the Kabīrpanthis. Rāmānanda also exerted tremendous influence on Nānak (1470–1540), the founder of Sikhism. Confronted with a diversity of religions, Nānak " proposed hopefully that hostilities should cease, that the warring factions adjust their differences and be reconciled through a method which he offered." [14] However, in 1899, the Sikhs established an independent kingdom in the Punjab, and played a prominent part in British imperial affairs. Another famous devotee of Rāma worship was Tulsī Dās (1532–1623), whose name is a household word among the Hindi-speaking people in northern India to this day. Although his poem, *The Rāmāyana,* is based on the story of Rāma, prince of Avadh in the Sanskrit literature, Rāma was understood by Tulsī Dās as the incarnation of God to whom all men pray.[15] The second wing of the Vaishnavite *bhakti* movement, the tradition of Krishna worship, was divided into the Rādhā-Krishna cult and the Rukmini-Krishna cult. From the Rādhā-Krishna tradition came Nimbārka, Vallabha, and Chaitanya; from the Rukmini-Krishna tradition came the so-called Saints of Mahārastra. The most famous of these men was Chaitanya (1485–1533). It is to be noted that while he did not attempt to harmonize Hinduism with other religions as Kabīr and Nānak did, he recognized no caste distinction within Hinduism.

Modern India

At the beginning of the nineteenth century, India came under British control. This marked a turning point in the history of India, because it was exposed for the first time to " modernity." In the classical period of India, Hinduism was conterminous with the state, culture, and society, while in its more recent past Islam provided the normative principles for the Mughal rule of India. The British, however, governed India by the rule of law, rejecting religion as a normative political principle. Not that religions did not concern the British colonial administration. Indeed, Hinduism, Islam, and other religions could not be ignored, but the British raj dealt with these religions politically and not religiously. It is ironic that under the British " secular rule," both Hindu and Muslim religious aspirations became closely identified with nationalism, which caused the separation of the subcontinent into India and Pakistan in 1947.

In all fairness to the British, it must be pointed out that, in the main, British rule in India was, following Pitt's injunction, governed by British ideas of liberty and justice.

Indian nationalists are correct to point out, however, that the British sense of liberty was confined to civil liberty at the expense of political liberty.

During the period between 1815 and 1885 the British were preoccupied with the task of consolidating their position in India. A controversy between advocates of educating Indians along indigenous cultural lines and those who advocated a policy of Anglicizing Indians was settled in favor of the latter in the 1830's. The next period, from 1885 to 1947, witnessed the emergence of Hindu and Muslim nationalism, which struggled against each other as much as against the British raj. This turbulent era was ushered in with the first Indian National Congress meeting in 1885 in Bombay. Its founder, an Englishman named Allan Hume, was an advocate of a representative government for India, and the Congress was at first marked by pro-British utopian idealism. By 1907, however, the Congress was under the leadership of anti-British revolutionaries such as B. G. Tilak and A. Ghose. The Muslim League also started as a pro-British, English-speaking, and conservative group in 1906 under the leadership of the Agha Khan; understandably, the League did not represent the sentiment of the Muslim masses in India for many years to come. World War I, which involved India by royal declaration, brought the Muslim League close to the Indian National Congress, and in 1916 the so-called Congress-League Pact outlined a proposed constitution for the self-government of India.

After World War I a Hindu-Muslim rift became noticeable. In 1929 an all-India Muslim conference formulated the Muslim Fourteen Points, which aimed at separate Muslim electorates. A new constitution proposed in 1935 farther separated the Muslim League and the Congress. While Gāndhi led the civil disobedience movement, the Muslim

League supported the British Government. In 1935 the League started demanding an independent, autonomous, and sovereign Muslim state in the northwestern and eastern zones of the Indian subcontinent. In the midst of this three-cornered struggle of the British, the Congress, and the Muslim League, World War II broke out. During the war, the Congress called upon Britain to quit India, while the Muslim League continued its demand for a separate state. On August 15, 1947, the British Indian Empire came to an end, and the subcontinent was divided into the Dominion of Pakistan and the Dominion of India. The Dominion of India became a republic in 1950.

THE HINDU FAITH

Religion and Life

In any religion, with the exception of the ecclesiastics and a small minority of educated and interested laymen, the majority of the adherents are usually indifferent to systematic understanding of dogmas and doctrines. This does not mean that most people are not intelligent about their own faith, however. In India, where four fifths of the people cannot read or write, religion usually implies not so much the acceptance of certain dogmas as what one does as an individual and a member of his family, village, and caste. One finds an inexhaustible variety of popular devotions, colorful festivals, moving pilgrimages, and elaborate rites on such occasions as birth, naming, initiation, marriage, sickness and recovery, death and burial. If you ask ordinary householders what their religion means to them, they probably will not be able to articulate their beliefs. More often than not they will tell you what they do, such as the daily acts of offering to the gods, to the holy men, to forefathers, to lower animals, and to humanity.

Underneath — and in spite of — this bewildering variety of religious rites, practices, and beliefs, one senses Hindu acceptance of life as it is. The meaning of life to the Hindus is life itself, and not an intellectual understanding of it. Man in Hinduism is not a sojourner in this world, as the ancient Hebrew psalmist thought of himself; he is not a foreigner or a guest in this world. He is an integral part of the cosmos with its seasons and changes. " Just as nature is not interested in truth, but in manifestation . . . so Hinduism is not really interested in religious truth but in the endless possibilities of religious realization and expression." [16] What the Hindu seeks is not an intellectual acceptance of doctrinal truths, but the integration of his conscious and subconscious self with the source and ground of existence. A Hindu does not become conscious of his oneness with the all-pervading Spirit of the cosmos by offering sacrifice (pūjā) ; it is the other way around. He knows and feels that he is one with the Cosmic Spirit; he offers sacrifice as an expression of this belief. The ordinary faithful refer to the Cosmic Spirit as the Lord (Isvara) ; only the philosopher perceives that the Lord is in essence the impersonal Absolute (Brahman) . " The reality conceived of as God is the cause of the universe — its sole and whole cause. The universe rises from, remains in, and returns to God. . . . It is God that has taken, as it were, all the forms that we see." [17]

All Hindus hold that the nature of Ultimate Reality, the impersonal Absolute (Brahman), is unknowable. Thus, they accept all doctrinal formulations about God only as tentative and relative truths. But God in Hinduism is not the " Wholly Other." He is everywhere, and he is in everything. Man may not grasp His ultimate nature, but man can realize his union with God because man is a part of God. In Hinduism, God is immanent, while man as well as the world of nature is transcendent. Running through this divinely created and divinely ordained monistic universe is an immutable law of hierarchy and change. Everything from inanimate and animate beings to gods are believed to be graded vertically in a cosmic hierarchy, while everything and everybody are subject to the law of rhythmic change on a horizontal line. The family, the village, the caste, the society, and the universe are regulated by the law of hierarchy and change. Inevitably, the predictability of the cosmic law fosters, at best, a sense of respect for the givenness of the existential situation and, at worst, a fatalistic attitude. In traditional Hindu society, everyone knows what is expected of him, how he should greet others, how he should be treated by others, who can call him by his name, and who can eat with him. When one is young, he can do certain things; in his middle age, he has certain rights and prerogatives; and in his old age, he knows what he can do and should do. The importance of life is to live it, and that is the meaning of the eternal law (*sanatana dharma*) of Hinduism. This is what ordinary householders believe, without systematic articulation, and this is what " philosophers " attempt to state on a more sophisticated level.

" Philo-ousia "

Philosophy is a Western term, derived from the Greek term *philo-sophia,* signifying love of wisdom, based on human reason, judgment, and discrimination. The Eastern mind has never been satisfied with conceptualization as the vehicle of philosophic thought. Instead, the East attempts to establish direct contact with the Real. William Haas appropriately coins a word, " philo-ousia," love of reality or essence, to describe the Eastern attitude toward Reality.[18] While we are compelled to continue using such terms as " philosophy " and " philosophical " in an Eastern context, these words must not be understood in the traditional Western sense. For example, in India, philosophy sides with religion to a far greater extent than does the critical, secularized philosophy of the modern West. This does not mean that Indian philosophy (or " philo-ousia ") and Hinduism are identical; they do differ, but they reinforce each other. The ancient Hindu's love of Reality led him to the realization of the Self (*ātman*) as the one non-dual reality behind the phenomenal world. In order to attain and actualize this Selfhood, one has to transcend the world of ignorance (*avidyā*) and illusion (*māyā*). In this sense, Hindus do not practice asceticism; they know that life itself is asceticism, because life properly lived means constant transformation of their empirical beings and constant re-evaluation of the phenomenal world in which they live. Radhakrishnan emphasizes similar points when he depicts the characteristics of Indian philosophy as concentration upon the spiritual, belief in the intimate relationship of philosophy and life, and an introspective attitude and introspective approach to Reality.[19]

Indian civilization, religion, and philosophy are deeply rooted in the assumption that man is a cosmic being in the sense that man is a part of nature. He is not the lord of nature, nor is he its slave; man is essentially one with nature. In the ancient Hindu world view, the lord of the cosmos was not a god but the cosmic law (*rita*) and the moral law of causation (*karma*), which regulate the cosmic processes of continuous generation and destruction. Betty Heimann suggests that Indian metaphysics has never lost a sense of physics. Indian metaphysics in its theological dimension may be characterized as " a second physics " in the sense that gods are regarded as heavenly counterparts of earthly beings; in reference to ontology (cosmic primeval physics) it becomes " extended physics "; and in reference to eschatology (or another " here ") it becomes a " renewed physics." [20] This type of metaphysical speculation is based on the assumption that this physical world, which is subject to change, is not really real (*māyā*).

The only reality that is ultimately real is Brahman, which cannot be explained except in negative language, such as *na-iti, na-iti* (it is not this, it is not that). According to Hindu orthoxody, Brahman in its essential nature is described as *Sat* (existence, reality, or being), *Chit* (consciousness or knowledge), and *Ānanda* (bliss). In theistic terms, Brahman becomes a personal god, the supreme Lord (*Īsvara*). In the eschatological dimension, Brahman becomes Nirvāna (eternal bliss). Brahman has no predicates; it merely exists. Man can neither attain it nor worship it; he can only be it.

The Bhagavad Gītā teaches that there are three paths leading to the realization of one's union with Ultimate Reality, or God — the path of disinterested service (*karma yoga*), the path of devotion (*bhakti yoga*), and the path of saving knowledge (*jnāna yoga*). There have been different theories as to which path is superior, but it is safe to assume that all three are valid paths to spiritual perfection. As to the first, the Gītā emphasizes that one should " never work for fruit, nor yet desist from work." [21] It is not the result of work that is important; it is the disinterestedness of the worker which enables him to act in such a way that his actions do not bind him. The second path is one of love and devotion. While the devotion (*bhakti*) taught in the Gītā implies an emotional attitude of the devotee toward the God of love and grace, such devotion must be kept in proper balance with disinterested service and saving knowledge. " The external accessories of worship are not important. What is essential is that we should offer ourselves to Him. . . . When one's love of God becomes constant and complete, one attains wisdom through his grace, the wisdom which liberates the soul from the bonds." [22] The third path implies a harmony of saving knowledge and spiritual insight. The Gītā emphasizes that " knowledge is attained through faith, and through knowledge supreme peace is gained." [23] The three paths are, however, not merely the means to attain union with God; they are ends in themselves to those who are united with God through every act of everyday life.

Cults

The two diametrically opposed tendencies — unity and diversity — within Hinduism are expressed in its conception of God. All Hindus worship one God through many gods, and God is interpreted as Ultimate Reality (Brahman) apprehended from a religious standpoint. Since God (or Brahman) is omnipresent, he can be worshiped in any form: " Thou art woman; thou art man; thou art the youth and also the maiden; thou as an old man totterest with a stick; being born thou standest facing all directions." [24] Thus, a modern Hindu saint, Srī Rāmakrishna, worshiped the Divine Mother both in the form of a chaste woman of respectable family and also in the form of a shameless and immoral prostitute of the town. In other words, the one Ultimate Reality (Brahman), which is devoid of attributes, takes the " provisional forms " of gods who appear in diverse human or animal figures. One can identify each god by his attributes, his gestures, the style of his hair, his clothes, and by the people who surround him. Each god has his consort; these two are one divinity.[25]

Historically, there have been five major deities, Siva, Vishnu, Sakti (the Divine Mother), Sūrya (the sun god), and Ganesha (or Ganapati, the elephant-headed god). Each deity is the object of worship by his or her devotees. The worship of Siva and Vishnu goes back to Vedic times. The followers of Saivism worship Siva, who is a member of the Hindu trinity together with Brahma and Vishnu. Siva is the god of destruction and creation. Siva has a thousand names, including a popular one called Mahādeva (great God). Siva is usually symbolized in the form of the phallic emblem (lingam). In art, he is portrayed together with his consort and sons. The devotees of Siva paint three horizontal lines on their foreheads. Saivism has numerous subsects.

The followers of Vishnu identify him with the highest reality; Vishnu is believed to be the preserver. In art, he is portrayed resting on the coils of the serpent with his wife sitting at his feet. Like Siva, Vishnu also has a thousand names. Among all the " incarnations " (avatāra) of Vishnu, ten are important. They are: the fish (Matsuya), the tortoise (Kurma), the boar (Varaha), the man-lion (Narasimha), the dwarf (Vamana), the human (Parasurāma), the warrior-hero (Ramachandra), the shepherd (Krishna), the Buddha, and the future incarnation (Kalkin). It is evident that the concept of Vishnu, like its cult, is a composite of diverse elements. The followers of Vishnu form the most powerful sect in India. They are distinguished in south India especially by the mark of the trident on the forehead.

The cult of Sakti (Divine Mother) worships many forms

of female deities, such as the goddess of supreme power (Mahāsakti), the ten-armed Durgā, the four-armed Kālī (Siva's consort), and the goddess of wealth and prosperity (Lakshmī, the consort of Vishnu). The cult of Sakti is divided into the right-hand path and the left-hand path, and the latter tends to be more extreme and vulgar.

The cult of the sun god (Sūrya) was very popular at one time, and there were many temples dedicated to him. Even today, the sun god is worshiped not only by the members of this cultic group but by Hindus in general, especially in the rural areas. The cult of Ganesha (the elephant-headed deity) is widespread in India. The origin of Ganesha as an object of worship is obscure. But his idols are found everywhere, in temples and in households, at crossroads and on hilltops. Many Hindus invoke Ganesha, who is known as the god of prudence and sagacity, at every undertaking — when building a house, when starting on a journey, or upon a safe return.[26]

The Four Ends of Life

The Indian attitude toward life and the world has been characterized by some as negative. For example, Schweitzer, while acknowledging certain affirmative elements in Indian thought, nevertheless concludes that world and life negation occupies a predominant position. Since life is essentially meaningless and sorrowful, the Hindu attempts " (a) to bring life to a standstill in himself by mortifying his will to live, and (b) to renounce all activity which aims at improvement of the conditions of life in this world." [27] Such an interpretation of Indian thought, however suggestive it may be, seems to be quite one-sided.

The *Mahābhārata* defines the ends of life as wealth (*artha*), worldly enjoyment (*kāma*), righteousness (dharma), and deliverance (moksha). The four ends are not of equal value; deliverance alone is the supreme goal of human life, but the three other ends are regarded as important intermediate goals. So long as one lives in the household, he has the duty to acquire wealth for the well-being of his family. A good example of the philosophy of wealth and prosperity is found in the Artha-sāstra, a treatise on politics and diplomacy, written by Kautilya; the work is dated 321–296 B.C. A householder must also go through the stage of life dedicated to the task of procreation. Accordingly, India produced a variety of kāma literature, manuals of the art of love and the psychology of the heart.

However, the goals of wealth and enjoyment must be seen in the context of the moral law (dharma). The term dharma denotes a variety of meanings, such as law, righteousness, duty, and morality, but in Hindu orthodoxy this term has the connotation of " fixed position." Hindu orthodoxy defines the " horizontal " phases of individual life in terms of the four stages: the student, the householder, the forest dweller, and the wandering ascetic or holy beggar. Hindus also accept the vertical hierarchical principle which divides human society into four major castes. In the ancient Rig Veda, four varna (" colors " or " castes ") are mentioned: the priest-teacher (Brāhman), the ruler-warrior (Kshatriya), the trader-commoner (Vaisya), and the worker-serf (Sūdra). In the course of time, these developed into numerous castes and subcastes. The caste system and the four stages of life are believed to be the expressions of the eternal dharma, and thus every conceivable problem one faces during his life can be solved by observing the laws (dharma) of the caste to which one belongs and the rules of the particular stage of one's life.

The relationship between the first three goals — wealth,

enjoyment, and righteousness — and the supreme goal of life (deliverance) involves a basic paradox. On the one hand, Hinduism affirms that everything one does in life is ultimately determined by and related to the eternal *dharma*, and yet the Hindu is taught to discard the pursuits of wealth, enjoyment, and even righteousness for the sake of the supreme goal of life. The term *moksha* implies the realization of a perfect spirit in positive language, and deliverance from the bondage of the flesh and the chain of finitude in negative language. All Indian religions — not only Hinduism, but also Jainism and Buddhism — as well as all schools of philosophy regard *moksha* as the supreme goal.

Hindu philosophers attempt to transcend contradictions and opposites (*namarupa* or " names and forms ") and to realize that the Self (*atman*) is the same as Ultimate Reality (Brahman). For example, Sankara (d. 820), the spokesman of the nondualist (*advaita*) Vedanta school, stressed that the Self is the sole reality and all else is ignorance. Thus, only the knowledge (*vidya*) of the *atman*-Brahman identity can release one from ignorance (*avidya*). What philosophers sought was not merely speculative knowledge about the nature of the universe; the knowledge of ultimate realities was sought in order to attain deliverance (*moksha*). " In India metaphysical knowledge always has a soteriological purpose. . . . Knowledge is transformed into a kind of meditation, and metaphysics becomes soteriology." [28] The soteriological basis of philosophy was clearly evident in Ramanuja (d. 1137), who felt that one had to be released, not from ignorance, but from unbelief. Thus, he stressed the importance of believing love (*bhakti*) toward God.

Throughout the long history of India, its religion, phi-

losophy, art, politics, and culture have not lost their soteriological concern. Philosophers meditated on the Formless
Brahman (*nirguna Brahman*) ; pious people venerated the
personal God. They all knew, however, that they were one
with Ultimate Reality; in this sense, Hinduism is " a truly
gigantic enterprise for self-release (*Selbsterlösung*) by self-
realization." [29]

HINDUISM AND INDIAN SOCIETY

Religion and Society

Important as philosophy is, philosophy or " philo-ousia "
is not the sole foundation of Hinduism. Hinduism is fundamentally a socioreligious order; it is concerned with the
Hindu's total life, including morals, economics, politics,
and all aspects of culture and society. Hinduism may be
characterized as the total socioreligious system, or way of
life, which developed in part from the Vedic-Aryan religion
accompanied by the Sanskrit culture, and in part from non-
Aryan elements which have stubbornly persisted in the
local village religious beliefs and practices. In short, Hinduism is a historic synthesis of the Vedic-Aryan religious
traditions and the non-Aryan religious traditions of the
small communities that comprise India.

Structurally, the unity of the diverse elements of Hinduism has been maintained by the caste system. The simplest
definition of the Hindu is a person who was born a Hindu
and is a member of a caste. " No profession of faith, no
manifestation of spiritual gifts, no moral attainment, has
the slightest value as a qualification for admission to the
Hindu fold. . . . The ground for excommunication is always breach of caste rules." [30]

The importance of the village in the life of the Hindus

is evidenced by the fact that four fifths of the total population of India live in approximately 550,000 villages, where the " pure " tradition of Vedic-Aryan religion is scarcely known. In spite of a recent trend toward urbanization — between 1921 and 1951 the urban population increased from 11 to 17 per cent of the total — India is still predominantly a rural nation, and roughly 70 per cent of the people still depend on agriculture. It has been estimated that of the 70 out of every 100 Indians in agricultural pursuits, 47 are mainly peasant-proprietors, 9 mainly tenants, 13 landless laborers, and 1 a landlord.[31]

India has known the joint family system from time immemorial. Normally, the Hindu family includes three generations. At the same time, the Hindu home is regarded as the dwelling place not only of the living members of the family but also of the ancestors under the protection of Agni (the guardian deity of the home).[32] Every stage of the individual's life is celebrated by a family ritual. Thus, the Hindu home is the center of social, cultural, and religious activities.

The complexity of the Indian social structure is readily seen in the interaction of the joint family system, the village, and the caste system. They in turn have influenced, and have been influenced by, the dominant religio-cultural tradition of India throughout its long history. It must be remembered in this connection that the diversity of religious and ethnic groups makes a general characterization of Indian social structure extremely difficult.

The Family

The Hindu family follows monogamous and patrilineal principles, although polyandry has been practiced in some areas, for example, among the Kannuvans of Madura, and among the carpenter and blacksmith castes in Malabar.[33] Such local and ethnic variations have been tolerated by the main tradition of Hindu orthodoxy, which derives its norms regarding inheritance, succession, and marriage from such classical Sanskrit works as the Dharma Sāstras and the Code of Manu. Normally, a Hindu family is composed of a group of natural or adoptive descendants held together under the eldest living male member. According to the traditional system, the living quarters are divided among the subunits of the joint family, but they share common family rites, common property, and a common kitchen.

In the Hindu home, the daily routine includes many religious rites, at least the early morning worship, midday prayers, and the evening worship. The orthodox Hindu fulfills his five daily obligations, including offerings to the gods, to seers, to forefathers, to lower animals, and to humanity; the last is often symbolized by the giving of alms to the poor. The life of the orthodox Hindu, from the time of conception to death, is marked by a series of sacramental rites. Important among them are the " fetus-laying rites " performed at the consummation of marriage; the rite of supplication for a male child (usually performed during the third month of the mother's pregnancy) ; the blessing at the child's birth; the name-giving ceremony on the tenth or twelfth day after the child's birth; dedication of the child to the sun god in the fourth month after the child's birth; the first feeding of cooked food in the sixth month; the first tonsure of the hair (the date varies according to families) ; the initiation (*upanāyana*) of the boy into the study of the Vedas (which marks the child's entrance into the first stage of life) ; the *brahmacharyāsrama,* or the stage of the student; the rite signifying the return of the student to his ancestral home; the marriage rite; and the funeral rite.[34] The central rite for a woman is the marriage rite, which corresponds to the initiation rite for the male child.

Marriage is a sacred obligation for orthodox Hindu men and women. Historically, there were various forms of marriage. In one form the father offers his daughter to a suitable young man. Another form involves the gift of a pair of oxen from the bridegroom to the bride's family. Only rarely does the initiative come from the bridegroom, however. In the Vedic period, marriage between an adult man and woman was not rare, but the Code of Manu prescribed the age of the husband and wife as thirty and twelve, or twenty-four and eight, respectively; later texts encouraged a younger age for marriage. As the custom of child marriage became widespread, the marriage ceremony was divided into two parts, the first ceremony following the betrothal and the second taking place when the bride, after she reaches the age of puberty, joins her husband's family. It is usually considered a disgrace for a family to fail to marry off a daughter by the time she is three years past the age of puberty. Marriage across caste lines is not acceptable, even though ancient scriptures permitted men to marry women of lower classes. Usually, family religious rites are specified by caste rules, and a woman married to a man of different caste than her own cannot perform the prescribed rites of her husband's family. In recent years, cross-caste marriages are legally permitted, but they cause difficulties socially. Also, the remarriage of widows, which was practiced in ancient times, was prohibited in the Code of Manu. The custom of widow-burning was often rationalized on the ground that a widow's lot was so miserable that she would rather be dead. It took the combined effort of modern Hindu reformers and the British Government to eliminate the custom of widow-burning. The Hindu tradition allows divorce on various grounds, but divorce has not been practiced very widely. The monogamous principle is violated only when the first marriage does not produce offspring. There are exceptions, of course, but in general the husband does not take a second wife if his first wife can fulfill the performance of religious obligations and also can bear children, especially sons. An exaggerated emphasis on the importance of the adult male child often causes tensions and conflicts within the family.

The affairs of the family are usually managed by the head of the family, or sometimes by the eldest son, who is empowered by the head of the family. It is the prerogative and duty of the family head to watch over the spiritual and material needs of all the members of the family, living and dead. It is he who is held responsible for the preservation of the family line. The wife of the family head manages the domestic affairs of the family, which include the purchase of kitchen utensils and food, keeping family accounts, and looking after the general welfare of women and servants in the household. She is usually the first one who goes to the family shrine in the morning and invokes the blessing of the deity over the house. She takes her bath, eats, and goes to bed after her husband. In the joint family system, interpersonal relationships are very complex. This is particularly true of the women, who spend so much time together in the home. It is up to the mistress of the household to maintain peace in the family.

The significance of family life may be seen in two ways. On the one hand, the orthodox Hindu matures as a member of society by discharging family obligations with the co-operation of other members of the family. On the other hand, family life is only one phase of his religious life. He enhances his *dharma* by fulfilling family obligations, by performing family rites, and by meditating on the teaching of the Vedas. Even while he is dedicated to the worldly ends of wealth and enjoyment, he is training himself for the spiritual goal of life. The householder is in essence a trustee of the family, which belongs to "all the members of the family — past members that are no more, present members that are living, and future members that are to come into being." [35] Although exceptions and variations may be cited about the family and kinship system, the joint family has been an important stabilizing factor in Indian society.

The Village

There is no doubt that the village is a basic unit of Indian society. The origin of village solidarity was closely related to the development of the *gotra,* a group based on blood relationships and traced to a common mythological ancestor. According to the exogamous rule of Hinduism, no man shall marry a woman from within his own *gotra.* The growth of the *gotra* solidified a large number of related people who held property in the same area. In the absence of a formal constitution or system of administration, social and economic relationships among villagers have always been regulated by customary patterns and practices. The convention of village owners is an informal governing body which looks after wells, ponds, reservoirs, groves, and cowpens. Historically, villagers in India were quite self-subsisting and self-contained. They paid a share of the village crops to local princes who, in turn, paid their taxes to the Hindu or Muslim ruler, depending on the time and place. Dynastic changes in the central government hardly touched the life of the village.

It is difficult to make general characterizations of the Indian village because of local and ethnic variations. For example, in the north a tenure system was widespread, while in the south individual holding of the land and individual payment of the land tax directly to the local princes were more common. Recently, an important work on the subject was published under the title *Village India*.[36] This symposium includes eight scholars' studies of different aspects of contemporary village life, covering territories of nine different language groups. Two studies in this symposium, one dealing with a village in the south and another with a village in the north, are pertinent for our purpose.

Srinivas' analysis of a south Indian village, Rampura in Mysore, is concerned with the structure of role and status relationships among various castes and occupational groups. Each caste in this village traditionally has been associated with a particular occupation; however, in actuality each caste may have more than one occupation, and also one can change occupation without too much difficulty. The peasant caste is the only one engaged solely in its traditional occupation, agriculture. It is the most numerous caste, including almost one half the village population; the biggest landowners belong to this caste. Many members of the Brāhman and Lingāyat castes, the two priestly groups, are engaged in secular professions, while every other caste has some members who are professional priests. Five castes (two smith castes, potters, washermen, and barbers) provide services to the cultivators and are paid in grain at harvesttime. Nine other resident castes (shepherds, basketmakers, swineherds, untouchables, etc.) do not provide regular services in the agricultural life, and are not paid at the harvest. The social life of the village centers around agricultural activities and Hindu religious festivals. The traditional concepts of pollution, endogamy (marriage within one's own caste), and the institution of separate caste courts tend to insulate castes from each other, while tenantship, debtorship, and clientship interrelate the different castes. Local disputes are settled by the elders of the dominant caste, who represent the vertical unity of the village against the separatism of caste. It is evident that even today occupational specialization compels each group to support the total interdependent village system.[37]

Marriott, in his study of the northern village of Kishan Garhi in the Aligarh district, finds numerous internal divisions following the lines of kinship, economic, and religious groups. Nevertheless, village identification determines one's place in society, and the sense of village loyalty is very strong. Two factors relate the village to the outside. First is the relation of the village to the state government, and second is the caste system. Marriott studied the relationship between the religious life of Kishan Garhi and the dominant Hindu religious tradition. His analysis of the festivals and deities of Kishan Garhi reveals a two-way interaction — of " universalization " and " parochialization " — between the Sanskrit (Vedic-Aryan) religious tradition and the village religious life.[38]

In spite of the recent trends of urbanization and modernization, the village continues to provide focuses for individual identification in Indian society, and this will be the case for a long time to come. The Community Development Program and the National Extension Service of the Indian Government are bound to change certain aspects of village life in India. However, it will be very difficult for the Government to alter the religious beliefs and attitudes of the people in 550,000 rural villages, who perpetuate the conservative Hindu orthodoxy.

The Caste System

The term "caste," derived originally from the Portuguese word *casta* signifying breed, race, or kind, indicates a hierarchical social order that freezes individuals at the various levels of society. In its narrow and technical sense, this term denotes a unique Indian system which is the basis of the social and religious structure. The caste system is based on three concepts: (1) that the whole of society is a composite of many parts which are mutually dependent on each other; (2) that each part is an autonomous social group which regulates the beliefs and customs of its members; and (3) that the cosmic, moral, and ritual order sanctions, and derives support from, such a stratified society. A caste is usually defined as a social unit that has internal forces of cohesion, separate from other castes, and has fixed relationships with other castes. There are more than two thousand castes and subcastes in India. Among the important features of a caste are endogamy, a common name, hereditary membership, traditional occupations, claim of a common origin, immobility outside its own group, and a common ritual practice. However, a certain amount of flexibility and local variations make it impossible to define the caste system in any rigid manner.

In the main, the three upper castes are: Brāhmans, or priestly caste; the Kshatriyas, or warrior and ruler caste; and Vaisyas, or commoners. These three castes have been called the "twice-born," because members of these groups are "reborn" ceremonially in the initiation rite (*upanā-yana*). The fourth caste is the Sūdras, or serfs, and the fifth is the "outcaste" or "untouchables," variously known as Panchamas, Harijans, or "scheduled class." Hutton insists, however, that the first four groups are *varna*, a Vedic term denoting "color," and should not be confused with caste (*jati* or *jat*). In ancient India, different colors were associated with different groups: white with the priest-teacher group, red with the warriors, yellow with commoners, and black with the serfs. Historically, *varna* was not a caste; rather, it was regarded as a "group of castes." [39]

There are many kinds of castes. Some of them are based on ethnic or racial background, as represented by the cowherds caste in upper India, known as the Ahirs, which probably once was a Scythian tribe. In the course of time, some of the ethnic castes have lost their original identities. Some castes developed originally from sectarian principles. For instance, the Lingāyat was founded by a reformer who challenged the Hindu social system, even though it too became a full-fledged caste. New castes were sometimes formed by migration, change of occupation, mixed marriage, or conversion of a non-Hindu group into Hinduism. [40] Hutton finds the fluidity of the caste system operating in two directions, some castes attempting to combine under a new caste, and others tending to split up. He finds a similar fluidity operating among subcastes. [41] Hutton also calls our attention to the existence of a southern Indian tradition by which castes are divided into Right Hand and Left Hand groupings, which further complicates an already complex society. [42]

The structure of any society is determined by the ways in which social groups are related to each other. In India, the traditional social structure was based on the interplay of the family, village, and the caste systems within the larger sociopolitical, cultural, and religious context. What distinguishes Indian social structure is the decisive role played by the caste system for the integration of society. The caste provides an individual with a permanent body

of associations which control every aspect of his actions
from the cradle to the grave. The caste determines its own
membership and maintains the continuity of skill, knowledge, and culture from one generation to the next. Despite
the disadvantages and inequalities involved in the caste
structure, no one can deny the historic role played by the
caste system in welding into one community the various
groups of diverse background in India.[43]

The caste system is often sharply criticized for its complete and rigid separation of castes in all aspects of life —
such as marriage, religious worship, eating, residence, occupation — and its treatment of the untouchables. To be
sure, the integration of any society involves some inequalities, but nowhere else in the world are the inequalities so
marked and so rigid, and nowhere else are they religiously
sanctioned as in India. Despite the efforts of modern reformers and government legislation, age-old beliefs and
customs die hard. Gradually, however, under the impact
of modernization of India, the rigidity of the caste system is
being counteracted by more fluctuating " class " groupings,
established along the lines of wealth, profession, education,
and position. While the individual's caste is fixed, his mobility in the class system of wealth and position and of
personal prestige is not so fixed.[44]

It is apparent that Indian social structure in the future
cannot remain what it has been, but at the same time it
cannot be divorced completely from its past, in spite of
industrialization, urbanization, and other internal and external factors of the contemporary situation. The past is
never lost completely, although its significance and value
are bound to be modified and seen from different perspectives.

MODERN HINDUISM AND THE CASTE SYSTEM

The Impact of the West

The development of Hinduism has been characterized by its tenacity in maintaining its distinctive character, even though it has been enriched by the diverse streams that have flowed into it. At one time it looked as though Buddhism would replace Hinduism in India, but Buddhism was repudiated in the long run from the land of its origin. Later, Muslim rulers tried to establish the religion of the Prophet, and indeed Islam, while it failed to convert the whole of India, gained sufficient strength to split the subcontinent politically. Under Muslim rule, India's contacts with the rest of the world were expanded considerably. While Hindus did not travel outside India, foreigners came to India, and some Indian Muslims went out of the country.

The situation was vastly different under British rule. Indian-Muslim culture never penetrated below the upper strata of Indian society. During the British rule the number of Indians knowing English was far greater than those knowing Urdu under the Muslim regime; in fact, by 1850 English had become the language of the country. Also, in comparison with Indian-Muslim culture, which after all did not represent the main stream of Islamic civilization, English culture was the bearer of modern Western civilization. In the nineteenth century, the Indian elite, who used English as their own language, believed in the superiority of the Western way of life. Through the English language and British contacts, the Indian intelligentsia drew on the storehouse of culture, science, and art of the modern Western world. Thus, in the nineteenth and twentieth centuries Hinduism had to come to terms with " modernity," which confronted all spheres of Indian life.

Historians remind us that the British regime followed a general decline in the cultural and political life of India. By the latter part of the eighteenth century, many thoughtful Hindus were concerned about signs of the disintegration of Hinduism and Hindu society from within. With the establishment of the British suzerainty in this situation, India inevitably came under the strong impact of Western civilization. While the administrative units of India under the British corresponded neither to economic regions nor to linguistic areas, " the British raj contributed a number of modern unifying forces: a common army and common civil service, a lingua franca in the shape of the English language, and a unitary network of means of communication." [45] Western scholars also contributed much to the study of the Indian classics. For example, Max Müller devoted a lifetime to the publication of the first printed text of the Rig Veda, the collection of hymns which are the Bible of the Hindu religion.

It is exceedingly difficult to characterize the modern development of Hinduism by any one of the four general types of religious movement: reform, revival, renaissance, or revolt. " From the dawn of the nineteenth century to the present day, all these four types of religious movements are found operating, but not necessarily in a chronological order of succession. . . . Quite frequently all four types of movements are present at any one time, making the situation altogether too complex." [46]

The modern development of Hinduism may be summarized meaningfully, for our purpose, in three periods. (1) During the nineteenth century and the early part of the twentieth century, the reformers were awakened to the decadence of Hindu religion and society (especially in regard to the evils of the caste system), and they were willing to draw inspiration and examples from Western culture. (2) Between the two World Wars, the leaders of Hinduism aspired for genuine co-operation and coexistence between the East and West, and between Hinduism and other religions. (3) Since World War II, Indian leaders seem to be split between two approaches. On the one hand, there is a genuine yearning for a Hinduism-oriented nation, whereas on the other hand, there is another, equally sincere desire for a " secular state " in which the historic importance of Hinduism is respected but is not to be the socioreligious framework of the Republic. Admittedly, this characterization is arbitrary, because in each of the three periods we can find exceptions.

The First Phase of Modern Hinduism

During the first period of modern Hinduism, reformers came under the sway of Western thought and Christianity. For example, Rām Mohun Roy (d. 1833), the founder of a reformed Hindu movement called the " Brāhmo Samāj," was an admirer of the precepts of Jesus, even though he rejected Jesus' divinity and the doctrines of Trinity and atonement. He advocated the abolition of widow-burning, idol worship, and the caste system. His successor in the Brāhmo Samāj, Maharhi Devendranath Tagore, even rejected the authority of the Vedas. Another reformer, Keshub Chander Sen, became an ardent admirer of Christ; he labored for the passing of the Civil Marriage Act of 1872 and for other social reform. More conservative in religious outlook but equally progressive in social reform was Swami Dayānanda (d. 1883), the founder of the Ārya Samāj; he strongly upheld the authority of the Vedas, while

denouncing the caste system and idol worship. The revival
of Hindu religion found an able spokesman in the person
of an Englishwoman, Annie Besant (d. 1933), a leader of
the Theosophical Society. Almost singlehandedly she established a Hindu college in Benares; she was also an advocate of the Home Rule scheme. Her popularity waned,
however, when she refused to support the Non-Co-opera-
tion movement of Gāndhi. By far the most important religious figure of nineteenth-century India was Srī Rāmakrishna Paramahamsa (d. 1886), who has been described
as a man of " depth in spiritual consciousness which tran-
scends time and space and has a universal appeal." [47] Being
a priest of Kālī (the Divine Mother), he proclaimed that
the Divine Mother of Sāktism, the god Vishnu of Vaishnavism, and the Ultimate Reality (Brahman) of Hindu
philosophy were one and the same reality. Furthermore,
Rāmakrishna was convinced that the diverse religions of
the world — including the several traditions of Hinduism
— were different paths to the same spiritual goal. His disciple Vivekānanda (d. 1902) translated the master's spiritual insights into concrete religio-social and evangelistic
programs. Vivekānanda organized a brotherhood of monks
in India, and he also established the Rāmakrishna Mission
centers in various parts of America and Europe. As a pa-
triot, he lamented the fact that the so-called social reforms
of his day touched only the two upper castes, and he inspired many of his followers to undertake a thoroughgoing
social and religious reformation in India. At the same time,
he was critical of Christian missions, which aimed at conversion of Indians to a foreign religion; he was convinced
that Hinduism at its best was superior to any other religion
in the world.

The reformers of the first phase of the modern development of Hinduism were keenly aware of social evils that had been perpetuated in the name of religion. For example, V. Kunhikannan condemned the traditional belief that one's sins will be washed away by bathing in the water of the Ganges and by visiting the sacred city of Benares. " Could any idea be more primitive? " he asked.[48] V. Sriniva Rao was convinced that social reforms would be impossible without attempting to reform the underlying religious beliefs. He traced the social evils of his day to the popular beliefs of undue reverence for the sacred books, idolatry, and the caste system.

The Second Phase of Modern Hinduism

The second phase of modern Hinduism was characterized by a deep appreciation of the Hindu tradition and also by a desire for equality and coexistence between the East and West. Three men who epitomize this spirit are Srī Aurobindo Ghose, Rabīndranāth Tagore, and Mahātmā Gāndhi. They were keenly conscious of the shortcomings of Hinduism and Hindu society, and yet to them Hinduism was not a thing of the past but an ever-growing, dynamic spiritual movement that was open to novel ideas and experiment. All three were passionate Hindus and at the same time genuine world citizens. Their struggle for the political independence of India was remarkably free from emotional bitterness against the British.

Aurobindo (d. 1950) was the most systematic thinker among the three. Well versed in German, French, English, Greek, and Latin, he attempted, at least theoretically, a synthesis of the ancient Vedānta and modern European political philosophy. Living as he did in the midst of political and social chaos, he came to believe that the solution of world problems was to be found in the establishment of a "gnostic" community. This belief led him to give up all practical political activities in 1910, and to establish an *āsrama* (hermitage) in the French settlement of Pondicherry. To Aurobindo, a Western-educated scholar, the ancient Sanskrit scriptures became the source of an esoteric religious discipline. During the last forty years of his life, he practiced yoga and instructed disciples in spiritual matters.

Tagore (d. 1941), undoubtedly one of the great poets of the modern world, gained acceptance in India, ironically, only after he had won the Nobel Prize. In his person, and in his lifelong activities, we find a happy blending of East and West, past and future, a genuine patriotism to India, and dedication to the cause of humanity. His philosophy was based on the perfect love between the Supreme soul and the soul of all created beings. Such a perfect love alone holds duality on one side and nonduality on the other. " In this love strength and beauty, form and emotion, the limited and the unlimited have all become one." [49] His spiritual outlook is succinctly expressed in a prayer with which he closed an article written on his eightieth birthday:

> He is one alone and one attribute, and
> yet by His union with many powers creates
> infinite attributes fulfilling their
> hidden meanings. Into Him the world is
> dissolved finally, who is God from the
> beginning of the creation. May He unite
> us with Mind that is auspicious.[50]

Gāndhi (1869–1948), whom John Gunther once characterized as " an incredible combination of Jesus Christ, Tammany Hall, and your father," was, in his own words, not a visionary but a practical idealist. It is well known that he drew spiritual insights from Sanskrit literature, the

New Testament, and the writings of Thoreau, Ruskin, and Tolstoy. His eventful career in South Africa and India was motivated by his "experiments with Truth," to use his famous phraseology. During Gāndhi's campaign in South Africa, long before his name became famous, Gilbert Murray is said to have prophesied: "A dangerous man to fall out with. In a fight he will surrender everything except his soul. And his soul will conquer in the end." Many Indians followed Gāndhi's passive resistance movement against the British rule, but many Hindus resented his stand on Hindu-Muslim unity and the abolition of untouchability. Gāndhi urged his Hindu followers to befriend Muslims as fellow men. He was convinced that there is room in Hinduism for Jesus, Muhammad, Zoroaster, and Moses. According to him, different religions must cooperate as equal partners. For example, he welcomed the contribution of Western Christians "to get rid of the admitted abuses and purify" Hinduism, but Gāndhi was against the Christian policy of proselyting Indians, because such a policy would uproot Hinduism from its very foundation. In his opinion, if a house is in need of repair, the owner of the house would welcome anyone who shows him how to repair it. "But he would most decidedly resist those who sought to destroy that house that had served well with him and his ancestors for ages." [51] On the question of untouchability, he was persuaded that unless "this blot on Hinduism" is removed, Hinduism itself is bound to perish. Yet, he was against the use of law or compulsion in order to remove untouchability; it can be brought about only by the "conversion" of millions of Hindus. "The silent, loving suffering of one single pure Hindu as such will be enough to melt the hearts of millions of Hindus." [52] Although many Indians were baffled by him, they followed his leadership throughout the long struggle for India's political independence from British rule. Gāndhi's death at the hands of a fanatic assassin dramatically ended the second phase of modern Hinduism.

Aurobindo, Tagore, and Gāndhi were faithful Hindus. They and many others like them, however, were keenly aware that the progress of modern India had been hindered by conservative Hinduism, mass illiteracy, technological backwardness, and by a lack of organic relationship between the government and the people. They were also cognizant of the fact that India benefited " by the irresistible march of science, by the utility of certain Western conceptions in organizing social relationships, and by a longing in many quarters to meet the West successfully on its own ground." [53]

The Contemporary Scene

Political independence in 1947 ushered in the third phase of modern Hinduism. We need not indulge in speculation or prophetic utterances as to what will happen to Hinduism in the future, but we must, difficult though it is, attempt to analyze and understand the nature of contemporary Hinduism. It is safe to say that the dilemma of modern Hinduism, which was implicit before political independence, is becoming more and more apparent. During the struggle for political independence, all Hindus were guided by this objective. Now that political freedom has been attained, differences are beginning to threaten the internal unity of the new republic. The central issue of contemporary Hinduism is "modernity." The Congress Party, which is in power today, accepts this and is proceeding to establish a modern nation-state in India. The majority of the Hindus, as well as the religious minority groups in India, seem to accept the idea of a "secular state" in which freedom of religion is guaranteed. The extreme Left Wing is impatient with the platform and administration of the Congress Party, while the extreme Right Wing cries for the establishment of a rigid Hindu state. The predicament of the Indian Government is that the rural areas, which have been the stronghold of the Congress Party, are slow to accept changes.

It is an irony of history that when India finally achieved political independence, the nation-state had lost much of its relevance in the international domain. Today, the importance of "power blocs" supersedes nation-states in world affairs. This may account for India's decision to stay within the British Commonwealth, and also its active interest in the so-called Bandung Front. While many Westerners seem to feel that India appeases the Soviet bloc too much and expects too many concessions from the democratic bloc, Taya Zinkin reminds us that the newly freed nonwhite world sees the cold war from its own perspective. To the West the cold war is a very simple linear equation. "The West (democracy) versus the Iron Curtain (totalitarianism) equals good versus bad. To the average Indian . . . the equation from linear becomes quadratic. The West (democracy plus color bar) versus the Iron Curtain (totalitarianism minus color bar) equals good plus bad versus bad plus good." [54] Also, there is no denying that India is watching Red China's economic progress. According to Chester Bowles, what interests India is the fact that "today the debris of China's violent revolution has been largely focused on China's extraordinary new drive to enroll all of her 450,000,000 rural population in 'productive co-operatives.'" [55] Nehru himself is reported to have commented in 1954 that "India's liberal constitution will only last if the Indian economic plan can engender a sense of economic progress at least equal to that of China." [56]

No one seems to be able to assess accurately the strength of communism in India. The Communist Party surprised Indians and outsiders by becoming the largest opposition party in the National Parliament and in the Assemblies of Hyderabad, Madras, and West Bengal after the 1951–1952 election. One newspaper commented that the " have-nots " in south India " are mostly from the middle class, and one has therefore regrettably come to the conclusion that an enormous middle class is today veering to the extreme Left in the south of India." [57] In the state elections of 1954 and 1955, the Communist Party made every effort to consolidate the opposition to the Congress Party. In this connection, M. R. Masani has observed that it is not the economic factors that primarily dispose men to the attraction of communism. " It is the psychological and emotional void created by the looseness of the hold of the traditional religions of India that provides room for what is essentially a new religion of materialism." [58]

Diametrically opposed to the Left Wing, but equally antagonistic toward the Congress Party regime, is the extreme Right Wing, represented by the Rastrya Swayamseval Sangha, commonly referred to as the R.S.S., and the Hindu Mahasabha. The R.S.S., which emerged in 1925, was not important in the Indian political scene until 1942, when the British raj jailed the Congress leaders. Many young Hindus, resentful of the powerful Muslim League, rallied around the R.S.S., which drew over 400,000 members at the time of the Partition in 1947. The R.S.S. is against all " foreign ideologies," including secularism, materialism, and Marxism. Equally militant is the Hindu Mahasabha, which refuses to accept Partition as a closed chapter in the history of India. Both the R.S.S. and the Hindu Mahasabha are against the Congress Party's separation of religion and the state. Both advocate the unification and revitalization of the Hindu community and the establishment of a rigid Hindu state, preserving the traditional socioreligious structure, including the caste system.

In addition to opposition from the Left and Right Wings, the Congress Party regime has to face the masses in ferment. The masses supported the Congress leaders during the struggle for independence with the happy illusion that political independence would automatically improve their living standard, which of course, was not realized. In spite of the seemingly insurmountable problems that had to be dealt with, the accomplishments of the Congress Party regime during its first ten years in power were not negligible.

The stated aim of the Congress Government is to establish a co-operative commonwealth based on equality of opportunity and on political, economic, and social rights. The constitution of India prohibits all discrimination on grounds of religion, race, caste, sex, or place of birth. The practice of untouchability is forbidden. The right to the freedom of speech and expression, assembly, association, movement, residence, acquisition and disposal of property, and practice of any profession is guaranteed by the constitution.[59]

Equally important are the directive principles, which, though not enforceable through courts of law, are regarded as " fundamental in the governance of the country." They seek to ensure (Article 39) that: " (a) the citizens, men and women equally, have the right to an adequate means of livelihood; (b) the ownership and control of the material resources of the community are so distributed as best to subserve the common good; (c) the operation of the economic system does not result in the concentration of wealth and the means of production to the common detriment." Furthermore, " the state shall take steps to organize village *panchayats* as units of self-government." [60]

Questions have often been raised as to whether or not the present regime can successfully put its objectives into practice, and how soon. It must be remembered that the Congress Party consists of many elements, including a large number of orthodox Hindu adherents. For this reason, the Congress Party regime cannot afford to ignore traditional cultural and religious values. For example, it is widely known that Nehru was eager to put the Hindu Code Bill into effect, which would have changed the divorce and inheritance laws, but Rajendra Prasad, a devout Hindu, threatened to resign from the Presidency, and thus Nehru did not push it. The crux of the matter is how to reconcile the socialistic pattern of society that the Congress leaders envisage with the religious beliefs and practices of the Hindus. To be more specific, the program of the Congress regime to eradicate untouchability and caste barriers faces great difficulties because Hinduism and Hindu society are grounded in the caste system. While some Indians feel that the caste system can never be eradicated, others advocate a regrouping of all the castes and subcastes into the four classical *varna* (" colors " or groups of castes) . Still others, including the Leftists, the Dravida Kazhagam (a movement of the non-Brāhman Dravidians in the south), and some communalists, advocate the wholesale elimination of the caste system. The basic problem is to determine what kind of social order can and should be established, because India cannot move forward without having some vision of the future.

One of the remarkable men in contemporary India is Vinoba Bhave, the founder of the Bhoodan Yagna (land-sacrifice movement) who is regarded as a saint in the Gāndhian tradition. He has two main messages, village sufficiency and elimination of all social and political distinctions. Vinoba Bhave is trying to bring about a silent ideological revolution by asking the rich to donate lands to the poor.[61] In five years he has walked literally fifteen thousand miles and has received over four million acres of land. But what kind of vision of the future does Vinoba Bhave have? While he advocates co-operative farming, increased village industries, basic education, and the betterment of health conditions in the village, his whole outlook is based on the notion that India is to become a loose federation of self-sufficient village communities. " To the extent that power changes hands from the Government to the people," he declares, " so nonviolence will grow and the power of the state will gradually diminish and ultimately disappear." [62]

Much more " modern " and sophisticated than Vinoba Bhave is Sarvepalli Radhakrishnan, philosopher and statesman, and an articulate spokesman of modern Hinduism. Radhakrishnan attempts to resolve the traditional oppositions between the Absolute and the nonabsolute, God and the world, appearance and reality, intuition and reason, philosophy and religion, and philosophy and life.[63] It is his conviction that the essential truth of all religions is the same. For him, religion is not a creed or code, but an insight into reality; religion is the life of the inner spirit — or the affirmation of the primacy of spiritual values. His synthesis, however, is grounded in Vedāntic tradition. He holds that all that is good is implicit in the Upanishads.

Radhakrishnan does not look back to the golden age of classical Hinduism. According to him: " There is vast need to speed up our social program, increase employment, obliterate illiteracy, combat disease. If we pour social and economic content into our political democracy and achieve a welfare state, our effort will be an example to Asia and Africa." [64] But if we examine the nature and structure of Radhakrishnan's " welfare state," he is not very consistent. In the main, he seems to accept the caste system without caste rigidity. Wadia points out that Radhakrishnan in his book *The Hindu View of Life* (1926) praises caste as a great achievement of the Hindu genius; and in his *Eastern Religion and Western Thought* (1939) he prefers to speak of the " class " rather than " caste " and justifies it philosophically; but in *Religion and Society* (1947) he bitterly criticizes the traditional caste system.[65] Radhakrishnan acknowledges the mistakes of many of the social reformers who offered the untouchables advice to improve their position, instead of active help. " We should ask for their forgiveness; for we have wronged them. . . . The only way in which we can repay is by devoting our lives to their service." [66] Nevertheless, Radhakrishnan's philosophical position is fundamentally rooted in the notion of " hierarchy," for according to him hierarchy is not a coercion but a law of nature, and the four " classes " represent four stages of development in our manhood. He states that " if one who is of a lower nature desires to perform the social tasks of a higher class, before he has attained the answering capacities, *social order will be disturbed.*" [67] In spite of his five reasons in favor of a hierarchical social order, one can hardly accept Radhakrishnan's thesis that his fourfold hierarchy is " democratic."

No one will deny that the most influential architect of

new India, with the possible exception of Gāndhi, is Jawaharlal Nehru. On January 29, 1948, when Gāndhi was assassinated, Nehru addressed the crowd: " We can best serve Bapu by dedicating ourselves to the ideals for which he lived and the cause for which he died." [68] However, today, some people wonder if Nehru is in fact working toward the ideals of Gāndhi. This question cannot be answered with a simple yes or no. " Gāndhi, it is true, was not in favor of industrialization. . . . Yet as Nehru leads India into a program of industrialization one finds Gāndhi's spirit very much in evidence, especially his belief that economic reform should be brought about by nonviolent means, that ' work is worship,' that an agrarian simplicity of life is to be preferred to ' the mad desire to destroy distance and time, to increase animal appetites and go to the ends of the earth in search of their satisfaction.' " [69] We might point out that while Gāndhi and Nehru agreed on many specific objectives and also on nonviolence as a means of attaining them, Nehru does not define the nature of the problems faced by India in the same way Gāndhi did.

Although Nehru comes from a distinguished Kashmir Brāhman family and was educated at Harrow and Cambridge, he is not orthodox in either the Indian or the Western sense. Nehru is a modern man who lives in " an age of disillusion, of doubt and uncertainty. . . . We can no longer accept many of the ancient beliefs and customs; we have no more faith in them, in Asia or in Europe or in America. So we search for new ways." [70] He has profound respect for classical Hinduism, but traditional orthodoxy as such has no relevance to him. Characteristically, Nehru once remarked: " For centuries we have been asking ourselves the question, ' What should we be? ' I think that now in the new free India the time has come to ask ourselves the

new question, ' What should we do? ' " [71] Basically, Nehru's
vision of India in the future is a modern, " secular," industrialized welfare state, an important member of the family
of nations, and yet distinctly Indian, rooted in the Hindu
tradition of tolerance and nonviolence. There is no question that Nehru accepts the fact of " modernity," a parlia-
mentary government system, respect for the law, and the
principles of political and civil liberty. Recognizing the
difficulties involved in central planning in a mixed economy, Nehru tried to maintain a balance among the three
main areas — agrarian, industrial, and welfare — of the
second Five Year Plan. He does not underestimate the
difficulties involved, such as the lack of skilled managerial
personnel and capital for economic progress, opposition of
the well-organized groups of the extreme Right and extreme Left, and the political aspirations of linguistic
groups.

Probably one of the most critical issues of modern India
is the tremendous gap between Nehru's vision of future
India and the realities of contemporary India. Indian farming is still primitive even by Asian standards, and despite
a gradual drift to the cities from the countryside, the villages will continue to be centers of the social, economic,
and cultural life of a large majority of the Indians for many
years to come. " The grinding and terrible poverty which
besets the Indian people arises from the pressure of population on the food supply — and this is getting worse, partly
from ignorance and superstition, partly from the lack of
social services." [72] While it is true that villagers are co-
operating in the Community Development and Extension
Service Programs of the central Government, the old customs and beliefs die hard in the village. It must be recalled,
in this connection, that the ancient religious traditions of

the village were never completely superseded by Vedic-Aryan Brahmanism or Sanskrit civilization. Marriott, who studied the village of Kishan Garhi in northern India, admits that the main tradition of Hinduism has achieved an integrated position in village life, but he also found on close examination that out of the nineteen festivals of Kishan Garhi four have no evident Sanskrit rationale, and even those which have Sanskrit names contain local rituals which have no connection with the Sanskrit tradition. Furthermore, in his observation, connections between the local festivals and Sanskrit tradition are often loose, confused, or distorted.[73] In fact, what we generally call Hinduism is a dynamic historic phenomenon, rooted, to be sure, in Vedic-Aryan Brahmanism, but which also has accepted and transformed many of the non-Aryan religious beliefs and practices that have persisted in the village to this day. The structural link between the Vedic-Aryan Hindu tradition and the village religious traditions is found in the caste system. The general Hindu feeling about the caste system is that it has been based on and sanctioned by the eternal cosmic order (*dharma*). " Observance of caste, therefore, is equivalent to *dharma*, that is, to religious observance, righteousness, moral obligation." [74]

Various theses have been advanced concerning the future of Hinduism. Some groups — such as the Rastrya Swayam-sevak Sangha and the Hindu Mahasabha — would like to see re-established in India a Hindu state, with its traditional socioreligious structure, including a more rigid form of the caste system. Others feel that Hinduism itself will be emancipated from the yoke of its social and cultural framework and develop, as some spokesmen of Western Vedānta advocate, into a genuine world religion. They would agree with Hocking's principle: " The religious community is by definition universal. . . . It speaks not primarily to the man-within-the-nation but to the man-within-the-world." [75] However, the difficulty is that historically Hinduism has not developed a norm of ecclesiastical structure except in terms of the caste system. Still others are convinced that a "secular state" is the answer for India, where the term "secular" is to be understood in a spiritual sense, and freedom of all religions will be guaranteed. The present Congress leadership, which incidentally includes some non-Hindus, falls in this group. They would probably agree that "it is clearly *not the destiny of the secular state to render the functions of a religious community superfluous.*" [76] In effect, however, the socialistic program of the present Indian Government is destined to undercut the sanctity of the caste system, which is the very structure of the traditional Hindu holy community.

While it would be unrealistic to ignore the importance of the state today in India, it would be just as unrealistic to overlook the spiritual tenacity of the Hindu religion. There is much truth in the statement of Vinoba Bhave: "The Government might be capable of capturing anything, but never the hearts of the people." And in their hearts Hindus still accept the sacramental view of the universe which is the core of historic Hinduism, and which sustained Hindu culture and society through the ages. " In the sacramental order," said Ananda K. Coomaraswamy, " there is a need and a place for all men's work: and there is no more significant consequence of the principle, Work Is Sacrifice, than the fact that under these conditions, and remote as this may be from our secular way of thinking, every function, from that of the priest and the king down to that of the potter and scavenger, is literally a priesthood and every operation a rite." [77]

Nehru, the statesman and philosopher, senses the need for some vision of the future, however vague that vision may be. The crucial question is whether Hinduism, with its sacramental view of life and its notion of a cosmic hierarchy can provide this vision.

Where the mind is without fear and the head is held high;
    Where knowledge is free;
    Where the world has not been broken
up into fragments by narrow domestic walls;
    Where words come out from the depth of truth;
    Where tireless striving stretches its arms towards perfection;
    Where the clear stream of reason has not lost its way into the dreary desert sand of dead habit;
    Where the mind is led forward by Thee into ever-widening thought and action —
    Into that heaven of freedom, my Father, let my country awake.[78]

4 Buddhism and the Samgha

❖ ❖

BUDDHA

The Great Enlightened

Among all the religions of the world, few have been more copiously described than Buddhism and perhaps few have been less thoroughly understood. It is not difficult to study the life and teachings of its founder, nor is it impossible to study certain segments of the voluminous Buddhist scriptures and the philosophical systems of Buddhism. But how can we grasp the character of the complex body of beliefs, practices, and institutions of Buddhism? This is not an easy task.

Buddhism, like Islam and Christianity, is a world religion, not only because it embraces within its fold diverse national groups, but more basically because it holds that the fundamental meaning of life and the world cannot be derived from the experience of any one group of people or culture.

In the actual study of Buddhism, two obvious factors must be kept in mind. First is the Indian origin of Buddhism. Clearly, Buddha was a child of his age and culture, and even his protest against Brahmanism (early form of Hinduism) must be understood within the Indian context.

Second is the Pan-Asianness of Buddhism. While Buddhism in the course of time lost ground in India, it became securely established as a Pan-Asian religion, spreading to other parts of Asia. In other words, we have to take into account its Indian roots, which are lasting marks in Buddhism, and yet recognize that Buddhism developed an autonomous religious system of its own, quite distinct from Brahmanism.

In spite of numerous legends about the founder of Buddhism, we cannot be very certain about the details of his life. The canonical accounts of Buddha's life were written centuries after his death, with definite dogmatic and apologetic interests. " The popular story of Buddha's life, as known to the West, is merely the modern version of one of these traditions, and it has been made plausible only by ignoring the other accounts and omitting all the marvels." [1]

Scholars agree that Buddha was born in Lumbini, near the Nepal-Indian border, but there are many theories as to when he was born. Some say he was born in 624 B.C., others say 567 B.C., and still others believe that he was born in 466 B.C. His father's name was Suddhodana, and his mother's was Maya. According to tradition, his family was a high Kshatriya (warrior) family and belonged to the Sākya (Sākiya) clan, which founded the city of Kapilavastu on the slopes of the Himalayas. The Sākya state was a small aristocratic republic governed by a raja, who was under the King of Kosala. (Kosala, Magadha, Avanti, and Vamsa were four great kingdoms of northern India at the time of Buddha.) There are many legends that say that Buddha's father was a king, but more likely he was a raja. Another unsolved question is whether or not Buddha's clan belonged to the Aryan race. According to Mookerji, the Sākyas followed some non-Aryan customs, such as marrying within the same *gotra*, but "they were in the outskirts of Vedic civilization." [2]

Later legends portray Buddha as a prince who in his youth was accustomed to the splendor and luxury of a royal family. No doubt this glorification of Buddha's lineage met the psychological needs of the faithful, who attributed special significance to Buddha's renunciation of the worldly life, but there does not seem to be any basis for accepting the account that he spent his youth in an atmosphere of sensual pleasure, luxury, and pomp. Most likely Buddha "belonged to a fighting aristocracy, active in war and debate, wealthy according to the standard of the times and yielding imperfect obedience to the authority of kings and priests." [3] Actually, little is known about his childhood and youth. His given name was Siddhārtha (Siddhattha in Pali), but he was called Gautama (or Gotama), which was the name of his *gotra*. He was married to a woman whose name has been variously given as Bhaddakachcha, Bimba, Gopa, and Yasoddhara, and they had a son, Rāhula. When he was twenty-nine, Gautama decided to forsake the world and become a mendicant. At first he visited the capital of the Magadha kingdom and studied under two masters, Alara Kalama and Uddaka Ramputta. Unfortunately, our knowledge about these two Yoga masters is scanty, but "it would appear," said Eliot, "that they both had a fixed system (*dhamma*) to impart and that their students lived in religious discipline (*vinaya*) as members of an order." [4] It is to be noted that Buddha developed his religion later along similar lines — with Dharma (Dhamma, holy law), Vinaya (discipline), and Samgha (Sangha, community).

What motivated Gautama's religious quest? We are told that he was distressed by the facts of human life, such as old age, sickness, death, sorrow, and impurity, and that his search for the meaning of life behind its transitoriness led him to the Yoga discipline. But, not being able to find answers, Guatama left his teachers and spent nearly seven years in a grove near Uruvela, not far from Bodh-Gayā, and there he led the life of a lonely ascetic. It is quite possible that his austere asceticism was associated with Jainism. Be that as it may, the extreme asceticism not only made him weak physically, but caused spiritual unrest. Realizing that asceticism also was not leading him to spiritual insight, he abandoned it, and after taking food to nourish his body he concentrated on meditation. One cool night he saw in a trance a vision of his previous existences. In the second watch of the night he saw another vision, which revealed how all beings pass away and are reborn according to the law of *karma* (moral law of cause and effect). Finally, he gained piercing insight into the meaning of existence and the way of deliverance from the transitoriness of the finite world. His mind was freed from sensual desire, desire for existence, and ignorance. " And in me emancipated arose the knowledge of my emancipation. I realized that destroyed is rebirth, the religious life has been led, done is what was to be done, there is nought [for me] beyond this world. . . . Ignorance was dispelled, knowledge arose. Darkness was dispelled, light arose." [5]

Thus he attained the supreme state of Enlightenment. This event took place when Buddha was thirty-six years of age. Buddhists believe that the exact spot of his Enlightenment was under the Bodhi tree at Bodh-Gayā. After his Enlightenment Buddha preached *sad-dharma* (Good Law) for over forty years until he passed away at the age of eighty.

Buddha's Ministry

Buddha preached his first sermon to five monks in the Deer Park (the present Sārnāth, known in old days as Isipatana or Migadaya) near Benares. He urged his disciples to follow the Middle Path, avoiding the two extremes of pleasure-seeking and mortification, as well as contradictions and opposites. In his view, the Middle Path alone would lead to insight, supreme enlightenment, and Nirvāna. Then Buddha expounded the Four Noble Truths of suffering (*dukkha*). According to this formula, firstly, the finite existence is analyzed in terms of suffering or the absence of bliss. Secondly, suffering is traced causally to its origin of " Tanha," which is thirst, desire, or craving for finite existence, pleasure, and success. Thirdly, cessation of suffering is possible, according to Buddha, only by overcoming the basic craving itself. Fourthly, the course to be followed for overcoming suffering is expounded as right views, right intent, right speech, right conduct, right means of livelihood, right endeavor, right mindfulness, and right meditation (the Eightfold Path).

According to the canonical writings, very early in his ministry Buddha found adherents among the wealthy mercantile families. A certain youth, called Yasa, who took mundane pleasures for granted, suddenly realized the meaninglessness of worldly life and joined Buddha's group. Yasa's father, a guild master of Benares, became the first lay disciple, and his mother and former wife became laywoman disciples. Four of Yasa's friends, later followed by fifty more of them, joined Buddha's group too. As soon as the little band of monks came into existence, Buddha urged his mendicant brethren to undertake missionary work: " Go forth, mendicant brothers, upon journeys for the help

of the many, for the well-being of the many, out of compassion for the world (*lokanukampaya*), for the sake of, for
the help of, for the well-being of spirits and men." [6] This
missionary commission was followed by Buddha's instruction regarding " ordination " of new monks. According to
the ancient ordination rite ascribed to Buddha, the aspirant
was to repeat three times the Three Refuge formula: " I
take refuge in the Buddha, I take refuge in the Dharma,
and I take refuge in the Samgha."

We have good reason to believe that Buddhist missionary
work was quite successful from the beginning. The con-
spicuous success of the work was largely due to the personality of Buddha and his penetrating sermons, as exemplified
in his famous Fire Sermon.[7] Two able Brāhmans, Sāriputta
and Moggallāna, were converted and played eminent roles
in the development of the order. On the occasion of Buddha's visit to his native place, his family, including his own
son, embraced Buddhism. Increasingly Buddha shouldered
greater responsibility of instruction and administration of
the growing Community. Able disciples were added, such
as Anuruddha, Ānanda, Upāli the barber, and Buddha's
cousin, Devadatta. Gradually, the number of female adherents increased, as evidenced by the establishment of the
order of nuns.

The rapid expansion of the Community inevitably
caused some internal problems. At first, those who gathered
around Buddha were known as his " disciples." They were
seekers, interested only in the attainment of Nirvāna, but
not all of them were capable of sharing life with others in
close quarters. A certain amount of personality conflict was
unavoidable. The situation became more complicated as
the Community accumulated worldly properties. The gradual change of atmosphere within the order was reflected in

accounts that the monastic discipline was violated by some monks and that Buddha's authority was resisted by others. Among all the troubles Buddha experienced in his relation to the Community, the most heartbreaking was the schism caused by his own cousin, Devadatta, who aspired for the position of leadership, displacing Buddha. All these accounts indicate that already in Buddha's lifetime the Buddhist Community faced some of the institutional problems common to all ecclesiastical organizations.

We are told that in his seventy-ninth year Buddha was taken ill in the village of Beluva, and he told his faithful attendant, Ānanda, that his earthly pilgrimage would soon come to an end. Then, realizing Ānanda's bewilderment, Buddha exorted him to be " reliant on the Law, taking refuge in the Law, not taking refuge in another." As soon as he was sufficiently recovered, he and Ānanda proceeded on their journey and went to the mango grove of Chunda the smith. There he came down with a severe dysentery, caused by food poisoning. Despite his critical condition, he continued his walk to Kusinārā, but could no longer move on. By that time some of his followers sensed the seriousness of his condition and assembled around his deathbed. His end was peaceful and serene, so characteristic of his personality. Addressing the assembled disciples, Buddha uttered his famous last words: " Decay is inherent in all component things. Work out your own salvation with diligence! "

Buddha's Teaching

The uniqueness of Buddhism among all religions of salvation lies in the fact that while accepting Buddha as the founder, it knows no savior in the usual sense of the term. There is no revelation or revealer behind Buddha's experience of Enlightenment under the Bodhi tree. He found the secret of Good Law all by himself. " I have no teacher; none is like me; in the world of men and spirits none is my compeer. I am a saint (*araha*) in this world, a teacher unsurpassed; the sole supreme Buddha. . . . And in the darkened world I will be the drum of the immortal." [8]

Throughout his life, all his sermons, exhortations, and counselings had only one theme, Nirvāna. " As the great sea, O disciple, is permeated by but one taste, the taste of salt, so also, O disciple, this doctrine and this law are pervaded by one taste, the taste of deliverance." [9] It is important to note in this connection that to him the primary question was not, " What is Nirvāna? " but, " How is Nirvāna attained? " He refused to discuss metaphysical questions such as whether the world had a beginning, or what is the nature of the Absolute. His mission was not to explicate theoretically the meaning of Nirvāna, but to " witness " for Nirvāna, which he experienced. According to him, one who has achieved Nirvāna " is like a deer living in a forest, who might lie down on a heap of snares but is not caught by it." [10] From this point of view, metaphysical theories were not too important. " The important thing in Buddhism," says de la Vallée Poussin, " is not dogma, but practice, not the goal, the mysterious and unascertainable Nirvāna (of Hindu background), but the Path." [11] In other words, the Path is not the means to an end; the Path is the goal itself.[12]

Nevertheless, Buddha's teaching was based on definite philosophical assumptions, and the ethos of Buddhism was uniquely conducive to philosophical inquiry. There is no denying that all the cardinal concepts of early Buddhism were derived from Indian religious and philosophical tradition. Various theories have been advanced concerning the

possible connections between Buddhism and Hindu philo-
sophical systems, as well as between Buddhism and Jainism.
But a careful examination reveals basic differences between
Buddhist concepts and the philosophical concepts of either
Hinduism or Jainism.

One of the basic concepts of Buddhism is the doctrine
of the *anatta* (nonego, not-self), which holds that " neither
within these bodily and mental phenomena of existence,
nor outside of them, can be found anything that in the ultimate sense could be regarded as a self-reliant, real ego-
entity, personality, or any other abiding substance." [13] The
anatta doctrine does not seem to have any similarity with
the Brahmanic concept of the *ātman* (substance), even
though Coomaraswamy and others have tried to minimize
the difference between the two. Coomaraswamy argued that
Buddha was against the conception of " the eternity in time
of an unchanging individuality," but was not against the
timeless spirit. Therefore, " in using the same term, *atta* or
ātman, Buddhist and Brāhman are talking of different
things, and when this is realized, it will be seen that the
Buddhist disputations on this point lose nearly all their
value." [14] His conclusion is that Buddhist and Brāhman
agree essentially that the soul or ego is complex and phenomenal. Admittedly, here is the basic philosophical ambi-
guity of early Buddhism. On the one hand, Buddha refuted
the existence of a self as a permanent individual entity; on
the other hand, he taught that one's deeds in this existence
will have definite consequences in future existences. In
other words, despite the nonself doctrine, the Buddhist
seems to be pushed back to acknowledge something like a
person or a " living, continuous fluid complex," to use de
la Vallée Poussin's phraseology, which continues to be born
again and again, crossing different existences. Nevertheless,

the Buddhist view was a rejection of the Brahmanic position which equates *ātman* with the Absolute (Brahman). Buddha rejected the Brahmanic metaphysics of the substance-view, which holds that the inner core of the individual self shares the same substance with the basic structure of reality. On this question, Murti argues persuasively that Buddha denied *ātman* " because he took his stand on the reality of moral consciousness and the efficacy of *karma*. . . . The *ātman* is the root cause of all attachment, desire, aversion, and pain. . . . *Sakkāyaditthi* (substance-view) is *avidyā* (ignorance) par excellence, and from it proceed all passions. Denial of Satkāya (*ātman,* or substance) is the very pivot of the Buddhist metaphysics and doctrine of salvation." [15]

In sharp contrast to the Brahmanic view, the Buddhist theory is that the Real is not a changeless, substantial entity, but flux or becoming. The empirical self is nothing but a part of the cosmic process of physical and mental phenomena, crossing many existences. This process has two aspects. Its active (causal) aspect consists of the *karma* (deeds with inevitable results) process, while its passive (caused) aspect consists of the rebirth process which is the result of *karma*. Thus there exists no real being which migrates from one existence to the next, but merely this twofold process of *karma* activities and *karma* results. That is to say, no finite self as such dies and is born again; there is only continuity of causes and conditions, to use the traditional Buddhist language.

It is to be noted that none of these doctrines was presented by Buddha as a metaphysical explanation of the universe. What preoccupied Buddha was not a theory about the world, but the salvation of finite beings from the wheel of birth and rebirth. To him. " within this body, some six feet high, but conscious and endowed with mind, is the world, and its origin, and its passing away." [16] In his view, doctrines were useful and necessary to make people understand the nature of finite existence, eliminating false knowledge and attachment to this transitory world. Equally important was Buddha's insistence on the importance of moral discipline and spiritual insight. He taught all Buddhists to refrain from (1) killing living things, (2) taking what is not given, (3) unchastity, (4) falsehood, and (5) intoxicants. He required monks and nuns to follow five additional precepts, refraining from (6) eating at unseasonable times, (7) seeing displays, dancing, singing, and music, (8) the use of garlands, scents, and unguents, (9) the use of a high or a big bed, and (10) receiving gold or silver. The purpose of these and other precepts was not merely to eliminate obstacles and hindrances from the path of liberation. Buddha was convinced that moral training, together with an intellectual understanding of truth, was imperative for the realization of a mystic intuition.

In a real sense, Buddha was a spiritual heir of Yoga. He expected his followers not simply to understand his gospel, but to realize liberation experimentally. Buddhist mental training takes it for granted that adequate moral discipline is necessary before one enters meditation, which in turn enables one to experience four stages of trance. Then one is in a position to acquire a mystical knowledge concerning his former existences, the death and rebirth of finite beings, and destruction of the *asavas* (bias) of ignorance. Buddha himself underwent such a mystical experience under the Bodhi tree, and he gave personal instruction to his disciples in the art of meditation. The early Buddhists aspired to see Nirvāna with the " eyes of the saints " in mystical contemplation, and an ancient master had a word of admonition to those who tended to belittle the mystical experience: " Blind men, because they do not see blue and yellow, have no right to say that those who have sight do not see colors and that colors do not exist." [17]

In retrospect, it is apparent that Buddha was a child of the Indian spiritual tradition, but his gospel had a universal message. He was one of the great thinkers in history, but his primary concern was not philosophical speculation. He was convinced that anyone can understand enough about the mysterious universe to know his or her relation to it, and that such a knowledge is important for one's salvation. He also stressed that right conduct is the prerequisite of meditation and insight, and both in turn are necessary steps in one's attainment of liberation and the experience of Nirvāna.

THE BUDDHIST COMMUNITY: THE SAMGHA

The Samgha

E. J. Thomas once stated that the Buddhist movement began " not with a body of doctrine, but with the formation of a society bound by certain rules." Buddha did not intend to hold a series of mass meetings for the purpose of general spiritual edification. He founded a community of men and women, who accepted the corporate life as the best path for salvation. Thus, " to begin by analyzing the doctrine without first examining the Community and the circumstances in which it originated would be likely to lead to quite arbitrary results." [18] However, the significance of the Samgha for understanding the basic character of Buddhism has not been always recognized.

The formation of a mendicant order was not a new creation of Buddhism. There had been other groups of ascetics and mendicants throughout the long history of India. The term *samgha* (*sangha* in Pali) was not specifically a religious term originally. Literally, it means a herd or association or a group of people living together for some purpose. As far as we can ascertain, it was during the Maurya period (ca. 322–185 B.C.) that the term "Samgha" came to be accepted as an official designation of the Buddhist Community. Before that time, a number of other terms seem to have been used. The early tradition implies that Buddha called his disciples "my people." Another frequently mentioned term was *savaka* (hearer, disciple), referring both to the monastics and laity, although later this term came to be used strictly for those who have realized one of the eight stages of holiness. Significantly, both Buddhism and Jainism often used the term *ariya-savaka* (noble disciples), referring to pious laity.

There is every indication that Buddha regarded the monastic life as the normative path in the Buddhist Community.[19] Nevertheless, early Buddhism took it for granted that the four groups — monks (*bhikkhu*), nuns (*bhikkhuni*), laymen (*upāsaka*), and laywomen (*upāsika*) — constituted the Buddhist Community. At first, there was no necessity to adopt an official name for the Buddhist Community. Non-Buddhists called Buddhists *Sakyāputta* or *Bodha-Bauddha* (followers or members of the Sākya or Buddha), and some of the monastic groups called themselves variously *bhikkhugana, bhikkhusamgha,* or *isisamgha* (congregation of monks). By the time the general term Samgha was accepted as the official name of the Buddhist Community, it came to be used frequently as a synonym for the monastic order because of the strong monastic emphasis of that period. But it should be remembered that the term Samgha in its origin and intention referred to the whole of the Buddhist Community, embracing both the monastics and the laity, much as the term *guna,* which had a similar general meaning, was adopted as the official designation of the Jain Community.

In the beginning, the only prerequisite for admission into the Buddhist monastic order was the *pabbajjā* ("going forth" or "leaving"), and after a period of instruction the aspirant was permitted to take the ordination vows. Very early in the history of Buddhism these two steps became united for all practical purposes. The *pabbajjā* in Buddhism meant more than the traditional Brahmanic practice of leaving home for a homeless life. According to traditional Indian metaphysico-social principles, the complex social system of the castes and the stages of life was divinely ordained by *dharma,* the cosmic moral law. While, metaphysically speaking, *dharma* transcended the empirical world, practically it was taken for granted that the correct manner of apprehending the cosmic *dharma* was to follow the particular laws *(dharma)* of one's given caste and of the given stage of life. The orthodox Hindu accepted the fact that one was born into one's own place, and that one's life was prescribed by the cosmic *dharma.* Zimmer astutely observed that there was an extreme one-sidedness in the static, departmentalized, mutually co-operative and hierarchical Indian society: "There is to be no choice, no floundering around, no sowing of wild oats. From the very first breath of life, the individual's energies are mastered, trained into channels, and co-ordinated to the general work of the superindividual who is the holy society itself." [20] Ideally, an orthodox Hindu was expected to go through the stages of the pupil and of the householder before he entered the stage of the forest dweller, followed finally by the stage of the wandering holy beggar. According to this scheme, one's " leaving home for the homeless " was prescribed by the *varnasrama* (the caste and stage of life) principle, derived from and sanctioned by the cosmic *dharma*.

But the Buddhist view of the *pabbajjā* ("leaving home"), despite its external similarities to the Brahmanic practice of leaving home, was a radical rejection of the Brahmanic notion of equating the cosmic *dharma* and the particular *dharma* of one's given caste and stage of life. According to Buddha, *dharma* could not be apprehended by observing the external religious principles and practices. Instead, the Buddhist held that the cosmic *dharma* was fully realized by Buddha's Enlightenment under the Bodhi tree, and that the *sad-dharma* (Holy Law) was integrally related, not to caste and the stage of life, but to the Samgha, the holy Community of Buddhism. Hence the threefold affirmation: " I take refuge in the Buddha, I take refuge in the Dharma, I take refuge in the Samgha." Thus Buddha and Buddhism have to be understood, not so much as a revolt against the corruption and ritualism of Brahmanism, but more basically as a rejection of the metaphysico-social basis of the Hindu holy community. In turn, Buddhism was repudiated by Hinduism, " not because of its peculiar, deviating doctrine, but by virtue of its having a different *dharma*, which *excluded conformity*. Hinduism sensed that Buddhism discarded one of its two indispensable foundations — its social conception of religion as a common *dharma*." [21]

This does not mean, however, that Buddha was a great social reformer, who fought against the evils of the caste-ridden Indian society. Although such an assertion has been made by some scholars, there is no indication that Buddha tried to fight against the caste system as such, or any other traditional sociopolitical institution, for that matter. What

he made abundantly clear was that empirical sociopolitical systems, important though they may be for the practical operation of human society, do not provide the path
for man's ultimate liberation. The corollary to this principle was that those who renounced the world were no longer
subject to caste restrictions within the Buddhist monastic
order.

As for the physical aspect of the monastic community, it
underwent many stages even during Buddha's lifetime.
In the beginning the monks had no buildings, and they
lived in the forests, in the valleys, in mountain caves, in
cemeteries, or in groves of trees. Gradually, for practical
considerations, the mendicants began to stay together either
in caves or in some resthouses during the rainy season. As
the number of members increased, the monastic orders
were compelled to secure buildings of their own. How this
came about is not certain, although there are many legends
about wealthy supporters of Buddha contributing buildings for the use of the monastic orders. Although some of
the old mendicants' poems praised the life in the forests
and mountains, such sentiments were quickly overshadowed by the glorification of the settled resident quarters
(*vihāra*).[22]

Once the *vihāra* were established, the Buddhist Community became a monastic-centered community, replacing the
earlier idea of the Samgha that embraced both the mendicants and the laity. Here we find a transition from the egali-
tarian ideal of primitive Buddhism to the monastic ideal
of Theravāda Buddhism, the latter epitomized by the spir-
itually aristocratic concept of the *arahat* (the holy ones).
Also, in contrast to the earlier emphasis on the " Path " as
the goal, the Theravādins shifted the emphasis to " perfection " as the goal. To them, the path was important but only

as a means. The goal was to attain Arahatship, by completing all the requirements to enter Nirvāna. To put it another way, the whole Buddhist Community was to exist for the monastic community, which in turn was to exist for the spiritual elite.

Institutionalization of the Buddhist Community (Samgha)

In the history of Buddhism, as in any other founded religion, the death of its founder marked a turning point. During his lifetime, Buddha was the final authority in the life of the Community, deciding all matters of doctrine and practice, even though he may not have meant his decisions to be binding in the years to come. It is said that Buddha on his deathbed urged his followers to depend solely on the Dharma as the guiding principle of their path. But the Dharma was not self-evident; it was the Dharma taught and interpreted by Buddha that his followers accepted. After his death, his immediate followers and companions assumed a new responsibility for the successful realization of Buddha's ideal. Inevitably, their memories and interpretations of Buddha and of Dharma became important traditions in the Buddhist Community.

The history of Buddhism from the time of Buddha to the period of King Asoka in the third century B.C. is clouded in mystery. Nevertheless, this was an important period in the development of the Buddhist Community. Two or three so-called councils were held, and eighteen sects were said to have arisen. The oral traditions were codified, modified, and interpreted; and thus the Pali Canon (Tipitaka, or the Three Baskets) came into existence. Shortly before the time of Asoka, the orthodox community, or the " Old Wisdom School," was split into the Theravāda and Sar-

vāstivāda schools, and the Mahāsanghikas, the precursors
of the Mahāyāna tradition, appeared on the horizon. Also
during this period, the monastic community was consolidated and stratified, and Buddha became " deified."

Concerning the councils there have been heated debates
among scholars. There is general agreement that the First
Council was held at Rajagaha shortly after Buddha's death;
some portions of the Pali Canon were approved and codified by the leaders of the Buddhist Community.

The Second Council is believed to have been held at
Vesali one hundred years after Buddha's death. The issues
discussed at this council were the ten points of the monastic
rules, such as the use of salt, liquor, and the flexibility of
the monk's daily schedule. We are told that the defeated
party at the Second Council held its own council and compiled its own Dhamma (or Dharma) and Vinaya. While it
is difficult to reconstruct the origin of the Mahāsanghika
school, which was referred to as the " defeated party," it
had a large number of followers ("ten thousand wicked
monks," according to the description of its opponents).

The accounts about the origin of the Sarvāstivāda school
are not at all clear. We know, however, that it was one of
the schools developed out of the Theravāda tradition, and
it held distinct doctrinal beliefs. The basic differences between the Sarvāstivāda and Theravāda positions centered
around the nature of reality and the question of being and
becoming. Unlike the Theravādins, the Sarvāstivādins affirmed the reality of elements, and also held the view that
the world is, over against the traditional view that the
world is a continuous process of becoming.[23] At any rate,
in the third century B.C., the Buddhist Community had
three major divisions, the Theravāda, Sarvāstivāda, and
Mahāsanghika.

The steady growth of the Buddhist Community before the time of Asoka was due largely to the activities of the monastic orders. The guiding principle of the monastic orders was the Pātimokkha (Prātimoksa), a collection of 227 monastic rules.[24] It is important to note that most rules in the Buddhist monastic orders were adopted from the Brahmanical Code, and this is particularly true of the observance of celibacy and the five precepts of good conduct.[25] Also significant is the way the traditional Brahmanical rules were rearranged to provide the normative principles for the Buddhist orders of monks and of nuns.

Codification of Doctrine (Dharma)

The internal consolidation of the Buddhist Community, and more especially the monastic order, was greatly aided by the codification of the hitherto orally transmitted doctrines and traditions into the form of the Tipitaka (Tripitaka, or the Three Baskets). This is divided into (1) the Vinaya-Pitaka, or the Basket of Discipline — rules and precepts of the monastic order; (2) the Sutta-Pitaka or the Basket of Discourses — dialogues between Buddha and his disciples; and (3) the Abhidhamma-Pitaka, or the Basket of Doctrinal Elaboration.

The Vinaya-Pitaka deals primarily with the monastic rules. For instance, the first section of the Vinaya, known as the " Classification of Offenses," is nothing but a commentary on the Pātimokkha. The Vinaya is a precious source material for understanding not only the conditions of early Buddhist monastic life but also the underlying doctrines of the Samgha. The Vinaya literature makes it clear that the monks were expected to act as members of the corporate body and not as individuals. The laity is not ignored, but the attitude of the Vinaya-Pitaka toward the laity is paternalistic, and there is no question in the minds of the compilers of this Basket that Buddhism is essentially a movement of the monastic ascetics.

The second Basket, the Sutta-Pitaka, deals with the Dhamma (Dharma) or doctrinal matters. Many scholars believe that the present arrangement of the Sutta-Pitaka, consisting of five portions, can be traced back to the third century B.C. The five portions are (1) Division of Long Discourses (Digha-nikāya), (2) Division of Medium Length Discourses (Majjhima-nikāya), (3) Division of Connected Discourses (Samyutta-nikāya), (4) Division of Numerically Arranged Discourses (Anguttara-nikāya), and (5) Division of Minor Discourses (Khuddaka-nikāya). Each portion is again subdivided into many *suttas* (*sūtras*) or *suttantas* (*sūtrantas*). Since all these parts were grouped together to facilitate memorization, they were not necessarily divided according to subject matter.

The third Basket, the Abhidhamma-Pitaka, was compiled after the Old Wisdom tradition was split into the Theravāda and Sarvāstivāda schools, and the latter school developed its own Abhidhamma literature. The word *abhidhamma* means " further " or " special " *dhamma,* and this Basket deals with metaphysical analysis and elucidation of Dhamma (or Dharma).

Deification of the Founder (Buddha)

Side by side with the institutionalization of the Buddhist Community and the codification of the doctrines, we find the gradual process of Buddha's deification. Anesaki observed that this " docetic " tendency made its progress in two ways — " one the way of mythical fancies about the Buddha's supernatural qualities, and the other that of metaphysical speculations on his personality as a Tathagata and on its relations with the truth (*dharma*) which he revealed." [26] In the course of time, devotionally Buddha and Bodhisattvas (beings destined for Enlightenment) became *de facto* deities, and philosophically " Buddhaness " was identified with the Dharma.

Early Buddhists did not regard Buddha to be different in any qualitative sense from other visionaries and ascetics, except that he was the discoverer and the teacher of the Path. The gradual deification of Buddha must be understood in terms of the external and internal factors involved. Externally, Buddhism was exposed to the Indian religious tradition and atmosphere, and it was but natural that Buddha came to be portrayed by the pious imagination as a semidivine being. Accordingly, he was addressed as Bhagavat (Lord), Bhagavat Buddha, and Tathāgata (" one who has gone thus "), and later he was elevated to the status of a celestial being. Internally, the Buddhist Community began to discover a deeper and greater significance in the person of Buddha. Not only was he the discoverer and teacher of the Path, he was " the actuality of the central doctrine, the one who has lived it and reached the goal." [27] Seen from this perspective, Buddha did not die; he entered Mahāparinirvāna. The believer becomes a *Sākya-putto* (son of Buddha), because the *pabbajjā* (" leaving the world ") enables him to become a " natural son of the Blessed One, born of his mouth, born of *dhamma,* fashioned by *dhamma,*" to use the phraseology of the Samyutta-nikāya (II, 221) . Thus, Buddha became immortalized as the object of the affirmation of faith: " I take refuge in the Buddha." In the faith thus uttered, his message and his being became one, and he came to be the crystallization of piety and spirituality of all those who constituted the Buddhist Community.

It is conceivable that from the beginning there were several kinds of oral traditions about Buddha's life. To these were added non-Buddhist lore, as evidenced by the Jātaka tales, providing ample resources to the pious biographers for describing the details of Buddha's birth, childhood, youth, religious search, Enlightenment, and preaching activities, as well as his previous existences. In this process, the historical figure of Buddha became increasingly " transparent," with the result that philosophically he became one with the Dharma (truth), devotionally he became deified, and culturally he became the spiritual and idealized world monarch (cakravartin). The idea of the mahāpurusa cakravartin (the Supreme who turns the wheel) is an old one; Zimmer thinks it can be traced to the pre-Vedic and even pre-Aryan traditions of India. At any rate, the ideal of a righteous world monarch has never been lost throughout the history of India. No one knows when the Cakravartin will make his appearance, but his arrival will be announced by the seven great symbols, including the cakra (sacred wheel), the divine white elephant, and the white horse. Also his figure is believed to have the thirty-two great marks. It is a matter of interest that the concept of the Cakravartin was adopted by the Buddhist Community as the secular counterpart of Buddha. Buddha and the Cakravartin were both universal kings, one in the spiritual and the other in the secular domain, but both have similar characteristics, including the thirty-two great marks. Just as the Cakravartin is believed to turn the wheel, so was Buddha believed to have turned the wheel of the Dharma. Buddha is supposed to have instructed Ānanda that his (Buddha's) funeral was to be patterned after the ceremonies traditionally reserved for a Cakravartin.[28]

To sum up: In the beginning the Buddhist Community

was a humble group of mendicants and lay disciples, but there soon developed within it tightly knit monastic orders. Buddhism began to meet the devotional, philosophical, and cultural needs of people in all walks of life. By the time of Asoka Buddhism was becoming a full-fledged institutionalized religion, with written scriptures, systematic doctrines, a deified Buddha, ethical precepts both for the monastics and the laity, and powerful and wealthy supporters. Buddhism was no longer just one of many sects, or a heretical wing of Brahmanism; it was becoming a powerful cultural force and a bearer of civilization. This new ethos of Buddhism was manifested under King Asoka, the Constantine of Buddhism.

The Development of the Samgha

From Asoka to Kanishka

The period from the third century B.C. to the second century A.D. was marked by two great Buddhist monarchs, Asoka and Kanishka. Asoka's grandfather, Chandragupta Maurya, founded the Maurya dynasty in northern India shortly after Alexander's departure from Indian soil in 325 B.C. He was ably supported by his prime minister, Kantilya, who advocated the famous principle: " *rājā rājyam* (king equals kingdom)." Accordingly, the Maurya kingdom was a highly centralized state, ruled by an absolute monarchy. During Asoka's long reign (274–232 B.C.) his empire extended to Afghanistan in the west, the Ganges in the east, and the Madras region in the south. In his ninth year on the throne, he annexed the kingdom of Kalinga, and according to tradition the horrors of the Kalinga campaign provided the occasion for Asoka's conversion to Buddhism. His career and ideology have been recorded in inscriptions on rocks and pillars of stone, commonly known as Asoka's inscriptions.

This is not the place to discuss Asoka's achievements as a ruler, but we must recognize his role as head of the Buddhist Community and propagator of the faith. In Eliot's considered opinion, Asoka's activity " was not so much that of a pious emperor as of an archbishop possessed of exceptional temporal power," [29] and there is a great deal of truth in this statement. As a ruler, he tolerated and protected Brahmanism and Jainism as well as Buddhism. As a pious Buddhist, he visited the holy places of Buddha in all parts of India, building stupas and monasteries, and engaged in various kinds of charitable activities. As an " archbishop," he sent Buddhist missionaries to all parts of his dominion, to the neighboring principalities, and to the Hellenistic kingdoms of Asia, northern Africa, and parts of Europe. It is said that Asoka's son, Mahinda, was the first missionary to Ceylon, and one of his daughters, Carumati, engaged in missionary work as a nun in Nepal.

According to the Pali Canon, the Third Buddhist Council was held at Pātaliputra (Patna) during the reign of Asoka. The date of this council is quite uncertain, however. There is good reason to believe that Asoka was disturbed by the division and corruption within the monastic orders, and he may have sponsored a gathering of monks in order to promote internal unity.

It is apparent that Asoka played a significant role in making Buddhism a world religion. He recognized the universal message in the Dharma, but the Dharma he advocated was quite different from the tenets of early Buddhism. Even though he must have known the orthodox doctrines, his inscriptions are conspicuously silent about the Four Noble Truths, the Chain of Causation, and even

about Nirvāna. What he stressed was a kind of applied Buddhist ethics, applicable to all men, Buddhist as well as non-Buddhist. Asoka did not formulate a new system of teachings, but instilled a new spirit into Buddhism. To him, Buddhism was a practical religion, capable of reshaping the traditional spiritual culture of India. He dared to dream that his vast empire could be transformed into a religious community and a missionary society by turning state officials into religious teachers and using monasteries as local centers of educational and charitable works. His appointment of " Ministers of the Dharma " meant that Buddhism for the first time in its history was shouldered with the responsibility of guiding not only individual seekers and believers but a complex society, nation, and civilization. In this situation, the Dharma had to be related in a significant way to the social, political, economic, and cultural dimensions of life. The Buddhist Community was no longer a small segment of Indian society; it was in effect the total nation and potentially a world-wide community, embracing peoples and nations outside India. Likewise Buddha was no longer portrayed as a local ascetic, discoverer and teacher of the narrow path. His teaching had a universal message, because he had set in motion the universal wheel, which had to be symbolized by a Cakravartin (an ideal universal monarch) and actualized in an ideal social and political order. Such was the ethos of Buddhism during Asoka's reign, and subsequent developments of Buddhism were greatly influenced by this vision of what Buddhism ought to be.

Critics of Asoka often state that he left behind him a growing religion and a declining empire. Probably his attempts were too novel, too premature, and too idealistic to be understood and followed by his contemporaries. In all fairness to Asoka it must be pointed out that the difficulties he experienced in realizing his dream were in part inherent in Buddhism itself, for it is not easy to reconcile the two seemingly unrelated objectives of " spiritual salvation " and " this-worldly welfare." At least Asoka made a bold attempt to actualize the Dharma in his own time.

The next great landmark of Indian Buddhism was the period of King Kanishka in the second century A.D. His people, the Kushans, or Yüeh-chi as the Chinese called them, migrated into India from Central Asia, where they had had some contact with Buddhism. The Kushan empire under Kanishka included Afghanistan, Bactria, Kashgar, Yarkland, Khotan, and Kashmir. Kanishka was a great patron of Buddhism and Gandhara art, which introduced the Persian and Greek influence into India. During his reign a Buddhist council was held, and although it was not recognized by the Theravādins, it came to be known as the Third Great Council by the Sarvāstivādins.

Kanishka's relation to the Mahāyāna tradition is not clear, even though we know that Mahāyāna ideas were growing during his period. During the time between Asoka and Kanishka, the upper classes favored Buddhism and Jainism, but the masses were gradually influenced by Brahmanism. With Kanishka's royal patronage, Buddhism tried to capture the masses. The significant development of Buddhism under Kanishka was not so much the geographical extension of Buddhism — although this occurred too — as the internal evolution of Buddhism: veneration of *sarisa* (bones of saints), stupas (burial mounds for relics of saints), Buddha's footprints, and the Bodhi tree became widely accepted; and likenesses of Buddha, unknown at the time of Asoka, became objects of popular devotion. The scriptures, especially those of the Mahāyāna tradition, were written in Sanskrit, the sacred language of Brahmanism. The monasteries, which hitherto had given only religious instruction, began to teach secular subjects. In fact, " the doors of the Buddhist Samgha which were open before only to those who had forsaken the world, were now thrown open to the students as well, who, if they chose, were at liberty to leave the monastery and embrace once more the life of a householder, after their education was over." [30] The development of the Mahāyāna tradition must be understood in this historic and cultural context.

Internal disintegration, and the rise of the rival Sasanian empire in Persia, resulted in the decline of the Kushan empire in the early part of the fourth century, and the Gupta dynasty was established ca. A.D. 320. The Gupta period witnessed the golden age of Hinduism, but Buddhism continued to produce some illustrious thinkers, such as Vasubandhu, Asanga, Harivarman, and Buddhaghosa, and Buddhist sculpture and painting flourished as visitors to Sārnāth and the Ajanta Caves can testify even today. In the field of education, the most influential institutions were the three monastic universities, Nālandā and Vikramasila of the Mahāyāna tradition, and Valabhi of the Theravāda tradition.

The Gupta dynasty began to decline toward the end of the fifth century A.D. Buddhism continued to be represented by thinkers like Dignāga, Dharmakīrti, and Sāntideva, but lack of royal patronage, increasing internal divisions, and strenuous attacks by philosophical and devotional movements of Hinduism resulted in the gradual decline of Buddhism in India. The situation was further complicated by the growth of the Esoteric tradition of Buddhism (Vajrayāna or Mantrayāna), which became popular after the middle of the eighth century. This form of Buddhism was destined to influence Tibet, Mongolia, China, and Japan, and spread as far south as Java. Finally, the decline of Buddhism in India was accelerated by the invasion of the Muslims.

It is true that Buddhism was not expelled, but absorbed by Hinduism. We can depict obvious Buddhist influences on Hindu beliefs and practices, and even Sankara, the greatest Hindu theologian, may be characterized as a crypto-Buddhist. Buddha is venerated by Hindus as one of the greatest Indians, and he is even recognized as an incarnation of Vishnu by many Hindus. Nevertheless, Buddhism as a living religious community lost ground in India; by losing its distinctive character, it was assimilated into the Household of Hinduism.

Three Traditions of Buddhism

In retrospect it is apparent that Buddhism became highly differentiated during its first fifteen centuries in India. The schools that developed, however, are not analogous to the ecclesiastical divisions of other religions. The Buddhist divisions of schools (yāna) are based on different conceptions of Buddhology (the nature of Buddha), the path for sanctification, the problem of metaphysics, and the interpretation of the monastic discipline. The historical development of the different schools cannot be ascertained with any degree of certainty. The history of the Buddhist councils, which had great bearing on the rise of schools, is unfortunately far from clear. We know that already at the time of Asoka the Buddhist Community was divided into the Theravāda, Sarvāstivāda, and Mahāsanghika groups. There were also philosophical and disciplinary disagreements within each of these schools, which may account for the traditional number of eighteen sects.

There are many approaches to the classification of schools of Buddhism, but here we will focus our attention on the three different " images " of Nirvāna apprehended and developed by the three main divisions: the Theravāda (Hinayāna), Mahāyāna, and Mantrayāna (Vajrayāna). Although these three divisions were further subdivided historically — especially after they were transplanted outside India, and under the influence of social, political, and cultural factors — it is our contention that the three " images of Nirvāna " can be traced to Indian Buddhism.

Briefly stated, the Three Jewels (Buddha, Dharma, and Samgha) must be seen as an interrelated and mutually dependent triad, while at the same time each one must be viewed as a philosophical and religious focus. Buddha, Dharma, and Samgha are not only objects of philosophical inquiry but also affirmations of religious faith: " I take refuge in the Buddha, I take refuge in the Dharma, I take refuge in the Samgha." Furthermore, behind the philosophical and religious concepts of Buddha, Dharma, and Samgha lies a beatific vision or the " image of Nirvāna," as the peak of the pyramid, as it were. Thus, the development of the concepts of Buddha, Dharma, and Samgha were colored by, and also influenced, changes in the image of Nirvāna. To be sure, throughout the history of Buddhism Nirvāna has been regarded as incapable of being expressed in words, unutterable and indescribable. Thirty years ago, Stcherbatsky confessed that " although a hundred years have elapsed since the scientific study of Buddhism has been initiated in Europe, we are nevertheless still in the dark about the fundamental teachings of this religion and its philosophy." [31] This is still true today. What seems to be needed in this connection is not a frontal attack on the concept of Nirvāna as such, but an attempt to catch a glimpse of the changing image of Nirvāna by following the development of the doctrines of the Three Jewels in relation to Nirvāna.

Slater, in his study of Burmese Buddhism, makes the important observation that both religious paradox and logical opposition are simultaneously involved in the notion of Nirvāna. Nirvāna as ultimate annihilation is negative, while as fulfillment it is positive.[32] Here is logical opposition on the philosophical level, but paradox in the religious realm. The image of Nirvāna can be expressed only symbolically in the language of religious paradox. Philosophy attempts to define Nirvāna, but religious paradox refuses this definition, because " there is an aspect of reality which is still unfathomed, beyond the capacity of intellect or the limitations of discursive formulation." [33] Slater quotes appreciatively Shwe Zan Aung, who speaks of " a very peculiar and complicated process to win a momentary flash " of Nirvāna, recognizing also that " a fleeing glimpse is a very different thing from the steady vision, the perfect understanding which betokens [Nirvāna]." [34] Indeed, the Buddhist seeks Nirvāna not only with the mind, but also by means of a discipline of the will and of the emotions.

A cursory glance at the three traditions of Buddhism, Theravāda, Mahāyāna, and Mantrayāna, may clarify what is meant by the changing image of Nirvāna. In the Theravāda tradition, Nirvāna or Nibbāna is seen as an antinomy to the phenomenal world (Samsāra) . The term Samsāra, which in the pre-Buddhist Hindu context meant a continuous stream of actual lives, was reduced by the early Buddhist to a collection of separate elements evolving gradually toward final extinction. Whether or not anything like a consciousness survives in Nirvāna was a matter of heated controversy among early Buddhists. In the course of time, one of the early schools, known as the Sautrāntikas, " cut down the list of artificially constructed elements, cut down Nirvāna itself as a separate entity, and transferred the Absolute into the living world." [35]

With the rise of Mahāyāna, epistemological questions began to be raised. Although Nāgārjuna, one of the earliest theoreticians of Mahāyāna, claimed to be reverting to Buddha's Middle Way, F. H. Smith astutely observes that " the fundamental issue for Gotama [Gautama] was the lust; for Nāgārjuna it was the theory of knowledge associated with lust." [36] Accordingly, Nāgārjuna's use of negative language must be seen as an attempt to stress the ultimate goal, which is the realization of perfect transcendental wisdom (prajñā). " Wisdom here is opposed to all partial knowledge," says Takakusu, " or rather is inclusive of all partial knowledge. Thus, by not clinging to the knowledge of special things, one can attain perfect wisdom; and by not adhering to one thing or another, one can attain perfect freedom. Perfect emptiness or void comprehends all things." [37] A second Mahāyāna school, known as the Yogācāra or Vijnāvādins, affirmed the reality of consciousness as the abode (alaya) of an objective-subjective universe. " Illusion has its source in, or subsists in, alaya-vijnāna (repository of latent consciousness), the subconscious life below the threshold of the waking consciousness. Full consciousness is continuous, with a potential latent subconscious repository of thought, whence, as from seeds (bīja) the manifested universe arises." [38] Thus, one can readily see that the Yogācāra position was very close to the absolute idealism exemplified by the famous Mahāyāna sūtra, Awakening of Faith, which accepts the totality of all existence as the Absolute.

In sharp contrast to the Theravāda (Hinayāna) tradition, the Mahāyānist equated philosophically both Buddha and Dharma with Nirvāna, now known as suchness, thusness, or Dharma-dhātu. Significantly, the term Dharma-dhātu (the realm of principle) signifies both the phenomenal world (Samsāra) and Nirvāna.[39] Religiously, however, the Mahāyānist found an infinite distance between the two. Even the Western Paradise, which is an intermediate state between Samsāra and Nirvāna, is believed to be ten trillion worlds away. This distance is further emphasized by the Bodhisattva conception, which implies the need of divine grace and compassion for man's deliverance. The Mahāyānist religious concept of grace (*karunā*) finds support in the philosophical concept of co-creation, which teaches that every being is self-created and self-creating, and that everything inevitably comes out of more than one cause. In other words, " all is mutually relative, a product of interdependence." [40] Thus, the Mahāyānist can hold simultaneously the lofty concept of attainment of Buddhahood or Bodhisattvahood and the belief that " even the householder in the midst of family life, the merchant, the artisan, the king, nay, the laborer, the pariah, can attain salvation." [41] Hamilton has this paradoxical ideal of Mahāyāna in mind when he states that " Enlightenment is no longer an end for its own sake," and that " it is the highest means of a selfless devotion to universal good." [42] In other words, one needs both philosophical insight and religious faith in order to catch a glimpse of the Mahāyānist's image of Nirvāna.

By far the most radical change in the image of Nirvāna took place in the Mantrayāna (Vajrayāna) tradition, of which Tibetan Lamaism and the Japanese Shingon school are the two living examples. To recapitulate for a moment: Nirvāna was regarded by the Theravādins as the antinomy of Samsāra; the Mahāyānist equated Nirvāna and Samsāra in void (*sūnyatā*), which alone was considered to be really real. In contrast, the Mantrayānist viewed the phenomenal world as the manifestation of the Cosmic Body of the Sun-Buddha, Mahāvairocana, who is believed to have the six elements or the material of every existence. In the words of a contemporary Shingon priest: " Since all beings and all things are of the same essence . . . one should, by thought and other means, by acts of mystical value, by the practice of our symbols, of our incantations, and of our formulas, strive to feel and to understand the cosmic life and become conscious of our intimate and universal communion. . . . We *are* the cosmos, and the cosmos *is* ourselves." [43] In the Mantrayānist tradition, paradoxical language is carried to its extreme. Philosophically, the only reality is the whole, known as Mahāvairocana. And yet, religiously, in this very phenomenal world one can become Buddha with one's own body. Or, to take another example, early Buddhism accepted the historic Indian notion of *kalpa,* which is a cyclical concept of time, divided into a variable number of incalculables. The only way to escape from this endless, cyclic time was to be emancipated from phenomenal existence and win Nirvāna. However, the Mantrayānist conceived of *kalpa* as the stages of one's spiritual growth in his lifetime; thus one could conquer the iron cycle of existence in this phenomenal world.

This is a very brief sketch of the main tenets of the three divisions of Buddhism. Their doctrinal differences in Buddhology, in the concept of Dharma, and in ecclesiology were derived from their different images of Nirvāna, and vice versa. The Theravāda Buddhist seeks Nirvāna in the liberation from ignorance which causes attachment and desires. Buddha, Dharma, and Samgha are viewed from this perspective, with emphasis on monastic discipline and Yoga meditation. The Mahāyānist seeks Nirvāna in a more positive way. Based on the doctrine of "cocreation," the Mahāyānist attempts to create a spiritual world for himself, and to him freedom is not something given but a task to be achieved. To him, the historic figure of Buddha is not so important as Buddhaness, or a transparent quality through which one encounters the Dharma, and Nirvāna and Samsāra are mutually interpenetrating. The Bodhisattva doctrine of the Mahāyāna tradition implies that the monastic orders exist not only — nor even primarily — for the salvation of monks and nuns, but also for the salvation of all sentient beings. Lastly, what the Mantrayāna Buddhist seeks is creation of a "new man and creating him on a superhuman plane, a man-god [Mahāvairocana], such as the imagination of historical man has never dreamed it possible to create." [44]

How these different traditions of Buddhism developed historically in various parts of Asia is discussed in the next section.

BUDDHISM OUTSIDE INDIA

Missionary Character of Buddhism

The history of Buddhism, at least from the time of its founder to the tenth century A.D., makes it plain that it was one of the great missionary religions in the world. Buddha himself, among other things, was an untiring evangelist, and to him the *raison d'être* of the Buddhist Community, more particularly of its monastic orders, was the conversion of the whole world. We may recall that the *pabbajjā* ("going forth" or "leaving the world") was required of all his followers, but those who joined the order were again commanded to "go forth" into the world "for the help of the many, for the well-being of the many, out of compassion for the world" (Mahā-Vagga, Khandhaka, I). That this missionary spirit did not die with the death of Buddha is evident in the work of King Asoka, who envisaged a gigantic evangelical enterprise three centuries before Christ. It is well said that "the missionary zeal which Asoka inherited from the great founder has characterized Buddhism throughout its history and marked it off from all the other religions of Southern and Eastern Asia." [45]

It has been pointed out by many historians that Buddha, in creating the Samgha, took the name and the constitutional form of the political *samgha* which existed in northeastern India in his time.[46] He seemed to have accepted the existence of the territorial state for the sake of the general welfare of society. While he uttered practically nothing about what might be called Buddhist social policy, he evidently hoped for a gradual transformation of society, not by legislation and coercion but by the permeating influence of the Buddhist Community, as well as by individual conversion and moral persuasion. In short, the ecclesiastical Samgha and the political *samgha* were to exist side by side without and official connection, and yet in a spirit of mutual trust and harmony.

In contrast to early Buddhism, which attempted to spread the gospel of Buddha by means of missionary activities, Asoka attempted to realize the ideal of a Buddhist state on a large scale. Indeed, he was a great missionary statesman, but he was also an empire builder. Thus, his missionary strategy was supported by the prestige and machinery of his great empire. He did not propagate any narrow orthodoxy, but it was clear that he intended to regulate the behavior of his subjects according to the ethical ideal of Buddhism. He even enforced the rule of *ahimsā,* or the prohibition of killing living things, by imperial edicts. Historians do not agree on how lasting his influence was, or to what extent his royal ordinances were intelligible to the diverse groups of people in the Maurya empire. Nevertheless, his subjects must have known that Asoka had "power enough to punish them for their crimes." [47] The royal favor of Buddhism during Asoka's reign gave tremendous impetus to Buddhist missionary activities. At the same time, the historic distinction between the political state and the ecclesiastical Samgha was no longer maintained. Two things happened in this situation. First, the early concept of the Samgha — consisting of monks, nuns, laymen, and laywomen — was lost, and the term Samgha came to be limited to the orders of monks and nuns, in line with the Theravādin monastic principle. Secondly, another aspect of the early Buddhist understanding of the Samgha, that it was existing in the world but not of the world, to use a Christian phraseology, also disappeared, because the Buddhist Community in the broad sense became conterminous with the state.

Asoka is often referred to as the first great missionary, next only to Buddha, in the history of Buddhism, somewhat analogous to the apostle Paul in the Christian tradition. But unlike Paul, Asoka stood in the Hindu tradition of the divine monarch, and he understood the missionary work, not in terms of preaching missions and charitable works by a handful of mendicants, but as a well co-ordinated venture of "conquest through Dharma," supported by a vast number of government officials stationed in key places. We read in his Rock Edict (XIII) : "And such a

conquest has been achieved by the Beloved of the Gods
[Asoka] not only here in his own dominions but also in the
territories bordering on his dominions, as far away as the
distance of six hundred Yojanas. . . . Everywhere people
are conforming to the instructions in Dharma imparted by
the Beloved of the Gods." [48] But what about the nations
outside of his sphere of interests? On this question, Asoka
was optimistic. " Even where the envoys of the Beloved of
the Gods have not penetrated, there too men have heard of
the practice of Dharma and the ordinances issued and the
instructions in Dharma imparted by the Beloved of the
Gods, and are conforming to Dharma and will continue to
conform to it." [49] Thus Asoka considered his empire as a
Buddhist-inspired Community, which was to serve as the
headquarters of the Dharma's peaceful mission throughout
the world.

At the risk of oversimplification, we can classify the expansion of Buddhism in two major categories. First, Buddhism penetrated India's immediate neighbors as a form
of Indian civilization. Not that India necessarily dominated
its neighboring states politically, but many of them were
in essence religio-cultural satellites of India. Even though
Buddhism was destined to be modified by local conditions
in these nations, it remained within the larger framework
of Hinduization. Second, Buddhism as a religio-cultural
movement penetrated many parts of Asia where non-Indian
cultures and civilizations were securely established. These
areas cannot be regarded in any way as religio-cultural
satellites of India, however strongly they were influenced
by Buddhism. Whereas in the first case Buddhist-Hindu
civilization provided the sole basis and structure of local
cultures, in the second case Buddhism was one ingredient

of a multi-value system. Parenthetically it may be added that these two types of movements intertwined in certain areas.

Expansion of Buddhist-Hindu Civilization

Historically, the Hinduization of India's neighboring states was accompanied by the transplantation of Brahmanism, and for centuries after Asoka's time this movement had a lively strain of Buddhism. This process was observable in varying degrees in Nepal, Kashmir, Java, Cambodia, Ceylon, Burma, and Thailand. Where Brahmanism was established as the religion of the natives, as in Nepal and Java for instance, Buddhism and Brahmanism were intricately amalgamated. On the other hand, in areas where Brahmanism maintained a stronghold in the courts while the masses adopted a Buddhist-oriented Indian civilization, Buddhism often became the rallying point of nationalistic aspirations, resisting the Brahmanic influence in the court. In both cases, we do not find indigenous civilizations strong enough to counterbalance the Buddhist-Hindu civilization as such.

In the north, Asoka sent monks and nuns to Nepal, and he sent Buddhist colonists to Khotan. Shortly after the beginning of the Christian era, Buddhism existed in Funan, Champa, and Sumatra. By the fourth century, Buddhism was established in Java, Borneo, and Celebes; by the fifth century, in Cambodia; by the sixth century, in Burma.

Undoubtedly, the rapid growth of Buddhism under Asoka was accelerated by social and economic factors. Nakamura points out that the mercantile class, which developed during the Maurya period, supported Buddhism,[50] and Kasugai finds an interesting parallel between the existence of gold mines and the concentration of Asoka's pillars

in south India.[51] Similarly, the expansion of Buddhism outside India did not depend solely on the work of monks and
nuns. In many parts of Southeast Asia and areas beyond the
northern borders of India, Buddhism was first introduced
by Indian colonists and traders. They brought with them
not only Buddhism and Brahmanism but also the art of
writing, technology, and commerce, as well as the Brahmanic concept of the divine king. Indeed, the Dharma
thus transplanted was more than the teaching of Buddha;
it was a Buddhist-oriented Hindu civilization. Let us take
the example of Ceylon, the acknowledged motherland of
Theravāda Buddhism.

The history of Ceylon goes back to the legendary north
Indian prince Vijaya, who colonized the island in the sixth
or fifth century B.C., and the dominant religion of the
island before the introduction of Buddhism was Brahmanism. In the third century B.C., at the time of King Tissa's
enthronement, Asoka sent Tissa the five ensigns of royalty
and other items necessary for the consecration of the king.
Asoka also sent the " gift of the Dhamma " with the message: " I have taken refuge in the Buddha, Dhamma, and
the Sangha, and I have declared myself a lay disciple in the
religion of . . . [Buddha]. Take delight, even thou, in
these three, in the supreme religion of the conqueror, and
come to the refuge with faith." [52] It was this king (Tissa),
enthroned in the manner of a Hindu divine monarch, who
accepted Buddhism as the religion of his kingdom. Tissa
fondly called himself " the Beloved of the Gods," imitating
Asoka's description of himself. Thus what Tissa wanted to
establish in Ceylon was a miniature Indian empire based
on Buddhist-Hindu civilization.

The history of Buddhism in Ceylon is noteworthy because it was started by an infiltration of Buddhism into the

Hindu colony, and then it was exposed to successive waves of invasion, as well as religious and cultural propaganda, from south India. It was Eliot's thesis that " the preservation of a very ancient form of Buddhism in Ceylon " was due to the fact that the Sinhalese had no speculative interest, and thus " they were content to classify, summarize, and expound the teaching of the Pitakas without restating it in the light of their own imagination." [53] This statement may be true in regard to the doctrinal aspect of Buddhism in Ceylon, but the historical development of the Buddhist Community in the island does not indicate " the preservation of a very ancient form of Buddhism " there.

During the third century A.D., the influence of Mahāyāna Buddhism penetrated the island, and we read about the constant power struggles between Theravādins and Mahāyānists. The eighth century witnessed the decline of Theravāda Buddhism and the growth of Esoteric Buddhism, as well as the rise of the Tamils to political power in the northern part of the island. Ceylon became one of the centers of Esoteric Buddhism, with such notable Tantric masters as Samantabhadra attracting seekers from far-off lands. Amoghavajra, one of the patriarchs of Chinese Esoteric Buddhism, was one of his students. At any rate, Esoteric Buddhism was widely practiced in its various forms in the island.[54] From the tenth to the thirteenth centuries — known as the Polonnaruva period — Ceylon maintained close relations with south India, and this fact accounts for the strong continental influence on the island's religion and arts.

The fall of Polonnaruva in the thirteenth century was followed by a period of political unrest. The northern part of the island came under the Tamils, while the Sinhalese Kotte kings established the capital near today's Colombo.

During the Kotte period Vaishnavism (or Vishnuism) penetrated the Buddhist Community, which was split between those who accepted the worship of Brahmanic deities and those who rejected it. In the sixteenth century, Portuguese gained control of the maritime provinces, and in the next century the Dutch replaced the Portuguese. In 1796 the Dutch were ousted by the British. In this situation, caught between the Hindu Tamils and European powers, the Sinhalese national consciousness began to rejuvenate Buddhism, which was at a low ebb. This trend coincided with the establishment of the Sinhalese Malabar dynasty in Kandy. In 1753, the Malabar king invited some Siamese monks to Kandy, and three thousand Sinhalese were ordained by them. This marked the beginning of the Siamese sect (Upali-vamsa) in Ceylon, from which later an offshoot, known as the Kelanis, developed. Early in the nineteenth century, two groups of Sinhalese monks, trained in two different regions in Burma, started the Amarapura and the Ramanya sects, respectively.

The complex development of Buddhism in Ceylon makes it clear that it is impossible to isolate Buddhism from the total Buddhist-Hindu civilization which penetrated the island. In reality, Theravāda Buddhism in Ceylon has incorporated many elements of Brahmanism, the Mahāyāna and Esoteric traditions of Buddhism, as well as local animism. Even Eliot, who was impressed by the Ceylonese preservation of a very ancient form of Buddhism, acknowledged that actually Buddhism in Ceylon " tolerates a superstructure of Indian beliefs and ceremonies which forbid us to call it pure except in a restricted sense. At present there may be said to be three religions in Ceylon: local animism, Hinduism, and Buddhism are all inextricably mixed together." [55] In one sense at least, Ceylon has been faithful to the Buddhism of Asoka's period: that is, it stands for the supremacy of Buddhism without rejecting the diverse elements of Brahmanism and Hindu civilization.

The situation in other parts of Southeast Asia differed from that of Ceylon for many reasons. In Java, the Hindu civilization was established before the fifth century A.D., and it had close cultural ties with the Hindu settlements in Cambodia, Sumatra, and Borneo. The main trend of Javanese Buddhism was Mahāyāna, with an Esoteric tinge. Unlike Ceylon, where Buddhism superseded and subjugated Brahmanism, in Java, Buddhism accepted Brahmanism as a partner on an equal footing, so that Buddhism and Brahmanism were seen as two aspects of the same religion. The Javanese thought that the superhuman Buddhas were different names of Hindu gods, such as Amitābha for Mahadeva, and Amoghasiddhi for Vishnu. Understandably, Buddhism shared the destiny of Hindu civilization in Java, and both were exterminated by the Muslims. It is to be noted that the Buddhist-Brahman amalgamation also took place in Cambodia, as evidenced by the ruins of the ninth-century art objects at Angkor Vat. In Cambodia, however, Mahāyāna Buddhism was replaced by Theravāda in the thirteenth century, and it has remained to this day as a stronghold of Theravāda.

Mention should be made of Buddhism in Burma and Thailand, the two leading Theravāda nations in Southeast Asia today. Both countries have a mixed religious heritage, including Brahmanism and the Mahāyāna and Mantrayāna traditions of Buddhism. Both of them accepted Theravāda as the orthodox system and as a national faith. In Burma it was King Dhammaceti in the fifteenth century who tried to unify the various schools under Theravāda, and it was he who invited Ceylonese monks to reordain Burmese monks according to the Theravāda rite. But the royal decision to adopt Theravāda Buddhism could not erase either the deep-rooted Brahmanic tradition or the popular animistic beliefs known as *Nats* worship. Also, the Burmese kings, despite their patronage of Buddhism, took the Brahmanic concept of divine kingship very seriously, and " so complete was the royal domination that neither hereditary courtier-officials nor strong middle classes were ever able to arise in Burma." [56] The records of the monarchic period reveal increasing tension between the Brāhmans, who surrounded the king in court, and the people who depended on the Buddhist ecclesiastics for spiritual guidance. With the gradual decline of the monarchy, Buddhism gained more strength.

Buddhism in Thailand has many things in common with Burmese Buddhism. And yet, dissimilarities between them are also apparent. Probably there are stronger Brahmanic elements incorporated in the religious life of Thailand than in Burma, as evidenced by the numerous Brahmanic festivals in Thailand. Also, as mentioned earlier, Burmese Buddhism became a rallying point of the people's reaction against the Brahmanic influences in the court. In Thailand, however, Buddhism developed into a state religion, and the ecclesiastical hierarchy became an important unit of officialdom, so that the tensions existed not so much between Brāhmans in the court and the people, but rather between high-ranking Buddhist ecclesiastics and the court Brāhmans. Even today, the Thai king plays an important role in Buddhist affairs.

In spite of all these differences, Buddhism in Ceylon, Java, Burma, and Thailand may be seen as a part of Buddhist-oriented Indian civilization. This point will become more evident as we examine the expansion of Buddhism in other parts of Asia.

Expansion of Buddhism in Other Cultural Areas

Not only did Buddhism penetrate India's immediate neighbors, but it also influenced areas where non-Indian cultures were securely established. Among them, the most important area was China. Though there are scattered references to the presence of Buddhism in China as early as the third century B.C., Buddhist missionary work there did not officially start until the first century A.D. In general, there were three waves of Buddhism into China, first by way of Central Asia, then by sea around the Malay Archipelago in the sixth and seventh centuries, and finally through mountain areas into Tibet during the Mongol period.

The importance of Central Asia or the Tarim basin in the history of Buddhism cannot be exaggerated. The geographical position of Central Asia is such that various ethnic groups — Iranian, Scythian, Turkish, and Mongolian — lived side by side in this area. They were nomads who had little cultures of their own, but acted as transmitters of other civilizations and cultures. Thus, Central Asia became a crossroads of religions — Brahmanism, Buddhism, Manichaeism, Zoroastrianism, Chinese religions, and Christianity. In such an an atmosphere each religion was bound to undergo a certain amount of transformation and reinterpretation. For example, Sylvain Lévi contended that some Mahāyāna *sūtras* were either written or re-edited in Central Asia, and Eliot felt that apocryphal *sūtras* were probably composed in this region.[57]

The records of Chinese Buddhism show that many early

missionary monks were in some ways connected with Central Asia. As early as the middle of the second century a Parthian prince, converted to Buddhism and known as An-shih-kao by the Chinese, founded a school of translation of Buddhist texts in the Chinese capital. In the third century, Seng-hui of Sogdian descent established himself as a teacher of Buddhism in Nanking. Probably the most colorful and famous was Kumarājīva, an Indian originally from Kucha, who studied Buddhism in Kashmir and became a Mahāyāna teacher in Kucha. Toward the end of the fourth century Kumarājīva was taken to China as a prisoner by Lü-kuang, who later became the ruler of the state of Southern Liang. We are told that Kumarājīva had more than three thousand Chinese monks as disciples, and that he translated numerous scriptures into Chinese with the co-operation of his disciples. Central Asia also provided the route for the Chinese pilgrims who undertook the perilous journey of visiting Buddhist holy places in India.

Two general observations may be made regarding Chinese Buddhism. First, although at first Chinese Buddhism very closely followed and imitated Indian Buddhism, in the course of time it discovered a new creative impulse and developed a unique form of Buddhism in the climate and soil of China. Secondly, Buddhism did not replace Confucianism, Taoism, and other religious and semireligious systems in China, but it did change the tenor of these systems sufficiently so that all these systems, including Buddhism, could coexist within the Chinese cultural context.

The phenomenal growth of Buddhism in China during the first three centuries of the Christian era is astounding. " By A.D. 65 it was already embraced by a prince of the imperial family; and by 165, it was accepted by the Emperor Huan Ti. By 200, we find it was defended by one of the native scholars in southern China. By 300, it was talked about by all Chinese intellectuals as the greatest system of philosophy ever invented by the genius of man." [58] Buddhism continued to prosper until it reached its apex during the T'ang period (618–907). Considering the fact that Buddhism in origin and in ethos was an alien religion, one might ask why and how it gained such wide acceptance in China. Latourette answers this question in the following way. First, there was a spiritual vacuum, and Buddhism filled it by meeting the basic demands of the human spirit. Buddhism was also a welcome relief from the rigid determinism of Confucian orthodoxy. Secondly, Buddhism with its philosophical systems, impressive liturgies, and new spirit expressed in art and culture greatly enlarged the spiritual horizons of the Chinese. Thirdly, unlike the aristocratic ethos of the Chinese spiritual tradition, Buddhism exalted the individual and presented its gospel to all men. Finally, the time was favorable for the growth of Buddhism. During the first three centuries of the Christian era, Chinese society suffered from civic strife and foreign invasion, and this was the time when Buddhism was a dynamic spiritual movement in the full flood of missionary enthusiasm and expansion.[59]

While accepting Latourette's analysis of this question, we are inclined to add another reason for the wide acceptance of Buddhism in China. That is, Buddhism did not shoulder the responsibility of being the sole bearer of civilization. Unlike the expansion of Buddhist-oriented Indian civilization in India's neighboring countries, Buddhism in China did not claim the totality of Chinese culture, nor did it envisage the establishment of a Buddhist state. Buddhism recognized the existing culture, which had been molded by Confucianism, Taoism, and other indigenous thoughts. In other words, the role Buddhism accepted and played in China was grossly different from the role it accepted and played in the religious and cultural satellites of India. As Hocking points out, Buddhism in China did not pretend to be a contestant, but rather a supplement to existing local religions.[60] To put it another way, the problem that Buddhism faced in China was not how to reconstruct Chinese culture according to its Indian image but rather how Indian Buddhism might be reconstructed so that it could become naturalized in China.

Inevitably Buddhism encountered many problems in China. First was the translation and transplantation of religious thought and doctrine into Chinese expression. This entailed both the technical linguistic problem of translation and transliteration, and also the cultural problems of utilizing and developing appropriate thought forms for Buddhist doctrines. Tang Yung-Tung describes the attempts of the earliest Buddhist translators to find traditional Chinese ideas and words for Indian Buddhist ideas by developing the so-called " Ko-yi " method.[61] The problem was not only how accurate the translation was, but also how literarily acceptable the translation was to the literati, and how meaningful the thought expressed in translation was to the Chinese mind. Thanks to the joint efforts of Central Asian, Indian, and Chinese monks, voluminous sacred scriptures were translated into Chinese, and the Chinese Buddhists did not feel the need of preserving either Sanskrit or Pali as the ecclesiastical language. While the use of the Chinese language tended to distort the original body of meaning, this also provided the freedom with which Chinese Buddhists could develop their own systems of thought. It is true that Chinese Buddhism did not intend to deviate from historic Indian Buddhism in doctrinal matters, but by putting different emphasis on such ideas as the universal Buddhahood, it resulted in recognizing more value in the phenomenal world than Indian Buddhism ever acknowledged.

The second problem faced by Chinese Buddhism was socioecclesiastical. The Indian emphasis on the monastic orders as the best path provided an avenue hitherto unknown and undeveloped in Chinese religious traditions. By and large, the monastic institution was not properly understood by the people in China, who valued the extended family system. Such notions as ancestor worship and filial piety imply that the succession of lineage is a Chinese counterpart of the Indian dogma of the transmigration of souls. Here the Buddhist doctrine of the rejection of any phenomenal social order and structure for the sake of liberation had to undergo a significant transformation. Besides, the autocratic government of China resented and suspected the growth of the monastic groups as potential secret societies, which might resist the ruling dynasties. The Chinese government gave permission for the first time to native monks to take monistic vows in A.D. 335, but subsequently the monastic orders often became the object of suspicion and persecution by government officials and rulers, some of whom were devout Buddhists themselves. Eventually, Buddhist apologists twisted the traditional concept and explained the monastic vow as meritorious to one's whole family, and thus a true act of filial piety. But in the main Chinese Buddhism developed as a layman's religion, never, however, rejecting the role of monastic orders. The term " Samgha " was often translated as *chung* (multitudes) and not " select few." Basically, Chinese Buddhism never developed an adequate theory of ecclesiology. In practice, it became a religion of the family, and it did not articulate the relationship between the Buddhist Community and the society or state.

Related to the second is a third, political problem. The growth of Buddhism in China depended heavily on royal favor, which enabled the Buddhists to construct temples and carry on literary work without financial struggle. It is significant, as Tsukamoto points out, that around A.D. 200 the Chinese Buddhists created a legendary tale about a dream of Emperor Wu Ti, which caused him to invite Indian monks to bring Buddhism into China. " By pretending that Buddhism was received at the center of government by command of the emperor, they sought to invest their religion with an authority that the people of China could not easily deny." [62] That this type of propaganda was effective is reflected in the report that in 381 nine tenths of the inhabitants of northwestern China were Buddhists. It is conceivable that at first Buddhism, being the religion of Central Asian peoples, received special attention from the diplomacy-conscious rulers. Furthermore, it was the consistent policy of the Buddhist missionaries from the beginning to endear themselves to royalty. This policy was certainly effective, because starting with Liang Wu Ti, some of the monarchs embraced Buddhism, and many others actively supported it.

With the rapid growth of Buddhism the political situation became more complex. For one thing, Buddhism often became involved in court intrigue. The royal favor was unpredictable, however. For example, in 471 the ruler of Wei constructed a great statue of Buddha and a few years later abdicated in order to devote himself to Buddist studies. His successor, being an ardent Confucianist, reversed the policy in regard to Buddhism, but his successor again reversed the policy in favor of Buddhism. The difficulties were not confined to the favor of the court only. Under the emperor served a large body of officialdom, which usually favored the traditional Confucian orthodoxy. During a period when the power of the Confucianists was weak, or when a pro-Buddhist emperor had the personal ability and power to keep his ministers under control, Buddhism seems to have fared better, but reactions often came, too. There were two basic difficulties. First, the role of the Chinese emperor was very ambiguous, whether a despot or a representative of his nation. Secondly, Buddhism lacked normative theories about the political order, except for the example of King Asoka. Thus is was logical for Emperor Wen Ti of the Sui dynasty to adopt a policy of state control of Buddhism and utilize it for political ends. " With the armed might of a Cakravartin king," stated Wen Ti in 581, " we spread the ideals of the ultimately benevolent one [i.e., Buddha]." [63] But to him, it was unthinkable for Buddhist institutions to exert any moral judgments regarding imperial policy. By accepting the role of a state or court-sponsored religion, Buddhism in China found an efficient way to be naturalized into Chinese culture. However, by the same token it failed to develop a moral and spiritual reservoir, so that with the loss of royal favor it declined after the T'ang period.

Despite these and other problems which confronted Chinese Buddhism, its contribution to the religious and cultural life of China is impressive. In turn Chinese culture helped develop the Mahāyāna tradition of Buddhism. The doctrine of transcendental Buddhahood (tri-kāya, or three bodies) and of many Buddhas, the paradigmatic ideal of Bodhisattvahood, its virtues and its stages, and metaphysical speculation as well as devotional practice were not entirely new creations of Chinese Buddhism, but they would never have blossomed so fully without the Chinese contributions. Chinese Buddhism also produced voluminous sacred scriptures, 1,662 works in all, including both the Theravāda and Mahāyāna writings. All the Chinese denominations claimed to be heirs to Indian prototypes, but some of them were definitely Chinese in origin. In all, there were ten denominations, each possessing its patriarchal successions, favorite texts, and special practices. It may be said that the common characteristic of all Chinese denominations is the practical problem of salvation. Here we will mention only three main approaches. First is the gospel of salvation by faith, stressed by the Pure Land School. Second is the magico-mystical approach of the Esoteric (Mantrayāna) School, which supplied elaborate funeral rites to Chinese life. Third is the Meditation School, Ch'an, better known as Zen. Zen, in short, tries to attain the immediate realization of Buddhahood by developing direct intuition into the heart (*hsin*). Yet these approaches were not considered contradictory. In the words of Wing-tsit Chan, " Chinese Buddhism has followed the Ch'an (or Zen) and Pure Land schools in practice and has adhered to the T'ien-t'ai and Hua-yen schools in doctrine." [64] It was this Buddhism, developed in China, which was introduced to Korea and Japan.

Little need be said about Buddhism in Korea, the religio-cultural satellite of China for centuries. The rise and decline of Korean Buddhism shows an irregular curve, reflecting favor at court alternating with disfavor, which in turn reflected a similar curve in China. Historically, Korean Buddhism, after reaching its zenith in the thirteenth century, began to decline, and finally it received a fatal blow by the pro-Confucian and anti-Buddhist government policy in the fifteenth century.

Buddhism was first introduced into Japan from Korea in the sixth century. Geographically and historically, Japan has been close to the Asian continent, but its island setting enabled it to enjoy a separate and independent life both culturally and politically. Like everything introduced to Japan from China and Korea, Buddhism too was acculturated in Japan. The Japanese accepted Buddhism " simply, humbly, in sincere and almost childlike fashion, and then they have laid the stamp of their own transforming genius upon it." [65] In this connection, Langdon Warner reminds us that Shinto, the native religious cult of Japan, " has always been the artist's way of life." [66] Nurtured by this way of life, the Japanese never made a clear-cut distinction between religion and art, and Buddhism was deeply influenced by this spirit.

The first period of Japanese Buddhism, say from the sixth to the eighth centuries, witnessed the rapid growth of this alien religion. Prince Shotoku, following the example of the Chinese emperor Wen Ti, attempted to integrate Buddhism as one of the state-sponsored religious systems. Thanks to royal patronage, the eighth century saw a tremendous influx of culture from the China of the T'ang period, and Nara became the center of the first flowering of various Buddhist schools, all imported from China. The second period of Japanese Buddhism began with the introduction of Esoteric Buddhism, which not only supplied elaborate rituals for all conceivable occasions of national and individual life, but also provided a basis for a synthetic religious system, embracing within it Shinto, Buddhism, and shamanistic folk religions. Even the Tendai school, the Japanese counterpart of Chinese T'ien-t'ai Buddhism, was swallowed into this synthetic scheme, in the form of Ryobu-Shinto. The third period of Japanese Buddhism, notably the thirteenth century, produced a number of remarkable Buddhist saints. It was during this period that Zen Buddhism influenced the code of *Samurai,* known as *Bushido.* The heightened nationalistic consciousness, dramatized at the time of the Mongol invasions, was reflected in Nichiren Buddhism, named after the passionate preacher of the Lotus Sūtra and Nipponism. Also, a pietistic movement, deriving its inspiration from the Chinese Pure Land teachings, but based on deep personal religious experiences of the Japanese saints of this period, received widespread support among the masses. From the seventeenth to the nineteenth century, the Tokugawa feudal regime adopted Neo-Confucianism as the guiding ideology, but it also tried to utilize Buddhist institutions for the purpose of national solidarity. All in all, Japanese Buddhism fared better than its counterparts in Korea and China, even though it was as much, if not more, involved in political entanglements. What saved Japanese Buddhism was also a delimiting factor, namely, its acceptance of the role of being one ingredient of a multi-value system, sharing cultural responsibilities with Shinto and Confucianism. " The most salient feature of Japanese Buddhism," said Eliot, " is its intimate connection with the general condition of the nation, both political and social. It has vibrated in response to many and abrupt political changes, it has registered them in its sects and expressed in its art the special note of each." [67]

Last, but not least, is the Buddhism of Tibet, known as Lamaism. Its unique ethos cannot be understood without considering Tibet's geographical position, its native shamanistic Bon cult, and the constant influence exerted by India, China, and Mongolia. Also unique is the fact that Esoteric Buddhism, which was swallowed by Hinduism in India and overpowered by Mahāyāna Buddhism in China and Japan, became dominant in Tibet and Mongolia.

Buddhism must have been known to Tibetans long before its official introduction in the seventh century. Buddhism in Tibet, like its language, was destined to be a hybrid of Indian, Chinese, and native elements. The invitation to the Indian teacher Padmasambhava, about 747, marked the establishment in Tibet of Tantric Buddhism, which, however, incorporated within it the monastic discipline of the Sarvāstivādins and the philosophical systems of the Mādhyamika and Yogācāra schools. Accordingly, we find both lofty philosophical doctrines and the prevalence of *dhāranīs,* magic, sorcery, as well as the adoration of female deities in Lamaism.

Following a period of political unrest and religious disunity, the eleventh century witnessed a renaissance of Buddhism in Tibet. The Sakya school, which was the most powerful political and religious force between the eleventh and fourteenth centuries, was instrumental in compiling the Tibetan Tripitaka in 329 volumes, including the Kanjur (mainly canonical texts) and the Tanjur (exegetical and other auxiliary subjects).

Tibet was invaded by the Mongol forces in the thirteenth century, and this marked the beginning of the Lāmaistic influence on the Mongols. Kublai Khan himself was converted in 1261, and he appointed Phakpa, the abbot of the Sakya monastery, the imperial preceptor and head of all Buddhists in the realm. In spite of the royal favor, or because of it, Lamaism became hopelessly corrupt. The much-needed reformation was undertaken by Tsonkhapa (b. 1357), who established the Gelukpa tradition under the Grand Lāma in Lhasa. This school became influential, and the third Grand Lāma of Lhasa was given the title Dalai (Ocean Tide) Lāma by a Mongol ruler in the sixteenth century. In 1641 the fifth Grand Lāma united Tibet politically, with the help of the Mongol army, and started the Gelukpa hierarchy and the unique Buddhist theocracy of Tibet.

In Tibet we find a curious mixture of the first and the second types of expansion of Buddhism. Because of its geographical proximity to India, Tibet could be regarded in one sense as one of India's cultural satellites, but the same argument may be made in its relation to China as well. On the one hand, Tibet adopted Buddhism wholesale and translated voluminous sacred scriptures far more faithfully than Chinese Buddhists ever attempted to do; on the other hand, Tibetans appreciated and applied very little of Buddhist ethics, doctrines, and practices. Unlike China, Tibet had very little culture of its own, and yet Tibet managed to put its own mark on the Indian and Chinese elements of Buddhism and produced a unique form of Buddhism. Probably the secret of Lamaism lies in the Tibetans' "genius for hierarchy, discipline, and ecclesiastical polity," [68] which enabled them to establish a gigantic superstructure of the Buddhist Community, regardless of the quality of the faith of the priests and laity in all other aspects.

THE MODERN WORLD AND THE SAMGHA UNIVERSAL

Pan-Asianness of Buddhism

It has been our purpose to understand the dual character of Buddhism, its Indianness and its Pan-Asianness, for as Snellgrove states: " Buddhism is not just the word of one master, promulgated and fixed for all time. It was part of India's religious experience, changing, adapting, developing through the centuries, yet at the same time retaining a certain continuity and independence in its traditions." [69]

Buddhism continued to grow in India's immediate neighbors and also in other areas where indigenous religions and cultures had been established. In both cases the genius of Buddhism enabled it to maintain and express its *Lebensgefühl*, which is distinct and unmistakable. Eventually, Buddhism developed into a Pan-Asian religion, closely identified with various cultures of Asia.

Some general characterization of Asian cultures may be useful at this point. It has often been said that while the ethos of Europe may be described as a conscious and unconscious desire for unity of diverse elements, the ethos of Asia may be described in terms of " juxtaposition and identity," to use Haas's phrase. For example, two great Asian cultures, the Indian and the Chinese, developed independently with very little sense of mutual dependence or interpenetration. They stand side by side in juxtaposition and have developed in relative insularity.[70] In this situation, Buddhism alone developed and maintained cross-cultural regional ties.

Haas is of the opinion that the ideological differences between the East and the West can be seen most clearly in their understanding of the concept of the " natural." The East takes it for granted that social and political institutions are rooted in the " natural," which is identified with the " original." This view may be contrasted to the Hebraic-Christian notion of the Fall of man, which implies that the " natural " is a corruption of the " original." " The East admits no reason, or logos, in opposition and superior to the natural. The natural possesses, so to speak, its own reason. And it is the part of human wisdom to recognize and submit to it." [71] What distinguishes Buddhism from other Asian religions is what while accepting the necessity of transcendental wisdom, it refused to accept the empirical

sociopolitical system as a path to the realization of the
" original." Instead, Buddha created a separate community
of the faithful (Samgha), which alone was integrally related to the Dharma. However, the early Buddhist concept
of the Buddhist Community, consisting of the monastics
and the laity alike, was soon overshadowed by the monastic
emphasis of Theravāda Buddhism, and eventually the secu-
larization of the monastic institutions closely involved them
in the sociopolitical systems of Asia. Also, this nontheistic
religion began to embrace local spirit-worship in Southeast
Asia and to create its own pantheon in the Far East.

The historical development of Buddhism in Asia shows
its intimate connections with the ruling classes. To be sure,
there were sincere Buddhists in all walks of life, who tried
to follow the footsteps of their master, seeking not worldly
success or prosperity but sanctification and liberation. And
yet the growth of the Buddhist institutions was marked by
a passionate attachment to this-worldly values and to monarchic, hierarchic sociopolitical systems. This phenomenon may be explained, at least in part, by the fact that the
early concept of the Buddhist Community was not taken
seriously. Consequently, while Buddhism developed on the
local level something analogous to the Western pattern of
the parish, with temples and lay adherents, it never developed on a national or regional level a sense of solidarity
of all the faithful. Instead, Buddhists remember the reign
of Asoka as the golden age of Buddhism, implying that the
ideal of Buddhism is the establishment of a Buddhist state.
Because of this aspiration, the ecclesiastical hierarchy often
became for all practical purposes servants of the state, with
the result that Buddhism reflected the ethos of powers that
were far greater than it ever acknowledged. There is a saying that Buddhism did not convert China but China con-

verted Buddhism, and this was often true in other Asian countries as well. In short, Buddhism came to share the strength and weaknesses of Asian cultures over a long period of time.

Impact of Modernity

During the eighteenth and nineteenth centuries, traditional Asian cultures were disintegrating from within, and this process coincided with the advance of European colonial powers in Asia. To put it another way, " it was not their own stagnancy which delivered the Eastern peoples into the hands of the West," but " it was a stagnation that developed inversely as a result of their contact with the West " [72] that resulted in the decline of the East. The driving force behind the expansion of the Western nations was " modernity," which was destined to remain in Asia even after the end of the Western colonialism. Initially, of course, the impact of modernity was most directly felt in the areas that were taken over by European nations, such as Ceylon, Burma, and Indo-China, but it also precipitated social and political revolutions in Japan, China, and Thailand.

This is not the place to discuss the complex problem of colonialism in the Asian scene, nor was everything introduced by the Western administration necessarily bad, as some emotional nationalists insinuate. In fact, by eliminating some of the worst features of traditional autocratic and irrational political systems, the Western colonial administration prepared the way for more modern national governments. At the same time, the Western administrations disrupted the traditional ways of life in Asia. For example, Margaret Mead points out that the traditional government of Burma was based on a dual system: the king had customary powers over local hereditary headmen, who in turn governed people mainly by means of arbitration and not by coercion. In this situation, law and order were based on an accepted pattern of living and were not dependent on external authority. The Western administration, by making these hereditary headmen government officials, changed personal authority to bureaucratic authority, and transformed the organic relationships among the people into new territorial entities based on space. " When the organic unity of the village was shattered, when external authority with penal sanctions was substituted for the authority inherent in a traditional way of life, the traditional guiding principle of social conduct was destroyed and there was nothing to take its place." [73]

The most far-reaching effect of modernity was felt in the field of education, which divided Asians into two classes, a minority of young intellectuals with Westernized education and the mass of people without it. This is what Coomaraswamy called the separation of literacy from culture. The modern elite in Asia were uprooted from their ancestral ways of life, leaving indigenous religions and cultures to those who were less sensitive to the challenge of industrialized modern civilization. During the nineteenth and the early part of the twentieth century, modern education provided an avenue for upward social mobility in Asia. The colonial administrators were not totally unaware of the possible repercussions of this trend. The Administration Report of Ceylon (1877) stated, " Whether the spread of . . . English education . . . is an unmixed benefit or not, there can be no doubt that one of its results is to create a large and daily increasing class of men who reject all means of livelihood which savor at all of manual labor." And this is precisely what happened. Everywhere in Asia there developed a new social group of native intelligentsia, and it was this group which later provided leadership in nationalist movements.

During the first two decades of our century, however, the young intellectuals — whether they were nationalists, socialists, or communists — failed to capture the masses. In the meantime, traditional religious leaders gained prestige among the masses as spokesmen of the old ways of life, against the advance of the West, against Christian missionary work, and against the culturally uprooted native intellectuals. Gradually the traditional religions, which at first served only as rallying points of the illiterate peasantry, gained strength among the lower middle class. In the 1930's, many Asian intellectuals who had Westernized educations suddenly recognized the strength of their ancestral religions and cultures which they had hitherto spurned. Recognizing the need of relating themselves to their own peoples, some young Asian intellectuals and leaders became converts to the traditional religions, and this explains why some of them talk at one moment like radical revolutionaries and at the next moment like dreamy mystics.

Early in the 1940's, Western colonialism in Asia came to a sudden end with the Japanese invasion. Japan, be it noted, was an Asian nation where modern civilization and education had been taken over and utilized by the traditional culture. As soon as Japan occupied Southeast Asia, it eliminated the Western and pro-Western elements from government positions in the occupied area, and made every effort to eradicate the myth of Western supremacy. The Japanese occupation authorities also offered administrative positions to those natives who had been denied such advancement under Western rule, and gave large-scale military training to the natives for the first time. Furthermore, the Japanese were not idle in courting religious and political spokesmen in the countries they occupied.[74] Although the period of Japanese occupation was very brief, it nevertheless accelerated the growing nationalist movements in Southeast Asia, and this trend could not be easily reversed after the defeat of the Japanese.

After World War II, many Southeast Asian nations gained political independence. In this situation, what happened in Burma was repeated in many other countries. In the words of U Kyaw Thet: " Painfully aware that their national pride — even their continued existence — was manifestly debatable, the Burmese had to produce something tangible and traditional to justify their future as a separate entity. They found what they needed in Buddhism." [75]

The Samgha Universal

Many books and articles have been written on the resurgence of Buddhism since World War II. Even the most casual traveler passing through the Far East and Southeast Asia cannot help being impressed by the vitality of Buddhism. Like any other vital contemporary movement, the resurgence of Buddhism has many facets, and no sweeping statements can be made because the situations vary according to different areas of Asia. Here we will discuss two major aspects of the resurgence of Buddhism. The first is the relationship between Buddhism and the nation-states, and the second is the problem of the supernational solidarity of the Buddhist Community.

The problem of the relationship between Buddhism and the nation-state is acutely felt by many Asian leaders, both political and religious, who are shouldering the responsibility of guiding their nations in this difficult period of history. In recent decades, Asian leaders were struggling for independence; they fought against foreign rule by resistance movements and revolutionary actions. During that time, the problem was simple: politics meant struggle against imperialism, and religion stood for the indigenous values and ways of life which were suppressed by the alien rulers. Now that the native leaders are in power, they have to re-examine the relationship between Buddhism and the nation-state in the light of the contemporary situations in various countries. For example, Burma envisages the establishment of a " Buddhist Welfare State," based on dual roots of Buddhism and a planned economy. The problem that confronts Buddhist Burma is stated succinctly by U Kyaw Thet: " Are these two concepts really compatible? Are they self-defeating? Can a convinced Buddhist, who knows that things of this world are insubstantial and worthless, bring to the hard and tedious task of developing a still backward and badly war-ravaged country the energy and perseverance the job will require? " [76] Similar searching questions are being asked by thoughtful people throughout the Buddhist world. On the one hand, they want to preserve the Buddhist tradition, and on the other hand, they have to develop a new sociopolitical order.

Admittedly, Buddhism, which was closely interwoven with the premodern cultures of Asia, cannot be emancipated from the past overnight. In many areas of life Buddhism still represents the ultraconservative elements in society. For example, Bryce Ryan, in his interviews with eighty-six monks and priests in Ceylon on the question of family-planning, found that the views of the scholarly monks were overwhelmingly favorable but that the responses of uneducated village priests were uniformly negative to the idea of family-planning. The latter's views conform to those of the village laity, and this is where the actual strength of Buddhism is found today. Despite Ryan's optimistic conclusion that with careful public relations "the Sangha [Samgha] through its intellectual leaders would be a far more positive force than it would be negative,"[77] it may not be so easy to counteract the deep-rooted religious and social conservatism of the village priests and laity. The author of *The Revolt in the Temple* is impatient with those who loosely and naïvely talk about Buddhism as the only remedy for all the political isms, or a new way of life to the world. "Have those who use these slogans ever thought what kind of Buddhism they mean to offer to a distracted world? If by 'Buddhism' they mean the kind of Buddhism that is practiced in everyday Ceylon and dosed out to the people from the temples, loud-speakers, and the Broadcasting Service, we think there is little likelihood of that Buddhism taking root in the West, or anywhere else."[78] This type of self-criticism is going on in various parts of Asia regarding the actual situations of empirical Buddhism.

One of the important features of contemporary Buddhism is a serious effort on the part of some scholars to re-examine the historical Buddhist doctrines in the light of modern philosophical and social thought. For example, Wijesekera tries to portray Buddha as a rationalist and empiricist, who held an evolutionary view of the world and society.[79] There are others who also attempt to reinterpret Buddha as a social prophet, and Dharma as an ideology for the new age. Such attempts are not welcomed by conservative Buddhists, who resent any kind of change, doctrinal or practical. The modernist wing, however, advocates a new birth of Buddhism, emancipated from social and religious medievalism. "The sponsors of this revitalized religion, the Sangha [Samgha], would pursue not a will-o'-the-wisp Nirvāna secluded in the cells of their monasteries, but a Nirvāna attained here and now by a life of self-forgetful activity. Theirs will not be a selfish existence, pursuing their own salvation whilst living on the charity of others, but an existence full of service and self-sacrifice. To bring about this transformation the Sangha [Samgha] must be reorganized and the *bhikkhus* trained not only in Buddhist theory but also in some form of social service." [80]

There is no doubt that Buddhism can develop a dynamic social consciousness, a social philosophy, and social action, as well evidenced by the example of B. R. Ambedkar (d. 1956), the spokesman of the scheduled class of India, and a crusader for the rights of the oppressed. He launched a movement for abolishing untouchability in India by turning toward Buddhism. Although his Buddhist movement among the scheduled class has not been taken too seriously by the Hindu majority thus far, it is creating a significant minority of dedicated Buddhists in India. Ambedkar was a visionary who knew how to translate his vision into concrete social, educational, and political programs, and by his own example he demonstrated that Buddhism can inspire people to fight for the cause of justice and freedom, even defying the existing order of things, without any encouragement from the government or outside groups.

However, Ambedkar's was an unusual case. In general, most Buddhists today depend heavily on the leadership and assistance of their Governments. Historically Buddhism has been closely related to the state, and there is little effort on either side to alter this. While many Asian nations affirm in theory the freedom of conscience as well as the practice and propagation of all religions, in practice they accord special consideration to Buddhism. Conversely, many sincere Buddhists are convinced that teaching and preaching

Buddhist doctrine and ethics is not enough, and that the political structure must be made consonant with the Law of Buddha. " The task which the Buddha left to his followers was to create on earth a polity ordered in accordance with his teaching." [81] U Win, onetime Minister for Home and Religious Affairs in Burma, is more explicit on this point. He says: " Our religion has been in a neglected state for the sixty years since the overthrow [by the British] of King Thebaw, Promoter of the Faith. The prosperity of a religion . . . depends on the presence of a ruler who is genuinely inclined to promote it. . . . Now the circumstances have changed. Independence is once more restored and the Government is duly elected according to the constitution. It is but inevitable that the Government become the Promoter of the Faith, on behalf of the people who elect it." [82] In accordance with this principle, the Government of Burma passed in 1950 the Pali University and Dhammacarya Act to promote Buddhist study and to train priests. The Government also established the Buddhist Sasana Council of the Union of Burma to promote the cause of Buddhism, including the restoration of temples, encouragement of Buddhist study and meditation, and the propagation of Buddhism within and without Burma.

Today, the vitality of the resurgence of Buddhism is expressed in its missionary and " ecumenical " concerns, which are, of course, inseparably interrelated. The missionary outreach was not a particular concern of modern Buddhists until after World War II. Of course, there were exceptions. For example, in the 1930's Abbot T'ai-hsu and the leaders of the Chinese Buddhist Association sought the co-operation of Buddhists in other lands for a world-wide evangelism. It was T'ai-hsu's conviction that " Buddhist doctrine is fully capable of uniting all the existing forms of civilization, and should spread throughout the world so that it may become a compass, as it were, for the human mind." [83] With this far-reaching objective in mind, he suggested the establishment of an international Buddhist university for the training of learned monks, as well as the publication of Buddhist literature and a training program for laymen and laywomen. Similar objectives were advocated by the Maha-Bodhi Society in India. However, organized Buddhist missionary work was not undertaken on a big scale until the Burmese inaugurated the work among their animistic peoples in 1946. Today there are several missionary societies that are dedicated to the cause of the Buddhist missions in Asia, Europe, and America.

The Buddhist counterpart of the Christian " ecumenical " movement is bringing together the Theravāda, Mahāyāna and Mantrayāna traditions for the first time in Buddhism's long history. The World Fellowship of Buddhists, which by the way elected an able layman, G. P. Malalasekera, as its president, has had conferences in Ceylon (1950), Japan (1952), Burma (1954), and Nepal (1956), and provided valuable ecumenical experience to the delegates from various parts of Asia and the West. Also, celebrating the twenty-five hundredth anniversary of the Buddhist era, the Buddha Jayanti was held recently in many countries, which contributed greatly to the cause of Buddhist unity. Probably the most ambitious and dramatic undertaking of contemporary Buddhism was the Sixth Great Buddhist Council held in Burma, 1954–1956. This council, known officially as the Chattha Sangayana, was made possible by the combined efforts of the Government and the people of Burma under the leadership of the then prime minister, U Nu. The council, among other accomplishments, re-edited the sacred scriptures of Buddhism, which were recited and formally adopted as the canonical texts. Based on these experiences, Malalasekera is quite optimistic about the future of Buddhist unity. " The Buddhist flag now flies in every country as the emblem of World Buddhism, Mahāyāna monks are entering monasteries in Theravāda lands and vice versa to learn each other's language and canonical texts. They are co-operating in Ceylon's Buddha Jayanti project of an encyclopedia of Buddhism." [84]

Thus, in less than two decades, Buddhism has made notable advances toward the twofold goal of missionary outreach and Buddhist unity. To be sure, the Buddhist Community is still divided by different traditions, cultural heritages, and national interests, and the Buddhist nations are haunted by almost insurmountable problems concerning industrialization, communism, and social and economic welfare. Besides, whether the spokesmen of Buddhism admit it or not, Buddhism is not yet a live option in the religious life of people outside Asia. Despite all these problems which confront them today, Buddhists are beginning to see " in faith " the possibility of relating their holy Community to the totality of the human community. This is another way of saying that today Buddhists are seeing a glimpse of the Samgha Universal in the midst of the brokenness of the empirical Buddhist Community.

5 Islam and the Ummah

◈ ◈

THE WORLD OF ISLAM

Perspective

Islam or Muhammadanism (Mohammedanism) is a spiritual cousin of Judaism and Christianity. While many Jews and Christians regard Islam as a corruption of the Judaeo-Christian religious tradition, Muslims consider their religion a purification and fulfillment of Judaism and Christianity. Historically, there has been very little genuine understanding between Muslims and Westerners, in spite of the geographic proximity of the Islamic world and the West. Europeans often forget that the so-called Dark Ages in Europe coincided with the ascendancy of Muslim civilization. Exaggerated and one-sided accounts of the Crusades, told and retold in the West, have remained to this day as one of the obstacles to a better understanding between Muslims and Westerners.

During the modern period, the rise of Western European nations in the seventeenth century coincided with the general decline of the Muslim nations. " The Western counterattack on the Islamic world," says Toynbee, " was delayed by long Western memories of the Turks' and other Muslim peoples' historic military prowess." [1] He attributes the success of the Europeans to their conquest of the ocean, thus " throwing a lasso round Islam's neck; but it was not till the nineteenth century that the West ventured to pull the rope tight." [2] After the Ottoman Empire's failure in resisting the European powers, the once glorious Islamic empire was shattered. During the last one hundred and fifty years, Europeans have tended to regard Muslims as uncivilized peoples, to be exploited by colonial powers and enlightened by Western culture.

Today, however, the whole world is keenly aware of the importance of Muslim nations. The Arab nations' fight against the Zionist in Palestine indicates, in part, the Muslims' emotional reaction against their former colonial masters. The Arab Muslims are not reconciled to the fact that the State of Israel was established in their midst, with the consent and support of Western nations, in total disregard of Muslim sentiments. Many Muslims, if pushed, would admit that Israel is there to stay. However, this does not change the fact that their pride was seriously wounded, just as the pride of the Western nations was wounded by Nassar's sudden nationalization of the Suez Canal.

While many people recognize the political importance of the Muslim nations, they often fail to understand the religious importance of Islam. Contrary to the common impression that Islam is an Arab religion, it is today one of the most widely diffused religions in the world. In this connection it is significant that over sixty-eight per cent of the Muslim population today is found east of Karachi. Recent estimates indicate that there are roughly 413 million Muslims in the world, of which 42 million are in the Far East; 79 million are in Southeast Asia; 107 million are in the Pakistan-India area, including Burma and Ceylon; 64 million are in Turkish areas, including Sinkiang, Afghanistan, the Soviet Union, Eastern Europe, and Turkey; 20 million are in Iran; 64 million are in the Arab world; 35 million are in Africa, excluding the Arab countries; and 800,000 are scattered in Western countries.[3] Although these figures are rough estimates, it is safe to assume that approximately one seventh of the human race belongs to the world of Islam.

In comparison with two other world religions, Buddhism and Christianity, both of which were repudiated in the lands of their origin, Islam has remained the predominant religion in the Arab world where it originated in the seventh century. The history of the Islamization of non-Arab peoples has been accompanied by conscious and unconscious Arabization of new converts to a greater or lesser degree, depending on the individual situation. John Gunther has analyzed the world of Islam in terms of three overlapping circles: (1) The largest circle represents the religious world of Islam, embracing parts of Africa, the Balkan nations, the Middle East, the Indian peninsula, parts of Russia and China, and Southeast Asia. Adherents of Islam in all these places, regardless of their ethnic origins, constitute the community of the faithful, known as the " Ummah " or " Umma." (2) The second circle is a linguistic one, and it may be noted that Arabic is one of the most widely used languages in the world. Here, however, we have to remind ourselves that some Arabic-speaking peoples are not Muslims, and that only one sixth of all Muslims speak Arabic, even though many of them read Arabic. (3) The third and smallest circle covers the so-called Arab nations in the Middle East.[4] To complicate matters further, we find non-Muslim religious minorities scattered in the Arab nations. In Lebanon, for example, Christians outnumber Muslims, fifty-five per cent as compared with forty-five per cent. At any rate, the three above-mentioned circles can keep us from the easy pitfall of identifying Islam with the Arab world.

In its original ethos, however, Islam was a Middle Eastern religion. By its own claim, Islam began with Ishmael, the father of the Arabs. Muhammad held that his religion was not against Judaism and Christianity. Rather, he regarded Judaism, Christianity, and Islam as steps in a unilinear development of one eternal revelation, even though he rejected the claims to final revelation of both Judaism and Christianity. Nevertheless, Islam was inevitably influenced by these traditions. The relation between Islam and Judaism, and the relation between Islam and Christianity, have been perplexing problems in the history of religions. Some scholars assert that the doctrinal foundation of Islam was basically Christian; this view was widely held by Christains of the Middle Ages. Others insist that the main themes of Islamic doctrine were Judaistic. While there is some basis for both views, we are inclined to agree with Gibb's statement that " Islam is an autonomous expression of religious thought and experience, which must be viewed in and through itself and its own principles and standards." [5]

The Arabness of Islam

No one simple characterization can do justice to the complex character of Islam. However, it is important to recognize that throughout its history Islam has been held together by what Ibn Khaldun termed *'Asabiyya,* or the social solidarity of the Arabs. Thus, one cannot attempt to understand Islam without taking into account its fundamental " Arabness," even though Islam was strongly influenced by Judaism and Christianity in its ethical, eschatological, ritual, and legal minutiae. In the course of time, Islam came under the influence of a variety of non-Arabic cultures, but its " Arabness " has remained to this day an important thread in the colorful tapestry of Islamic religion and civilization.

Unfortunately, our knowledge of ancient pre-Islamic Arabia is very limited. Historically, Arabia was the homeland of the Semitic peoples — Babylonians, Assyrians, Hebrews, and Arabs. In the sixth century B.C. the Semitic peoples came under the domination of the short-lived Persian Empire. In 539 B.C. Babylon fell to Cyrus the Persian. " If Cyrus claimed to be sent by Marduk," writes Finegan, " the Second Isaiah felt that the conqueror was anointed by Jehovah himself for the task of releasing the Jewish exiles and returning them to their home (Isa. 45:1; cf. 44:28) ." [6] With the decline of the Persian Empire, Arabia came under the sway of Hellenistic culture. " Stimulated into maturity by the pressures of the Persian Empire's universality, Greek culture flowered and produced a dynamic that awaited only the appearance of an Alexander to go crusading to the ends of the East." [7]

In the first century B.C. the Romans became the rulers of the former Hellenistic states of Egypt and Syria. In A.D. 106 Trajan destroyed the northern Arabian kingdom and created a Province of Arabia. Subsequently, Arabia underwent a general transition from city to nomadic life. The international trade that had brought wealth and culture from abroad was almost paralyzed. The shift from urban to nomadic life coincided with a general decline of the old Arabic religion. In its stead, Christianity and Judaism found many proselytes. For example, Judaism became the state religion of the Himyarites' kingdom. [8]

The " Arabness " of Islam can be traced to the " nomadization " or " Bedouinization " of Arabia in the pre-Islamic period. Although there existed some old cities, such as Yathrib (later Medina), " they were more or less under pressure from the Bedouins who encamped around and about them, never strong enough to conquer them and expel their rulers, but sufficiently strong to compel them to pay tribute for their security." [9] Very few cities escaped the Bedouin encroachments. Mecca, the caravan center, was an outstanding exception.

Caskel states that the geographic and climatic conditions of Arabia forced the Bedouin to live according to a definite cycle of migration. " The same conditions force the Bedouin in spring (and possibly in autumn) to split up into small units of fifteen to twenty tents, while the other seasons permit a larger concentration. However, the need for security also forces these small units to remain within a distance of a few hours from one another in the spring, so that they can meet a hostile raid with a strength of about five hundred tents." [10] This natural association of the Bedouin was based on real or fictitious blood relationships. It is to be noted that within their sociopolitical organization — the tribal system — only the smallest unit and the next larger group, that is, the clan and its branches, form " solidarity groups." [11] This type of tribal organization was found not only among the Bedouins, but also among the nomadic Arabs, though with minor deviations. The most prominent features of Bedouin life were aversion to change and an isolationist, hyper-individualist attitude. " The nomadic Arabians were so jealous of their freedom (or, if we like it better, were so deep-rooted in their anarchy), that they regularly ousted or killed the would-be monarchs." [12] Evidently, public opinion was the supreme judge of Bedouins and nomadic Arabs. Their sense of unity was found in pilgrimages to Arafa and in intertribal fairs held at a place called Ukaz. " Even before Islam, the Arabs felt as one people, if not as one nation. This unity is due to Mecca and the Bedouins." [13]

Mecca is one of the oldest cities in Arabia. Its importance can be traced to the fact that it was situated at the intersection of great commercial routes in pre-Islamic times. Mecca " was advantageously placed at the extreme ends of the Asia of the whites and the Africa of the blacks, near a breach in the chain of the Sarat, close to a junction of roads leading from Babylonia and Syria to the plateaus of the Yemen, to the shores of the Indian Ocean and the Red Sea." [14] The religious importance of Mecca in the pre-Islamic period was due to its sacred shrine, the Kaaba, also known as " the House of Allāh." The Arabs possess no historical records of the origin of the Kaaba. Evidently an older sanctuary was destroyed and a new edifice was erected in the second half of the sixth century. At any rate, the worship of the sanctuary had developed into a cult several generations before Muhammad. This cult consisted of marching around the Kaaba and the accompanying rites of procession between the two great stones, called Safa and Marwa.

While we have no way of knowing what kind of deity Allāh was understood to be before Islam, we are certain that the Arabs worshiped a god called Allāh — " the *ilah*," or the god. It is also known that an earlier god called Hubal was worshiped at Mecca, and his idol stood in the Kaaba. Despite some scholars' suggestion that Hubal is identical with Allāh, this question has not been settled. Shortly before the time of Muhammad, Allāh was worshiped together with his three daughters, al-Lat, al-'Uzza, and Manat. " Each of these well-known female deities was worshiped elsewhere, independently of Allāh, so that there is no doubt that the setup of the Meccan worship was the result of a syncretistic development." [15] While Meccans accepted Allāh as creator and supreme provider, they worshiped on all ordinary occasions other subordinate gods. Meccans also held that there was a " kinship " between Allāh and the *djinn,* or spirits, and they made offerings to the *djinn* as Allāh's partners. Our information is not clear as to whether or not Meccans regarded angels as Allah's partners. Nevertheless, it is safe to conclude that the religion of Mecca in Muhammad's time " resembled much more a form of the Christian faith, in which saints and angels have come to stand between the worshipers and God. And Muhammad naturally regarded himself as a reformer who was preaching an earlier and simpler faith and putting angels and *djinn* back into their true places." [16]

Della Vida states that the religion of Muhammad was foreign to the Bedouin Arabians at first, because the Islamization of Arabia was directed against the nomadic pattern of life. " All that was characteristic in it and dear to the Bedouin's heart was bitterly assailed in Muhammad's preaching: the tribal organization, the individualistic freedom, and the coolness toward regular worship." [17] However, it must be remembered also that Muhammad did not reject pre-Islamic religious beliefs and practices altogether. For example, " the ceremonies of the great feast at Mecca were embodied by Muhammad into Islam, and therefore an old heathen, pre-Islamic ritual has been preserved up to our days, almost unchanged." [18] Indeed, Muhammad was successful in binding the Bedouins to his new religion, and in so doing he built his new religious community on the foundation of *'Asabiyya,* or the social solidarity of the Arabs. To be sure, much of the nomadic pattern of pre-

Islamic Arabia was changed under the leadership of Muhammad. But at the same time, Islam has never been completely emancipated from its "Arabness," which has remained an important ingredient of the Islamic religion and community to our day.

THE PROPHET OF GOD

His Life

Among the major figures in the history of religions, the founder of Islam is a controversial and complex personality. To some he was a bloodthirsty conqueror, to others the benign spokesman of a compassionate and merciful God. "Mohammed," says Nabia Abbott, "the prayerful and perfumed prophet of Islam, was avowedly a great lover of ladies, for whom, in turn, he held no small attraction." [19] Western historians often characterize him as cruel, lustful, shrewd, and vain, whereas Muslims regard him as *the* prophet of God and the highest image of humanity.

Many biographies of Muhammad have been written, and there are as many theories about Muhammad as there are biographers. And yet it is extremely difficult to find an "objective" life of Muhammad. "So far as the greatest monument to Muhammad's memory — the Qur'ān — is concerned, that is not difficult; but his biography is much more difficult to deal with. To translate without comment the statements of his biographers without historical criticism would be misleading; on the other hand, to generalize as some Western scholars have done would be rash." [20] The biography of Muhammad the man is inseparably interwoven with the pious legends of Muhammad the prophet, as is the case with all founders of religions.

Some basic vital statistics are ascertainable. Born in

Mecca about the year A.D. 570, Muhammad was the posthumous son of Abd Allah and the grandson of Abd al-
Muttalib, whose father was Hāshim. " Hāshim had married
a woman of Medina who belonged to the clan of 'Adi ibn
al-Najjār, which formed part of the tribe of Khazraj, and
thus Muhammad had blood ties with Medina. Mecca was
held by the tribe of Quraysh, and Muhammad belonged to
a well-established but impoverished family there." [21] Except for the fact that his mother died when he was very
young and he was brought up by his grandfather and uncle,
reliable accounts of his early childhood are scarce. While
Muhammad was working in the caravan trade as the agent
of a widow named Khadījah, he was deeply concerned with
religious questions. However, it was not until he " had
stirred the heart of his elderly but well-to-do employer —
the widow Khadījah — that he had the opportunity to
devote himself to his dreams. His marriage to Khadījah
brought him freedom from economic care and leisure for
spiritual contemplation." [22] Evidently, Khadījah was a devoted wife, and she bore him two sons and four daughters.
Unfortunately, their sons died young, but their daughters
played important roles in the early history of Islam. Among
his daughters, Zaynab married Abu'l-As; Ruqayya married
Uthmān, the third caliph; Fātima married Ali, who is
specially revered by the Shī'a branch of Islam; and Umm
Kulthum married Utayba.

Prophetic Call

The turning point of Muhammad's life was the prophetic
call that came to him when he was about forty years of
age. The first revelation took the form of a commandment:

> Recite thou, in the name of thy Lord who created; —
> Created man from CLOTS OF BLOOD: —

> Recite thou! For thy Lord is the most beneficent,
> Who hath taught the use of the pen; —
> Hath taught man that which he knoweth not.[23]

It is said that Muhammad was not certain whether it was a genuine revelation or a sign of mental disorder. After three years, a second vision commanded:

> O THOU, ENWRAPPED in thy mantle!
> Arise and warn!
> Thy Lord — magnify him!
> Thy raiment — purify it!
> The abomination — flee it!
> And bestow not favors that thou mayest receive
>   again with increase;
> And for thy Lord wait thou patiently.
> For when there shall be a trump on the trumpet,
> That shall be a distress day,
> A day, to the infidels, devoid of ease.[24]

From then on, revelation came to Muhammad regularly. His first converts were his wife Khadījah and adopted children, Alī and Zeid. Soon prominent citizens like Abu Bakr and Uthmān accepted the new faith. As the number of his followers increased, Muhammad began to preach publicly, stressing that God (Allāh) was one, and that there was to be a judgment day. His dedication to the prophetic calling is evident in his willingness to risk his own life, as well as the lives of his own fellow kinsmen, for the cause of Allāh.

Initially, Muhammad's claim to a prophetic ministry was ridiculed by his fellow Meccans. Gibb contends that " the resistance of the Meccans appears to have been due, not so much to their conservatism or even to religious disbelief (though they ridiculed Muhammad's doctrine of resurrection) , as to political and economic causes." [25] They rightly suspected that " their acceptance of his teaching would introduce a new and formidable kind of political authority into their oligarchic community." [26] At any rate, the Meccan leaders persecuted Muhammad's followers, so that he had to find a refuge for his adherents. Fortunately for them, the King of Abyssinia was under the impression that Muhammad's followers were persecuted Christians, and he offered them asylum in his domain. In the meantime, under continued persecution by Meccan leaders, Muhammad retracted some of his early utterances which had offended the Meccans. In the midst of his struggles with the Meccan leaders, Muhammad lost his wife, Khadījah, and a faithful follower, Abu Talib. Exhausted, Muhammad fled to the neighboring oasis of Taif, where he contemplated on the future of his community.

About this time, Muhammad spoke by chance to six men from the Khazraj tribe in Yathrib (later known as al-Medina or " the City "), a town about two hundred miles north of Mecca. Yathrib then was involved in internal tribal wars. The six men who heard Muhammad were so impressed by his message and personality that they initiated an arrangement whereby Muhammad was offered the suzerainty of Yathrib to establish peace and order. " With his habitual prudence, he first exacted guarantee for the security of his own position and for the right of his followers to precede him to Medina." [27] The negotiations between Muhammad and Medina took nearly two years and resulted in the famous formula which says in part: " We will not worship any but the one God. We will not steal. Neither will we commit adultery. Nor kill our children. We will not slander in any wise. Nor will we disobey the Prophet in anything that is right." [28] After the completion of negotiations, Muhammad fled secretly from his Meccan pursuers and established himself in Medina. It is said that he

arrived at the outskirts of Medina on the Jewish Day of
Atonement in A.D. 622. The migration of Muhammad from
Mecca to Medina, known as *hijra* or *hejira*, marks the be-
ginning of the Islamic calendar.

Prophet and Statesman

The Hijra, no doubt, was an important landmark in
Muhammad's mission. Gibb, however, rejects the oft-repeated thesis that the Hijra represented a great change in
Muhammad, from the persecuted prophet of Mecca to the
warrior theocrat of Medina. Rather, what happened at
Medina was that the religious community was translated
from theory to practice. While externally the Islamic movement assumed a new shape at Medina, " this merely gave
explicit form to what had hitherto been implicit." Fundamentally, Islam was " conceived of as a community organized on political lines, not as a church within a secular
state." [29] It was no simple task that confronted Muhammad
in Medina. " The months which followed [the Hijra] were
busy and critical ones for Mohammed and his followers,
the *muhājirūn,* or ' fugitives ' of Mecca. They had to make
a place for themselves in the new order without alienating
or imposing too much on the accommodating but ambitious *ansārs,* or ' helpers ' of Medina." [30] He had to undertake simultaneously the tasks of consolidating his own community at Medina, dealing with non-Muslim tribes, and
coercing Mecca to come under his domain. Muhammad at
first seems to have courted alliance with the Jews, but find-
ing no possibility of obtaining their support, he reacted
against Judaism. Gradually he began to " Arabianize " and
nationalize Islam by eliminating Jewish and Christian elements. Thus, " Friday was substituted for Sabbath; the call
from the minaret was decreed in place of trumpets and

bells; Ramadān was fixed as a month of fasting . . . the pilgrimage to the Kaaba was authorized and the kissing of the Blackstone — a pre-Islamic fetish — sanctioned." [31]

Muhammad's dealings with Mecca showed determination and astute statesmanship. Despite his own personal bitterness against the Meccan leaders, he recognized the supreme importance of the city and the necessity of incorporating it into his religio-political community. When peaceful means of persuasion failed, Muhammad began to use other means. For this cause, he went so far as to violate Arab tradition by attacking a caravan during the sacred month of Rajab. Exercising great military skill, he fought successfully with only three hundred men against a far greater Meccan force in the battle of Badr in A.D. 624 (A.H. 2); this event is celebrated as the " Day of Deliverance." While Muhammad's forces were defeated by the Meccans in the battle of Ohd, A.D. 625, and Muhammad was barely able to defend the city of Medina the next year, in A.D. 628 he managed to make a truce whereby Meccans agreed to let Muslims make the pilgrimage to Mecca in the following year. The pilgrimage in A.D. 629 (A.H. 7) converted many Meccans to Islam, and by the time Mecca finally surrendered to Muhammad in A.D. 630, Mecca came " not as a beaten and resentful enemy but as a willing, if not enthusiastic partner." [32] Muhammad himself went on the next pilgrimage to Mecca, believing that God's promises had been fulfilled in the brotherhood of Islam. " Entering its great sanctuary, Muhammad smashed the many idols, said to have numbered three hundred and sixty, exclaiming, ' Truth hath come, and falsehood hath vanished! ' " [33] Muhammad then declared that the territory around the Kaaba was sacred, forbidding non-Muslims to enter it.

With Mecca securely under his control, Muhammad now

faced the task of converting and conquering other parts of Arabia. He followed the simple formula that the pronunciation of belief in Allāh (God), and in Muhammad as God's prophet, was sufficient to indicate conversion. At that time, the northwest and southeast parts of Arabia were provinces of the Byzantine and Persian empires, respectively. Recognizing the impossibility of immediate conversion of the whole peninsula, Muhammad resorted to diplomacy. Thus, in the year A.H. 9 Muhammad concluded treaties of peace with the Christian chief of al-Aqabah and the Jewish tribes in the south. Muhammad assured protection to those Jews and Christians within the Islamic territory who paid a tax, which was later called *jizya* (land and head tax). It is understandable that while some Christians and Jews accepted this arrangement, others were not reconciled to being subject to Muslim rulers. " It is indeed quite possible," observes Gibb, " that Mohammed's later change of attitude toward Christianity reflects his growing hostility to the Greeks and their Christian Arab allies, Orthodox or Monophysite." [34]

In Medina, Muhammad the Prophet had to bear the burden of being the architect and leader of his religio-political community, which now faced the necessity of formulating laws concerning fasting, almsgiving, and other religious activities, as well as political ordinances. " His responsibilities had changed and so had his methods. His Lord was forgiving only to the believer; the ethics of his faith applied only within the community. To make Islam secure, assassination and compulsion, trickery and bribery, were legitimate means." [35] Muhammad's personal life was complicated by an increasing number of wives. There is every reason to believe that basically he was a man of simple tastes. Even when he was the supreme ruler of the state, he is said to have mended his own clothes. But the age-old custom that the conquest of a state was consummated by possession of the former monarch's wife or daughter was politically useful. And the expansion of Muhammad's domain " was reflected in the growing size of his harem of young girls and mature aristocratic women that now graced, now plagued, his private life." [36] Among all the women who shared in his life, two particularly played important roles. Khadījah, Muhammad's first wife, gave faithful support on the threshold of his prophetic career. Aishah, daughter of Abu Bakr, " with her lively temperament and pert charm, brought a refreshing air of romance into the closing years of his life." [37]

In 632 (A.H. 10), Muhammad went to Mecca for what turned out to be his " farewell pilgrimage." Three months after his return to Medina, he fell into a fever. He was taken to Aishah's apartment and died there. Inevitably, Muslims later developed idealized views of the figure of the Prophet, but " Muslim thought never quite lost touch with the human figure of Mohammed ibn Abdullah, the man of Mecca." [38]

THE UMMAH, THE CONGREGATION OF GOD

The Ummah

Even a superficial knowledge of Muhammad's career makes it clear that throughout his life he had two great religious aims: to proclaim Allāh as the only God, and to found the congregation of Allāh called the Ummah.

According to the *Shorter Encyclopaedia of Islam*, etymologically the term *ummah* (or *umma*) was not of Arabic origin, but was probably borrowed from Hebrew or Aramaic. The Qur'ānic use of this word varies widely, but essentially it refers to an ethnic, linguistic, or religious group of people who are the objects of the divine plan of salvation, which in some instances includes not only human beings but all living creatures. In some passages of the Qur'ān, Abraham is called Ummah, probably as the head of his community. In Sūra X, 19, it is taught that men were originally a single Ummah. The disunity of mankind is explained only in terms of God's inscrutable decree. Evidently, Muhammad at one time was convinced that each Ummah had the benefit of a messenger of God, and that he was the messenger to the Arab Ummah. Later, however, his understanding of Ummah changed so that all those who surrendered to Allāh and his prophet were to be included in the congregation of Allāh.[39]

When Muhammad arrived at Medina as the ruler of the city, he drew up a charter of guiding principles for the believers and Muslims of Medina and also for those who followed them. According to this charter, they were one Ummah (community) over against mankind: " A believer will not slay a believer for an infidel nor will he aid an infidel against a believer. The security [given by God's community] is collective. The protection granted by the least of believers involves [all] in the duty." [40] Some sections of this charter reflected the pre-Islamic Arab ethos. For example, believers were held responsible to avenge blood spilled on an errand of God. Of particular interest also were references to the Jews in Medina, for they were regarded as a " community alongside the believers (the Jews keeping their faith and the Muslims theirs) ." [41] However, after the Islamic community was more securely established, Jews and others who had not adopted Islam were excluded from the Ummah.

This charter is often described as the germ of the Islamic

state. At the time when the charter was written, Muhammad was clearly attempting to preserve old Arabic tribal traditions. Law and order were to be maintained within the family group, and the old chiefs were to retain their traditional authority. The novelty of the charter was that " ultimate authority for the doings of the community rested not with the chiefs or the collective voice of the people, but with Muhammad, and, beyond him, with Allāh." [42] Actually, during Muhammad's lifetime, the Muslim community was a haphazard group he had brought together by the unity of the faith and by his claim as a prophet. Till his death, Muhammad needed no code, for his own will was enough. He followed the traditional law of the Arabs when it suited him. When suitable laws were not available, Muhammad depended on revelation. " God's interest in detail, and particularly in detail concerning the Prophet's personal life, occasionally bewildered the faithful; but the principle that the whole existence of man should conform to divine ordinance was never put to doubt." [43] Muhammad could not depend on revelation to solve all the problems, however. He had to make decisions on such matters as the conflicting claims of heirs in an estate and questions pertaining to divorce, but jurisprudence was not one of his strong points.

The significance of the Islamic community lay not in the superiority of its legal system, but in the idea that religion implied a definite social and political system and organization. The traditional tribal kinship of the Arabs was replaced by a bond of faith. The uniqueness of the Ummah was that it had no priesthood and no special holy community apart from society. " Its mosque was its public forum and military drill ground, as well as its place of common worship. The leader in prayer, the *imām*, was also to be commander in chief of the army of the faithful." [44] In the Islamic community every moment of the faithful's life was subject to religious ruling. Von Grunebaum finds six reasons for the success of Muhammad: (1) His was the most consistent religious system developed by an Arab; (2) Islam had satisfactory answers to the problems of the Arabs of his time; (3) Islam raised the Arab world to the level of other civilized nations; (4) by placing himself at the end of a long line of prophets, Muhammad asserted the finality of his teaching; (5) Muhammad increased the Arabs' articulateness; and (6) " he taught the lesson that a community under God was more meaningful and thus of greater political promise than a community under tribal law." [45]

The death of Muhammad brought about a great crisis in the infant Islamic community. He had been a tribal Shaykh, a supreme judge, but without the authority that dynastic tradition and political custom can confer on a king. His revelations had not declared who should succeed him, and the " hereditary idea, foreign to the political habits of the Arab, was, moreover, excluded by the fact that Muhammad left no male child." [46] In this situation, the Muslim community had to find a basis of solidarity. The emphasis now rested on the message and the tradition left by the founder.

One important source of the solidarity of the Ummah was the memory of the Prophet, from which developed lavish legends. For instance, one legend states that Muhammad was confirmed a prophet " when Adam was between soul and body." According to another account, " when God created the great throne and expanded the heaven and the earth . . . he, by means of the pen, wrote on the foot of the throne, ' There is no God but Allāh: Mohammed is the apostle of Allāh and the seal of the prophet.' " [47] During his lifetime Muhammad the Prophet and lawgiver did not claim any superhuman power. After his death, however, miracle tales derived from Christian, Persian, and Indian sources were freely incorporated into the so-called biography of the Prophet. Understandably, the Muslim theologians were under a twofold pressure: " Popular imagination insisted on changing the apostle of God to a wonder-working prophet," and the Christians challenged them " to set forth the supernatural evidences of the Prophet's claim." [48]

The Qur'ān and the Sunna

The main record of the life and teaching of the Prophet is the Qur'ān, the sacred book of Islam. It is to be noted that the Qur'ān as we have it is not an accurate record of Muhammad's revelations. One passage of the Qur'ān implies that the Prophet could not read, and certainly he did not write a book. His disciples must have written down what was revealed to him on palm leaves and stones. It is said that the collection of all these scattered materials was undertaken first by Abu Bakr, the first caliph. We are told that before an authorized version was established under the caliph Uthmān (644–656) there were four rival editions in use. It is difficult to understand the basis of the compilation of the authorized version, which is still used today, as there is no apparent rationale in the organization of its 114 *sūras* (chapters) .

Once formulated and codified, the Qur'ān was accepted by the Ummah as the immutable word of God, mediated through the angel Gabriel. Passages from the Qur'ān are quoted with the prefix " God has said." According to the Qur'ān, Muhammad's early messages were very simple, lacking the ritual and legal elements which concerned him later. The Sūras (chapters) ascribed to the early part of Muhammad's prophetic career emphasize four major topics: " (a) the coming of Judgment; (b) the divine nature of his message; (c) argument from creation; (d) argument from past history." [49] While the basic topics of the early messages remain in evidence in later teachings, " in proportion, the substance of his Jewish and Christian materials assumes ever wider dimensions, growing in volume and variety with nearly each new Sūra." [50]

Not being trained in speculative thinking, Muhammad was not greatly concerned with logical consistency. It was his conviction that " Allāh would if expedient revoke one or the other verse of the revelation and replace it with a more appropriate one." [51] This theory of " abrogation," no doubt a useful doctrine during the Prophet's lifetime, resulted in contradictions within the Qur'ān, and raised difficult questions for Muslim theologians and jurists. These questions, in the course of time, led to the development of the theory of *mu'jiza* (the miracle of the Prophet) , which held that the inconsistencies in the Qur'ān were " the miraculous proof of Mohammed's mission." [52] According to Kraemer:

> The foundation of Islam is not, The Word became flesh. It is, The Word became book. It is quite logical and intelligible that Islam should have developed its own species of Logos speculation in the well-known dogma of the uncreated, pre-existent, and celestial Qur'ān.[53]

Next only to the Qur'ān, the " custom " (*sunna*) of the Prophet and his immediate circle played an important role in the Muslim community. In this connection, Gibb reminds us that every Arabian tribe in pre-Islamic times took pride in the *sunna*, the system of social and legal usages, of its ancestors. It was only natural, then, for the Muslim com-

munity to develop its own *sunna;* " but in the strict sense
the term was applied to those usages only which were not
laid down in the Koran [Qur'ān]." [54] Whether the term
sunna should include the usage of the whole Muslim community, or refers only to the usage of the Prophet, has
never been agreed upon by all Muslims. The Sunnīs
claimed to be the followers of the " Sunna," using this term
to refer to the usage of the community as well as the usage
of the Prophet; whereas " the Shī'a, the ' partisans ' of Alī,
gave allegiance to the Sunna of the Prophet, but held the
subsequent conduct of the Community to have been il-
legal." [55]

The Sunna of the Prophet is recorded in the Hadīth, or
the Tradition. The word *hadīth* is a noun from the verb
hadatha, meaning " to be new." " The Hadīth literature
as we now have it provides us with apostolic precept and
example covering the whole duty of man: it is the basis
of that developed system of law, theology, and custom
which is Islam." [56] Although initially the Hadīth was
looked upon by the faithful as the religious guide for the
individual and the community, " the growing importance
of tradition as an authoritative force in the establishment
of the legal and ritual life of the community created a demand for *hadīth* on every conceivable subject, a demand
which . . . produced an unfailing supply." [57] The foundation of the Hadīth is an *isnād* or chain of guarantors
going back to a Companion of the Prophet in the following
manner: " A told me, saying that B said C had informed
him, saying D mentioned that he heard E relate, ' I heard F
ask the Apostle of God so and so.' " [58] As early as the
eighth century, it was declared: " The Sunna is judge over
the Qur'ān, not the Qur'ān over the Sunna." Ahmad Ghu-
lam Halil (d. 888) went so far as to say that the Sunna " is

the foundation on which the community is built. . . . Whoso fails to follow them, errs and commits innovation. Whoso deviates from the Companions of Mohammed in any religious matter is an unbeliever." [59] Thus, by the ninth century, the Hadīth provided the norms of beliefs and practice of the Ummah.

The Sharī'a (Law)

The Ummah, however, was more than a religious community; it was also a religio-political community and a theocratic state. From its inception, the Muslim community took its political, legal, and cultural responsibilities as seriously as its religious responsibilities. It was only natural, then, that Muslims took a keen interest in the formulation of the Sharī'a, or law. Unlike the Western European tradition, which differentiates the law (derived from Roman jurisprudence) and religion (derived from Christianity), the Islamic tradition found no distinction between the " religious " and the " legal," the latter being interpreted as the practical aspect of the former. According to Fyzee, there is in Islam a doctrine of " certitude " that differentiates good and evil, or in the technical language of the Muslim doctors, a differentiation of *husn,* beauty, and *qubh,* ugliness. " What is morally beautiful, that must be done; and what is morally ugly must not be done. That is law or *shariat* [Sharī'a] and nothing else can be law." [60] The sources of the Sharī'a are the Book (Qur'ān), the Sunna (Tradition), and *fiqh,* or a body of rules developed by the legal experts. According to Fyzee: " If there is nothing either in the . . . [Qur'ān] or in the Hadīth to answer the particular question which is before us, we have to follow the dictates of secular reason *in accordance with certain definite principles,*" and " in law, independent judgment, *within certain limits,* is not only permissible but even praiseworthy." [61] Thus, *fiqh,* literally denoting " intelligence " or " understanding," requires a certain amount of independent judgment and *qiyās* (analogical deduction) of one form or another. " This science [*fiqh*] combines with that of *kalām,* or dogmatics and scholastic theology, to form the science of *shar'* or *sharī'a,* which means literally the ' path ' or ' road ' (of the theocracy of Islam, of which Allāh is the head and inspiration) , and hence ' the law ' of Islam." [62]

In addition to the Qur'ān, the Sunna, and " analogical deduction," the doctrine of *ijmā* or " consensus " also played an important role in the Sharī'a. There is a well-known saying of Muhammad to the effect that " my people will not agree in error "; this tradition provides the basis for the doctrine of " consensus." Not only did *ijmā* guarantee the authenticity of the text of the Qur'ān and Sunna, but it was " erected into a theory of infallibility, a third channel of revelation." [63] In fact, according to the Sunnī doctrine, the spiritual prerogatives of the Prophet were inherited by the community as a whole. While the doctrine of *ijtihād,* or the right of individual interpretation, was never ruled out in theory, " the great majority of Muslim doctors held that the ' gate of *ijtihād* ' was shut once and for all." [64] Originally, the doctrine of " consensus " implied a certain amount of flexibility and development, but quickly it became *de facto* agreement of learned doctors, known as Ulamā, who for all practical purposes rigidly upheld the principle of conformity, discouraging innovation as heresy. In brief, the Sharī'a, which was based on the Qur'ān, the Sunna, consensus, and analogy, reduced the acts of believers to five categories: " (1) Obligatory, (2) Recommended but not obligatory, (3) Indifferent,

(4) Disapproved but not forbidden, (5) Prohibited." [65]

The development of the Sharī'a may be discussed in terms of the different schools of the Sunnī and the Shī'a traditions, respectively. In the Sunnite tradition, there are four recognized orthodox schools. The first is the Iraq school, also known as the Hanafi school. This school " arose after the older Iraqi *sunna* and legal schools, adapted to the later growth of Prophetic Tradition, but retained a considerable element of personal reasoning." [66] The Hanafi school has remained to this day the most influential among the four Sunnite schools, especially in India, Lower Egypt, and parts of Western Asia. The second is known as the Medinian school, having developed in Medina; it is also known as the Malikite school. This school stressed the importance of the doctrine of " consensus." The Malikite school has many followers in various parts of Africa, especially in Upper Egypt. The third is the Shafi'ite school. In addition to the concept of " consensus," this school also stressed the doctrine of analogical reasoning. The Shafi'ite school is influential in parts of the Middle East, India, and Indonesia. The fourth is the Hanbalite school. While this school was relatively insignificant for many centuries, " in the eighteenth century it was revived (under the name of Wahhābi) in central Arabia, and is now the dominant school in most of central and northern Arabia." [67]

Every Sunnī Muslim must belong to one of the four Sunnite schools of law. The political rulers — caliphs and sultans — have no jurisdiction over the formulation of religious law. " The secular authorities were bound to recognize it and to provide for its due administration by the appointment of judges (*qādīs*) in all parts of their territories." [68] In the event that cases not already provided for in the Sharī'a come up, the *muftī* (jurisconsult) " is asked to give an opinion, and his pronouncement . . . then provides the judge with material on which to base his decision." [69] Traditionally, the Chief Muftī of Constantinople was regarded as the highest religious authority in the Ottoman Empire, enjoying the glorified title of the Shaikh al-Islām. Understandably, the collections of legal pronouncements by eminent jurisconsults are considered an important supplement to legal textbooks.

The Shī'ite rejection of the four Sunnite schools of law is based on the former's concept of *imām* (" one who goes before "). The term Shī'a is an abbreviation of *Shī'at 'Alī* or the party of Alī, the son-in-law of Muhammad. The Shī'ites hold that the Prophet appointed Alī as his successor; hence their rejection of the first three caliphs. Contrary to the Sunnite doctrine, which accepts the principle of election of the caliph as the temporal ruler, the Shī'ites accept their *imām* as a divinely ordained leader and the final interpreter of the law on earth. There are a variety of interpretations of the *imām* among the Shī'ites, however. For example, the western Ismā'īlis consider the *imām* hidden but not immortal, while the eastern Ismā'īlis identify their *imām*, for all practical purposes, with God.[70] Regardless of the different interpretations of the *imām* among the Shī'ites, they all subscribe to the notion that the *imām* is the lawgiver himself, and that the doctors recognized by the *imām* can still exercise individual interpretation (*ijtihād*). Apart from the doctrine of the *imām* and the significance of *ijtihād*, the difference between the Sunnite and the Shī'ite understanding of law is not significant.

The Five Pillars of Faith

All Muslims agree that law is the practical rule of religion. The privilege of belonging to the Ummah requires the faithful acceptance of religious duties, of which there are five, commonly known as the five pillars of faith. " Each of these duties is known as an ' essential duty imposed ' on the individual, as opposed to . . . a duty, such as that of the election of a sultan." [71]

The first duty or pillar is the profession of faith: " There is no god but Allāh: Muhammad is the messenger of Allāh." Once the formula is accepted and uttered, the person is considered a Muslim.

The second duty is prayer, to be offered five times a day facing toward Mecca. All adult males are required to participate in the congregational assembly, which takes place every Friday noon. On this occasion the leader (imām) delivers a sermon. All Qur'ānic regulations regarding prayer " were expanded and multiplied in the books of fiqh so as to provide answers to the widest possible range of queries that might be addressed to the legist, many of the points raised being casuistical in the extreme." [72]

The third duty is almsgiving. The Qur'ān simply states that of booty one-fifth part is to go " to God and his apostle, to near of kin and orphans, and to the poor and the wayfarer." [73] With the development of the Islamic empire, what was originally considered a voluntary act of love and charity became an obligatory tax.

The fourth duty is fasting. The Qur'ān gives minute regulations concerning Ramadān, or the month of fasting. " It is lawful to you on the night of the fasting to have intercourse with your wives . . . and eat and drink until by the [light of] dawn a white thread is distinguishable by you from a black thread. Then make your fasting strict until the night, and have no commerce with them, secluding yourselves in the mosques." [74] However, those who are on a journey or sick during the month of Ramadān can observe fasting at other times.

The fifth duty is pilgrimage. The Qur'ān states: " The first house [temple] that was founded for mankind was that at Bakka [Mecca]. . . . In it are clear signs; even the standing-place of Abraham: and he who enters it is safe. And a duty to God incumbent upon all mankind is pilgrimage to the house — all who can perform the journey thither." [75] Hitti estimates that the average number of pilgrims annually, between the two world wars, was about 172,000. It is not difficult to understand " the socializing influence of such a gathering of the brotherhood of believers from the four quarters of the earth." [76]

In addition to the five pillars of faith, the Islamic community teaches the duty of holy war, known as *jihād*, which has been regarded as a sixth pillar by some Muslims. The concept of *jihād* is based on the fact that, according to Islam, the world is divided into the *dār al-Islām* (regions under its control) and the *dār al-harb* (regions not yet subjugated) , and that there can be no peace between the two. " Practical considerations may induce the Muslim leaders to conclude an armistice, but the obligation to conquer and, if possible, convert never lapses." [77] The individuals who participate in the *jihād* are assured of religious merits in paradise.

Ideally, Muslims believe, mankind must become one community of God. Practically, however, the human community is divided, not only along social, political, and economic lines, but also along religious lines. In this situation, the fundamental duty of the Islamic community is to bring about the oneness of mankind under Allāh, preferably by peaceful measures.

Let us turn now to the historic development of the Islamic community — its successes and failures — through the ages.

THE UMMAH IN HISTORY

Early Expansion

Pascal, we are told, once said that Muhammad chose the way of human success and Jesus that of human defeat, and there is much truth in this characterization. The Ummah that Muhammad founded was not only a holy community but also a new society, empire, and civilization. As a result, religious, social, political, and cultural factors have been closely interwoven in the development of the Ummah. Before his death, Muhammad claimed most of the inhabitants of Arabia under his domain. Within ten years after his death, Syria, Iraq, and Egypt were added to the Muslim empire. In less than a century, Islam converted or conquered the Christian belt of North Africa and reached the Iberian peninsula. In the eighth century A.D., the Muslims crossed the Pyrenees into France, but their advance farther into other parts of Europe was checked by Charles Martel in 732.

The expanding Muslim community, however, faced a serious internal problem in connection with the caliphate. Immediately after Muhammad's death, his father-in-law, Abu Bakr, became the first caliph (Khalifa). Abu Bakr was succeeded by Umah, who had been an able lieutenant of the Prophet. Umah appointed a council to select his successor. The council chose Uthmān, a member of the Umayyad clan and a son-in-law of the Prophet, rejecting Alī, who also was a son-in-law of the Prophet. When Uthmān was assassinated, Alī became the fourth caliph, even though he was opposed strongly by Aishah, the widow of Muhammad, and others. Uthmān's nephew, Mu'āwiya, then governor of Syria, defied Alī's authority and proclaimed himself the caliph in Damascus. Thus, until Alī was assassinated in A.D. 661 there were two caliphs, Alī at Medina and Mu'āwiya at Damascus. Mu'āwiya attempted to perpetuate the caliphate in the Umayyad family, and appointed his son Yazīd as his successor. Yazīd was challenged by two contenders, Husain, son of Alī, and Ibn Zubayr. Although Husain was killed by Yazīd's forces in 680, the followers of Husain and his father, Alī, continued to regard Alī's descendants as legitimate *imāms* (heads of Islam); the followers of this group came to be known as Shī'a (the Partisans of Alī). The second contender, Ibn Zubayr, was acknowledged caliph for a short period of time in Egypt and its vicinity, but he also was killed by the Umayyads. The Umayyad family managed to stay in power until 750, when the caliphate was taken over by the Abbāsid dynasty.

The change of power from the Umayyads to the Abbāsids was more than a political change; it was a symbol of the new spirit instilled by non-Arab Muslims. During Muhammad's lifetime, his teaching of the equality of all believers never quite replaced the pre-Islamic Arab concept of tribal aristocracy. Ironically, soon after Muhammad's death, members of his own family became, for all practical purposes, the aristocrats (the *ashraf,* or "those of distinguished descent") in the Muslim community. With the rapid expansion of Islam, its vast empire had incorporated many non-Arab believers by the end of the eighth century. In this situation, the Arab Muslims regarded themselves as superior to the non-Arab believers, who came to be known as "clients" (*mawālī*). The Arab Muslims in effect envisaged a hierarchic society with themselves as a ruling class. It is reported that "while the Arab escaped with a small income tax known as *zakāt*, 'alms,' the non-Arab *mawlā* was made to pay the *kharaj*, a land tax that might amount to as much as a fifth of the product of his fields." [78] Ironically, however, the non-Arab Muslims had a higher culture than the Arab Muslims, and with the decline of the Umayyads arose the Abbāsid dynasty, which was "Arab in name, but . . . relied on the *mawālī* [non-Arab Muslims] for its support." [79] The Abbāsid caliphs ruled the Islamic world, except for North Africa and Spain, for the next five centuries, until the fall of Baghdad to the Mongol invaders.

Under the Abbāsid caliphs, a strong middle class came into being, and Muslim merchants engaged in foreign trade. Although the Arabic language continued to be used, the caliphate at Baghdad resembled a traditional Oriental autocracy, with harems and eunuchs. "Gradually Persian titles, Persian wines and wives, Persian mistresses, Persian songs, as well as Persian ideas and thoughts, won the day." [80]

In the West, Spain prospered under the "Umayyads at Cordova" (756–1031). While the early rulers of Cordova were known as "*amīr*" (ruler, or commander), Abd-al-Rahmān III assumed the title of caliph in the tenth century. Resisting the encroachment of Charlemagne and the Abbāsids, the Umayyad caliphs in Cordova made Spain one of the richest nations in Europe. The universities of Cordova and Granada, as well as other schools and libraries, attracted Muslim, Jewish, and Christian students from other parts of Europe and Africa.

Meanwhile, the Ismā'īli (one school of the Shī'a sect) expansion in North Africa resulted in the establishment of the Fātimad dynasty (969–1171) in Egypt. The Fātimad rulers established the city of Cairo (" al-Qahira," or the Victorious) and erected the Mosque of al-Azhar. The civilization that prospered under the Fātimads influenced Sicily, southern Italy, and North Africa. With the decline of the Fātimad dynasty, Saladin, the Muslim hero during the period of the Crusades, established the Ayyūbid dynasty and restored orthodox Islam in Egypt.

The world of Islam, under the Abbāsids in Baghdad, the Umayyads in Cordova, and the Fātimads in Egypt, made extraordinary progress in commerce, industry, and culture. The intellectual awakening of the Muslims was greatly aided by Jewish and Syrian Christian scholars who translated the works of Greek philosophers and Persian and Indian scientific books into Arabic. Significantly, Christian Europe first became acquainted with the works of Plato and Aristotle through the writings of Muslim scholars, such as Avicenna and Averroes.

The Greek Influence

Among the factors that contributed to the intellectual awakening of the Muslims, the primary inspiration came from Greek antiquity. The Greek influence on Muslim thought is particularly noticeable in the Hellenistic theology of the Mu'tazilite school, and also in Islamic mysticism, known as Sūfism, which incorporated many elements of Neo-Platonism.

The Mu'tazilites (rationalistic theologians) attempted to formulate the Islamic faith for the benefit of non-Arab intellectuals. In so doing, they took seriously the free will of man and tended to give more value to human reason than to the Word of God. With philosophical astuteness, the Mu'tazilite thinkers criticized the orthodox doctrine of God's attributes as inconsistent with God's unity, while they acknowledged that the divine power did not penetrate the realm of accidents.

Orthodox counterattacks against the Mu'tazilites came from the " scholastics " (Mutakallimūn), or the " people of the Tradition (Hadīth) ." They came to be known as " Mutakallimūn " because they used the *kalām* (literally, speech) in order to defend the orthodox faith against the *kalām* of the Mu'tazilites. Notable among the scholastics was al-Ashari (d. 942), a seceder from the Mu'tazilite school, who accepted literally the Qur'ānic doctrine that God has hands and eyes, and that God's power controls every event that appears to be accidental to human eyes. Rejecting the Aristotelian view of a fixed universe, the Asharite view affirmed that " the energy of God is in perpetual motion, vitalizing the very particles or atoms of all created objects, which therefore live and move and have their being by the constant flow of divine life." [81] Also, according to the Asharite view, man is morally responsible for his actions even though they are basically predetermined. In the eleventh century, the Asharite system became the normative school of Sunnite orthodoxy. One by-product of scholasticism was the activity of such thinkers as al-Kindi (d. 873), al-Fārābi (d. 950), Avicenna (Ibn Sīnā, d. 1037), and Averroes (Ibn Rushd, d. 1198). " Though many of them were far from orthodox, their works are among the glories of the Islamic civilization." [82]

The influence of Neo-Platonism on Islamic mysticism has been debated by many scholars. The Muslim historian Ibn Khaldūn traced the origin of Sūfī mysticism to the Companions of the Prophet. The name " Sūfī " was probably taken from the garment of wool (*sūf*) which the mystics wore. The Muslim mystics held that God is the only agent and the sole cause of all existence, and that only one's love for God enables one to attain union with the Divine. In this connection, Margaret Smith reminds us that a Neo-Platonic work, *The Theology of Aristotle,* was translated into Arabic in the ninth century. " This might have supplied the Sūfīs with their monistic conception of God and the universe, with their idea of the pre-existence of the soul in a state of perfect unity, with some of their psychology, and with their conception of God as the Light of Lights." [83]

Essentially a religious movement, Sūfism nevertheless was also a reaction against the sociopolitical abuses of the rulers and learned doctors (Ulamā). In the course of time, this nonecclesiastical, spiritual movement developed its own orders and liturgy, with a keen missionary spirit. One of the famous Sūfīs, al-Hallāj, taught that the uncreated Divine Spirit becomes united with the created spirit of the ascetic, so that in a true sense the saint *(wali)* is the personal witness of God. Thus, he asserted, " I am Creative Truth " (" *Anā 'l-Hakk* "). For this view, which was considered blasphemous, he was flogged, mutilated, and finally burned in A.D. 922.[84] Even such extreme measures failed to halt the expansion of Sūfī mysticism, because people found great comfort and satisfaction in the personal approach to God which characterized Sūfism.

The greatness of al-Ghazzālī (d. 1111) lay in the fact that he synthesized the three main trends of Islamic theology, the Asharite and Mu'tazilite systems and Sūfism. He gave up his professorship at Baghdad and plunged into mystical training for many years. " His is a reasoned, philosophic type of mysticism, able to appeal to the intellectual type among his readers, while its sincerity and the use which he makes of familiar illustrations made it equally comprehensible to the common folk." [85] His work and influence " led men back from scholastic labors upon theological dogmas to living contact with, study and exegesis of, the Word and tradition," and also through his effort " Sūfism attained a firm and assured position in the church of Islam." [86]

The Decline of the Abbāsids, the Crusades, and the Mongol Invasion

Al-Ghazzālī and others tried to save Islam from internal spiritual decay, but the gradual disintegration of the Islamic community could not be halted, and the classical period of Islam ended dramatically with the fall of Baghdad in 1258.

During the first four centuries after its emergence, the phenomenal expansion of Islam was based on a belief in the divinely ordered Ummah, in which Islamic religion and Muslim political dominion were united under the rule of the caliphate. " The Muslim conquests had been directed, at least in name, by one central power whose seat was moved, owing to shifts in the internal situation, from Medina to Iraq, then to Damascus and again back to Iraq." [87] However, in reality the unity of the Ummah under the caliphate was more an aspiration than an achievement. As early as the eighth century the central caliphate lost control of the Muslims in Spain, and in the ninth century it lost control of North Africa. In the tenth century, the central caliphate came under the domination of a pro-Shī'ite group. Beginning with the eleventh century, Christendom began to overpower Muslims in Sicily, Sardinia, and later in the Iberian peninsula. In the eastern part of the Muslim world, new ethnic groups assumed important roles. For example, Mahmūd of Ghazni, ruler of a small Turkish kingdom in Afghanistan, conquered northwestern India in the name of the Prophet during the eleventh century. Equally important was the rise of the Seljūq Turks, a nomadic group originally from the Turkestan steppes, who defeated the Byzantine forces in the eleventh century and captured Emperor Romanus Diogenes. The Seljūqs' mistreatment of Christian pilgrims to Jerusalem provided Christendom with a convenient excuse for undertaking the Crusades.

The term " Crusades " refers to a series of campaigns undertaken by the West European princes from 1096 to 1291, ostensibly to recover the Holy Land from Muslim rule, but mixed with other motives. Pope Urban's message had an emotional appeal to restore the Holy Sepulcher to Christ, " nor did Urban neglect the gains, temporal as well as spiritual, which accrued to the Crusader." [88] " The Crusades were served with a devotion that, had it been as wise and true as it was fervent and undaunted, would have blessed the Eastern world. But devotion was ill-served, misused, misguided, and betrayed." [89] From the military standpoint, the Crusades did not threaten the Muslims. In fact, many Western Christians settled in Syria and lived peacefully among the Muslims. Among the personalities involved in the Crusades, one of the most curious was Frederick II, who was personally an agnostic. When he finally joined the Crusades, he went " as the ally of a Moslem prince, in a fleet manned largely by Moslem sailors." [90]

In retrospect, it becomes evident that not only did the Crusades fail to accomplish their objectives, but they left many unpleasant memories on both sides. The Muslims were certainly not impressed by the Crusaders. And " the false reports brought back by those who returned from the wars filled the West with popular misinformation about Islam that Western mass education has not yet been able to remove." [91] Only in a few isolated cases — for example, men like Peter the Venerable (d. 1156) — did men attempt a serious study of Islam, and usually for the purpose of refuting the Muslims. Later, Thomas Aquinas (d. 1272) wrote *Summa contra Gentiles* with a similar objective in mind. Despite the sincere efforts of Francis of Assisi (d. 1226) and Ramon Lull (d. 1316) to convert Muslims, the Muslims were not impressed by medieval Christianity.

More disastrous than the Crusades, from the standpoint of Islam, was the Mongol invasion that captured Baghdad. In 1216 Jenghiz Khan and his forces appeared on the scene, and subjugated Muslims from the Oxus frontier to the Euphrates. (It was only the death of Jenghiz' son that saved Western Europe from the invasion of Mongol forces.) In 1258 Baghdad fell to Hūlāgū, grandson of Jenghiz. " For the first time in its history the Moslem world was left without a caliph whose name could be cited in the Friday prayers." [92] Hūlāgū founded the Mongol kingdom of Persia and become its first Il-khān (king). On the whole, Christian Europe rejoiced in the Mongol victory over the Baghdad caliphate. However, the seventh Il-khān accepted Islam as the state religion, which crushed some Europeans' hopes for a Christian-Mongol alliance. In the meantime, the Muslims in Spain were gradually overpowered by the Christians, and the colorful history of Muslim Spain came to an end in the latter part of the fifteenth century.

In the thirteenth century the Mamlūks, originally a Turkish or Armenian slave family, defeated the Mongol forces and established a dynasty in Egypt. The Mamlūks dominated North Africa from 1250 to 1517 as a great commercial power, but the discovery of the sea route to India by the Cape of Good Hope ruined the Mamlūk economy. " Though on the whole uncultured and bloodthirsty, [the Mamlūks'] keen appreciation of art and architecture would have been a credit to any civilized dynasty." [93]

Near the end of the fourteenth century a Transoxian, Tīmūr Lang, known also as Tamerlane, led his Tartar hordes across the Volga territory, Persia, and Mesopotamia, and captured Baghdad. Tīmūr Lang destroyed Damascus and defeated the Ottoman army in Ankara. Only his death in 1404 spared the Mamlūk empire in Egypt from invasion. However, the Mamlūks were conquered by the Ottomans in 1517.

The Ottoman Caliphate

The Ottomans, a tribe of the Ghuzz Turks, had been driven from their homes in Central Asia by the advancing Mongols, and for centuries they provided soldiers to Muslim rulers. In 1284 Osman I was recognized as the Ottoman sultan, and in 1453 Sultan Muhammad II, known as the "Conqueror," defeated the last Byzantine emperor. Muhammad II was the architect of the Ottoman administrative system. He also established the Palace School, a great military institution that offered "one of the most formal, systematic, and arduous courses ever devised in preparation for a public career." [94] In 1516, the Ottomans defeated the Mamlūk forces, and the following year the puppet caliph, al-Mutawakkil, was brought from Cairo to Constantinople. The prince (Sharīf) of Mecca sent the keys to holy places — the traditional emblem of the caliph — to the Ottoman sultan, although the Ottomans did not claim the caliphate until 1774. At any rate, the death of al-Mutawakkil in 1543 closed the last page of the nominal Arab caliphate. In the sixteenth century, the Ottoman Empire became a great sea power. Internally, power was maintained by the military class and the Muslim doctors. In the seventeenth century, the Ottomans attempted a siege of Vienna; this aroused an anti-Turkish movement in Europe, and an alliance of Austria, Venice, the papacy, Poland, Russia, Malta, and Tuscany was formed in order to check the Turkish power.

In the eighteenth century the Ottoman rulers began to adopt Western techniques in an attempt to reform their army. During the war with France, Napoleon attacked Egypt, and the Ottomans appointed Muhammad Alī, a young officer, as the *pasha* (high-ranking officer) in Egypt. Muhammad Alī destroyed the remnants of the Mamlūks in 1811 and became the new master of Egypt. His prestige rose after his successful campaign against the Wahhābi uprisings.

During the nineteenth century, European powers closed in on the Islamic world, and began to divide among themselves the former Islamic territories. Greece declared its independence from Ottoman rule, and Muhammad Alī Pasha of Egypt almost took over the Ottoman Empire. Faced with internal and external crises, Sultan Mahmūd II (1808–1839) initiated a wholesale reform program, abolishing the feudal system and reforming the tax law. While Russia lost the right to protect the Christians in Turkey after the Crimean War (1856), Russia's Pan-Slavism continued to agitate the Slavic elements within the Ottoman Empire. In this situation there emerged a secret society called the Young Ottomans, which was later transformed into the Young Turks.

The Ottoman Empire was a multilingual and multisect dynastic state. Throughout the history of the Ottoman Empire, there were two related but different movements, Turkification and Muslimization. Both of these movements were greatly stimulated by the impact of Western civilization during the period between 1850 and 1918.[95] The Young Turks advocated Pan-Ottomanism at first, but later changed their slogan to Pan-Islamism. During World War I, the Young Turks advocated *jihād* (holy war) in order to influence the Muslims who were under Western rule, but their attempts failed.

After the defeat of Turkey in 1918, Kemal Atatürk led the nation toward Turkish nationalism with the motto " Turkey for the Turks." In 1922, the caliphate was separated from the sultanate, and the latter was abolished. In 1924, the National Assembly expelled the Ottoman dynasty and abolished the caliphate. Thus ended the visible symbol of the " unity of the Ummah." Though the unity of the Ummah never has been realized in the history of Islam, it has always been envisaged by all Muslims.

THE UMMAH IN THE MODERN WORLD

Islam and the West

At the risk of oversimplification, we may divide the history of Islam into four periods. The first period was characterized by the phenomenal expansion of the Islamic community. It was also a period of absorption of non-Arab peoples into the Muslim fold, and of Persian and Greek influences into Islamic thought. During the second period, corresponding roughly to the age of the Crusades, the Islamic community suffered from a loss of prestige and territory. While the Crusades as such did not threaten the core of the Islamic community, they were nevertheless a symbol of the new spirit of European Christendom which regained Spain, Sicily, and other parts of Europe from Muslim rule. The prestige of the caliphate was shattered by the invasion of the Mongols, who destroyed Baghdad in the thirteenth century.

The third period, from the fifteenth to the eighteenth

centuries, witnessed the rise of non-Arab Muslim empires, such as the Turkish Ottoman Empire, the Shī'ite Persian Empire, and the Mogul or Mughal Empire of India. All of these were multi-racial empires ruled by military dynasties. The historic myth of the " unity of Ummah " under the rule of an Arab caliphate was no longer a reality. Although the Ottoman sultans inherited the caliphate, they could hardly extend their influence to Muslims outside the Ottoman Empire. Throughout this period, the Ottomans fought against Persia, and Persia fought against Mughal India. The fact that each of the great empires was ruled by a Muslim monarch did not foster the unity of the Islamic community as such.

The fourth period of Islamic history, from the eighteenth century to the 1920's, marked the disintegration of these Muslim empires and the Western domination of the Islamic world. For example, the decline of the Ottoman Empire resulted in the gradual encroachment of Russia and other Western powers into its domain. Not only did Greece and the Balkan nations declare independence, but many of the former Ottoman territories were ceded to Western nations. Most of North Africa was taken over by France; the British came to rule Egypt and Arabia; and East Africa was parceled out among France, England, Germany, Italy, Spain, and Portugal. The Persian Empire suffered from internal political instability and constant interference by Russia, Germany, France, and England. The Mughal Empire crumbled, and British supremacy over India was established. Also, Indonesia, where Islam was growing rapidly, came under Dutch rule.

During this period, the impact of the West was strongly felt in all parts of the Islamic world. Initially, Muslims adopted Western civilization for military purposes, in order to defend themselves from possible extinction by Western nations. As Toynbee points out, the typical revolutionary Westernizer in the Ottoman Empire in the eighteenth and nineteenth centuries was a young military officer.[96] Inevitably, Western thought and culture were also introduced, but in the main the contact between the West and the Islamic world was confined to technological matters, and the Muslim attitude was "marked by a desire to defend the theological precepts of Islam against modern sciences." [97]

Gradually Western science, Western philosophy, and Western political ideologies influenced young Muslims. In all parts of the Islamic world, "a new elite of political thinkers, trained in Western schools and animated by a passionate faith in the ideals held up before them by Western education" developed.[98] Muslim intellectuals were keenly aware that the world of Islam was parceled out among European colonial powers, but they accepted their "temporary" subservience because they anticipated genuine co-operation and coexistence between the West and the Islamic nations in the not too distant future. Side by side with the political progressives arose a small group of religious modernists. Outstanding among them were Muhammad Abduh (d. 1905) of Egypt and Muhammad Iqbāl (d. 1938) of India. Abduh "attempted to rejuvenate Islam by a clarification of its fundamental principles and an elucidation of its doctrines in modern terms. He refuted the attacks of Western scholars against Islam by showing that there is no contradiction between Islam and reason; rather, that for Islam reason is the key to faith in God." [99] Iqbāl, a poet-philosopher, was greatly influenced by Bergson and Nietzsche. Refuting the "philosophy of self-annihilation which had led the Muslims to despise the conquest of material forces," he taught that "Islam is a doctrine of self-assertion which teaches man to work for the attainment of worldly power and to attempt the conquest of the self and the nonself." [100] Some of the religious modernists felt congenial not only with Western philosophy but also with Christianity. Syed Ahmed Khan, founder of Aligarh Muslim University in India, went so far as to say: "We . . . [Muslims] hold that Jesus Christ is honorable in this world, and in the world to come. . . . The apostles of Christ were inspired men. . . . The *Injeel* [the Gospels] are all true and sacred records, proceeding primarily from God." [101]

After World War I, however, Muslim thought, both political and religious, changed. At the outbreak of war, some of the Muslim leaders wondered whether to support the Turks who were fellow Muslims or to rise in revolt with the Western nations against the Turkish Ottoman power and insist on their independence as a reward from Western colonial rule. Their aspirations were bitterly crushed by the postwar peace settlement, and an anti-Western sentiment began to replace the earlier idea of co-operation with the West. "Western political and economic controls in the Near and Middle East, and the disregard of Western political leaders for human and social interests, forced the nationalist leaders to develop all their energies to the struggle against Western domination." [102] The anti-Western sentiment quickly allied with social and religious reform movements. The Muslim leaders felt that to live under foreign rule was not only politically humiliating but religiously wrong; and religious, social, and political reformers hoped to see Islamic society " once again flourish as a divinely guided society should and must." [103] Numerous reform movements developed in various sections of the Islamic world, such as the Indian movements led by Sharī'at

Allāh and Sayyid Ahmad, the North African movement led by Muhammad Ibn Alī al-Sanūsi, the Mahdist brotherhood in the eastern Sudan, and similar movements in Nigeria and Sumatra. Many spokesmen of Islam agreed with Syed Ameer Alī, who advocated that " in every department of life, the teaching and example of Muhammad is superior to that of Jesus Christ." [104] These reformers and reform movements at first did not receive popular support. Al-Banna, the founder of the Association of the Muslim Brethren in Egypt, wrote:

> No one but God knows how many nights we spent going over the state of the nation and its present relation to various aspects of life, the effect of its sickness and the various remedies. . . . How shocked we were when we compared ourselves in our violent emotional discussions to the complacent and indifferent people who were loafing about the cafés.[105]

Undaunted by frustrations and discouragement, the reformers continued to gain followers by utilizing the popular resentment caused by poverty and foreign rule. In one of the magazines issued by the Muslim Brethren we read: "People shall find that Islam is not only a religion of worship, fasting, and prayer. . . . They shall find that it requires the Moslems to fight if their land is trespassed or occupied by the enemy." [106] In the course of time, anti-Western sociopolitical and religious reform movements took on a strong nationalistic character.

Islamic Nationalism

Islam, which affirms in principle that all believers constitute the Ummah, has never officially and theologically acknowledged nationalism or the autonomous nation-state, even though in reality, throughout the history of Islam, the sultans' governments exercised political control of their territories. The Muslim doctors (Ulamā) traditionally took the position that the only legitimate political authority rested in the caliphate and that the territorial governments were " no more than organizations of force for defense against external enemies and the maintenance of internal order." [107] In the history of Islam there were times when more than one caliph existed, and the Shī'a sect has never acknowledged the orthodox caliph's authority. Nevertheless, in theory, all Muslims upheld the caliph as the supreme head of the whole Islamic community.

During the period of the non-Arab Muslim empires, from the fifteenth to the eighteenth centuries, the institution of the caliphate was used not for the purpose of uniting all Muslims, but simply to rule the various religious and ethnic groups within the Ottoman Empire. The Ottoman sultan-caliph would have claimed that as sultan he controlled only the Ottoman Empire, but as caliph his authority extended beyond the Ottoman domain; however, no one outside the Ottoman Empire would have taken such a claim seriously. Also, the Mughal monarch who ruled India was in a precarious position from the Islamic religious standpoint, because the overwhelming majority of his subjects were non-Muslims.

A new concept of a Muslim empire developed in Mughal India, where under King Akbar (d. 1605) the traditional poll tax on non-Muslims was abolished and a policy of tolerance of all religions was proclaimed. In this situation the historic belief in the Ummah as the community of all believers broke down. The term " Ummah " came to refer to the Muslim elements within the empire. While the empire was Islamic in the sense that it was ruled by a Muslim ruler with Islamic principles, not all its citizens were adherents of Islam.

It is interesting to note that the Young Turks, who had advocated Pan-Ottomanism, aimed at integrating all religious and ethnic groups within the empire, and changed their slogan to " Pan-Islamism " when the end of the Ottoman Empire was in sight. But, apart from the theological principle of the unity of the Ummah, there never was any practical basis for uniting all Muslims until the twentieth century when at least three factors aided the Pan-Islamic movement. First was the encroachment of Western powers into the traditional Islamic world; second was the disintegration of the Muslim empires; third was the disappearance of the caliphate, a nominal but nevertheless a visible symbol of the unity of the Islamic community. It was an anti-Western revivalist and an advocate of the theocratic ideal, Jamāl ad-Dīn al-Afghānī (d. 1897), who " brought inspiration and a popular program to the Pan-Islamic movement by restating the bases of the Islamic community in terms of nationalism." [108]

Islamic nationalism is not a simple phenomenon; it has undergone many stages. For example, in the Arab world the initial impulse of the nationalist leaders was not to establish an independent Arab nation but only to establish an Arab province within the Ottoman Empire. In this connection, " it must be remembered that during the greatest part of the Turkish rule the Arabs did not consider the Turkish rule as a ' foreign ' rule. . . . The world in which the Arabs and the Turks lived together was, in the nineteenth-century sense of the term, *politically* a nonnational world." [109] Only in the last years of the Ottoman rule did the Arabs begin to resent its misgovernment. It is equally true, however, that the Arab Muslims had never lost a communal solidarity based on regional proximity, conservative religious beliefs and practices, and a common language.[110] The Arab sense of solidarity was greatly strengthened when the Ottoman policy catered to Turanian (Ural-Altai peoples) elements at the expense of the Arabs. During World War I the Turkish commander of the army in Syria ordered the hanging of prominent Arab leaders in Beirut and Damascus, which further alienated the Arabs from the Ottoman rule. Meanwhile, Sharīf Husain of Mecca advocated the establishment of an Arab Muslim state with an Arab Muslim king and on Islamic religious foundations. The promise of the Western powers to emancipate the Arabs from the Ottoman rule prompted the Arab revolt which started in Mecca in 1916. Thus, the Arab religio-communal movement developed into a political nationalism during World War I.[111]

After the war the spokesman of the Arab Muslims presented a memorandum to the Peace Conference, asking " that the Arabic-speaking peoples of Asia, from the line Alexandretta-Diarbekr southward to the Indian Ocean, be recognized as independent sovereign peoples under the guarantee of the League of Nations." [112] But the peace settlement, which inaugurated a mandate system instead of giving outright political independence, disappointed and angered the Arab Muslims. " Arab opposition was now directed against the Western ' liberators ' of the Near East and not toward the Turks, whose empire had ceased to exist." [113] The disappearance of the Turkish-Ottoman Empire was followed by the disappearance of the caliphate. While Muhammad Iqbāl and other modernists advocated a new type of caliphate as a spiritual office, such a romantic notion was not entertained seriously by most Muslims. Instead, most Muslims began to accept the formation of Muslim nation-states as the only practical alternative under the circumstances. In this situation, some Muslims envisaged the establishment of several large, regional Islamic states, while others emphasized the importance of smaller political nation-states. Both groups, however, were seriously disturbed by their inability to reconcile theologically the basic tenets of Islam with nationalism.

Since World War II, many Muslim states have come into being. They all chant in unison that nationalism is a means of ejecting Western colonial control, and thus the only practical steppingstone toward the eventual formation of one great community of Islam. However, today, the Household of Islam is incurably divided by the political and economic interests of independent and semi-independent Muslim states. Even the Arab world, the smallest and most homogeneous unit of the Islamic community, is threatened by internal disunity. A few years ago Michael Adams observed that the Arabs had their own cold war. On one side of the Arab iron curtain stood Egypt, which claimed to be the champion of the " free Arabs " against the West-dominated Arabs; on the other side stood Iraq, which also claimed to be champion of the " free Arabs," in this case in opposition to " fellow-traveling Arabs." [114] The situation has changed recently. Iraq is now regarded as the stronghold of the Arab communists, while Egypt has begun to part with Moscow. It is likely that the balance of power in the Arab world will continue to shift back and forth, but internal disunity will remain for many years to come. If we look at the entire world of Islam — Turkey, Pakistan, Indonesia, the North African states, and the Arab nations, to say nothing of the Muslim communities in India and those behind the Iron Curtain — it is clear that the unity of all Muslims in one great community is virtually impossible.

The Ummah and Modernity

Even a casual visitor passing through Muslim nations is impressed by the multiplicity of problems that confront the world of Islam today. Surrounded by Europe, the Soviet Union, South Africa, and new, independent nations in Asia, the Islamic world has a difficult course to steer in today's world if it is to survive at all. While Islam has a religious kinship with Judaism and Christianity, politically the Muslims, especially in the Arab world, regard Israel as their archenemy and Western nations as their former colonial exploiters. Ironically, in spite of their emotional reaction against the West, the Muslim nations have been influenced by Western culture and civilization more than they are willing to admit. Caught between the two powerful blocs of the communist world and the free world, the Muslim nations have been compelled in recent years to cast their lot with the Afro-Asian nations that constitute the so-called Bandung Front, which itself is suffering from internal disunity.

Internally, the Islamic community is threatened by a growing secularism and scientific materialism, in addition to extreme forms of nationalism. Underlying all these problems is the fundamental issue of " modernity," which was a by-product of the Western culture and civilization that have penetrated the Islamic world for the past two centuries. Initially Muslim leaders wanted to introduce only the technological aspects of Western civilization, but they " were deluding themselves when they imagined that they would be able to fit their country out with adequate Western armaments and then to arrest the process of Westernization at that point." [115] Inevitably, in the process of adopting Western techniques, education, and business methods, the Islamic world " inhaled " consciously or unconsciously the ethos of " modernity," which was the driving force behind the advance of the modern West.

Ironically, the world of Islam used modernity, the gift of the West, as an effective weapon and means for its emancipation from Western domination. It was not the historic community of Islam, under the leadership of the caliphate, that successfully arrested the advance of the West. Rather, it was the new Muslim nation-states, which developed out of the blending of Islam and modernity, that emancipated Muslims from further domination by Western nations. Indeed, today we are witnessing the last phase of the process of emancipation of the Muslim peoples. The basic frustration of Muslims, however, lies in the fact that while they are politically freed from the West, they are deeply caught in " modernity."

For example, in the Arab world, Muslims seem to be caught between their memory of the past and their vision of the future. " Unable to glorify their present, the Arab nationalists projected themselves in the past and made it a reality," for there was a time " when their language was the language of arts, sciences, and the civilized peoples; their religion was the religion of the socially favored." [116] Those who share this sentiment reject Western civilization and its by-product, " modernity." The extreme wing of this group confuses civilization with imperialism and social evils. Thus they hope to turn the clock backward to return to a truly Qur'ānic nation, reuniting all the Islamic sects and reintegrating all the Arab states. On the other hand, there are some Arabs who wish to be emancipated from the past. Just as they were liberated from Ottoman rule and from Western domination, they want to be emancipated from the feudalistic spirit and institutions which are inherent in Arab society, and envisage the establishment of a "secular," socialized Utopia. They are not against Islam, but they do reject any religiously conceived nation-state. The advocates of secular nationalism are small in number, but they are articulate. The advocates of romantic Qur'ānic theocracy are greater in number, but they suffer from the fact that they do not understand the problems of the modern world. The problems that confront the Arab world are many: Israel, communism, economic and social backwardness, but above all the underlying fact that "those who in the fullest sense know the religion have lost contact with the modern world, and those genuinely oriented to modernity have largely lost contact with their religion." [117]

In comparison with the Arab world, Turkey seems to be cognizant of the issues involved in the problems arising from modernity. It is an irony of history that Turkey, the heir of the Ottoman Empire, has oriented its policy along pro-Western lines. Internally, however, there is every indication that Islam continues to exert influence. Although the Turkish Republic abolished the caliphate, closed the Sūfī mystical orders and *tekkēs* (Sūfī community centers), and substituted Western jurisprudence for the Islamic law (Sharī'a), in recent years the Government has encouraged the training of new types of Islamic leaders — the *muftī* (canonical jurist), the *imām* (leader in mosque prayers), and the *hatip* (preacher). The Government office of the Director of Religious Affairs is resposible for general supervision of Islamic affairs.[118] It is reported that between 1950 and 1957 the Government built mosques in 15,000 villages with public funds.[119] Yet Turkey is not accepted by the Arab world, and Turkey feels the necessity of setting aside almost forty per cent of its budget for defense against the communist threat and also, ironically, against its Arab Muslim neighbors. It is interesting to speculate which way Turkey will move from now on, politically and religiously. In the meantime, those who visit Turkey may be impressed by the numbers of people who flock to the mosques and by the intellectual awareness of the young Turks. " They are no longer satisfied with the mere observance of the outward form of their religion, but are looking for spiritual and moral guidance in Islam compatible with modern civilization." [120]

The Muslims in Asia have been caught in the whirlwind of a multidimensional sociocultural and political revolution. The Asian revolution is a revolt against Western colonialism; it is also a movement to rectify internal economic inequalities. Furthermore, it is a " revolt of the East against the West, a determination that . . . the new nations of the East will be ends in themselves, not means to Western ends." [121] The driving force behind the Asian revolution is nationalism, accompanied by resurgence of religions, both of which have been greatly influenced by " modernity." The three important Muslim areas in Asia are India, Pakistan, and Indonesia. In India, there are forty million Muslims. Before the Partition, many Indian Muslims supported the Muslim League's agitation for the establishment of Pakistan, but there were also a considerable number of Muslims who opposed the League. Muslims who have stayed in India suffer emotionally because of the division of the Indian subcontinent into two states which view each other with hatred and fear. Muslims in India have a difficult problem of adjusting to a non-Muslim republic, in which their civil rights are guaranteed but they are a religious minority. Some of them are trying to find a new meaning in their situation by translating Islamic literature into Hindi, and discontinuing the use of beef. Others are inclined toward mysticism or rigid orthodoxy. The insecurity of Indian Muslims is accentuated by their inability to relate their faith to the very existence of a secular state of which they are a part.

The problems that Pakistan faces are also complex: economic instability, residual feudalism, the division into East and West Pakistan, and a lack of unity among peoples of different linguistic and cultural backgrounds. " It is one of the greatest frauds on the people to suggest that religious affinity can unite areas which are geographically, economically, linguistically, and culturally different." [122] Nevertheless, the purpose of the existence of Pakistan is clearly indicated in the Objectives Resolution (1949), which says in part: " Wherein the Muslims shall be enabled to order their lives in the individual and collective spheres in accord with the teachings and requirements of Islam as set out in the Holy Qur'ān and the Sunna." [123] A recent visitor to Pakistan reports that this new Islamic state, which manifested an outburst of interest in the meaning of Islam during the first six years after independence, seems to be losing this very enthusiasm. Among many reasons for this phenomenon, he cites the disillusionment of the Pakistanis resulting from the inability of the religious leadership to state precisely what it was that they envisaged in the Islamic state. " In a sense Pakistan can be characterized as the failure of an ideal," and yet, " it may be that the very fact that such an ideal existed is a matter of some significance." [124]

Islam penetrated Indonesia in the thirteenth century, but Islamization was a very slow process. For example, southeast Java was not converted until the middle of the eighteenth century. In the twentieth century, nationalist leaders agitated for political independence from Dutch rule. During World War II, the Japanese who occupied Indonesia established a native committee to prepare for Indonesia's independence. This group proclaimed the independence of the Republic two days after the collapse of Japan in August, 1945. " Most Dutch officials in Java at the end of 1945 seemed sincerely to believe that the overwhelming majority of Indonesians would be glad to return to Dutch rule once the Republic had been disposed of. It was a historic miscalculation." [125] On December 27, 1949, complete sovereignty was transferred from the Netherlands to the Republic of the United States of Indonesia. Although ninety per cent of the population are Muslims (74 million), Indonesia considers itself a " national " and not an " Islamic " state. The state is based on five principles: the belief in the divine One, humanity, nationalism, democracy, and social justice. However, since 1952 a movement called Mūbaligh Islam (Missionary Islam) has been urging the adoption of an Islamic constitution for the Republic. Following the example of Egyptian reformers Muhammad Abduh and Rashid Ridā, some Indonesian modernists have established Muslim societies for evangelistic, educational, and social welfare purposes. More conservative Muslims follow the Nahdlatul Ulamā (the Rising of the Ulamā), which in recent years has organized a political party based on strict Islamic principles. The Masjūmi party (the Indonesian Muslim League) is dedicated to the preservation of the state and the Islamic religion; it attempts to blend the modernist outlook of political leaders and the conservative views of the Muslim masses.

Situations vary in other Islamic nations, say in Africa and Iran, but the fundamental problems that confront them are similar. The modern nation-states that have emerged in the world of Islam support the resurgence of Islam, but modernity, which is a parent of modern nationalism, is a mixed blessing to the Household of Islam. " Even in Muslim countries . . . the appetite of the modern national states is not easily satisfied short of the total allegiance of its population." [126] Consciously or unconsciously, Muslim nations are preoccupied with political values at the expense of other values.

Ideally, the Household of Islam is both a holy community and a body politic. Theologically, the " unity of God " should find its correspondence in the sociopolitical ideal of the " unity of mankind." Thus, Islam envisaged the establishment of a comprehensive sociopolitical order in the name of religion which would control all aspects of man's thinking, belief, and behavior. This does not mean that Muslims have been unaware of the tension between theory and practice. Historically, both the idea and the fact of autonomous governments and states have existed in the world of Islam. What is new today is the character of modernity which tends to accept a secularist interpretation of the state and the law, rejecting the supremacy of the sacred law of Islam.

While political leaders of the new Muslim states justify the existence of the nation-states as a necessary step toward the eventual establishment of the Islamic ideal of the universal Ummah, the very nature of modernity challenge. the theocratic basis of an Islamic community that accepts the sovereignty of the sacred law in all spheres of human life. While Muslims rejoice over their political independence, modernity dichotomizes their life, differentiating the sacred from the secular, and political values from sociopolitical and religious values. The crucial issue for the

Islamic community is whether or not Islam can maintain its ideal and vision — against seemingly insurmountable obstacles and difficulties — to weld together all aspects of human life within one religious, social, and political order under Allāh.

◈ ◈

EARLY SHINTO

The Land of Kami

Japan is a small island archipelago off the Asiatic continent, stretching north and south in the western Pacific.
Its total area is less than that of California, and it is not
rich in natural resources. But, Japan has been blessed by
temperate climate and natural beauty, decorated by vol-
canic peaks, rivers, small plains, lakes, and coastal lines.
Undoubtedly, the beauties of nature played no small part
in nurturing the belief in the minds of the inhabitants
that Japan is a divine nation, a land permeated by numerous *kami* (gods, spirits, sacred and superhuman nature
or beings).

The indigenous religion of Japan is called Shinto, which
is usually translated as the " way of the *kami* or gods." The
beginnings of Shinto are clouded in the mist of the prehistory of Japan, and elude such simple and oft-repeated
characterizations as polytheism, emperor cult, fertility
cult, or nature worship, although these features are embodied in it. Having no historic founder, no official scriptures, and no fixed systems of ethics or doctrines, it has
nevertheless preserved its abiding, if nebulous, ethos

throughout the ages of Japanese history.

Historically, due largely to its geographical proximity to the Asiatic continent, Japan was destined to be influenced by various aspects of Chinese civilization and Buddhism. It would be a mistake, however, to consider Japan simply as a museum in which each of the diverse religious traditions as such has been preserved side by side. Rather, the history of Japanese religions might be seen more as a sort of brocade in which indigenous and foreign religious and cultural traditions have been intertwined following the design which was based on peculiarly Japanese patterns of beliefs, sentiments, and approaches. Thus, we must attempt, not so much to delineate the beliefs and practices of each one of the different religious traditions, as to understand the character of the underlying religious experiences of the Japanese people, which to be such have undergone a series of changes from the prehistoric period to the present.

Unfortunately, not much is known for certain about the prehistory of Japan,[1] so that we can only speculate where the original inhabitants of Japanese islands came from. Most scholars, however, accept the appearance of pottery marks around the fourth millennium B.C. as the beginning of the earliest phase of Japan's prehistory, which lasted until about the third century A.D. During the long prehistoric period a number of ethnic groups infiltrated into the Japanese islands from the north, east, and south of the Asiatic continent, bringing with them various cultural, religious, and linguistic traditions. In the course of time, these different traditions coalesced, so that by the end of the prehistoric period the inhabitants of the Japanese islands attained a degree of self-consciousness as one people sharing an emerging culture. They also developed a

common religious outlook, based on the notion of *kami,*
and accepted a common mode of social cohesion, based on
the *uji* (clan) system.

Kami *and* Uji

The term " *kami,*" as intimated above, has a wide range
of meanings such as gods, spirits, sacred and superhuman
nature or beings.[2] It has been traditionally accepted as an
honorific term for the object of Shinto worship, especially
sacred and noble beings and spirits. It must be noted that
while all beings are endowed with *kami* nature, and as
such could become objects of worship, there is no absolute
deity in Shinto in the Judeo-Christian or Islamic sense.
The term " *kami* " is also used to designate the mysterious
life force which brings about growth, fertility, and production as well as natural phenomena, natural objects, and
animals.

More important, perhaps, is the fact that the notion of
kami provides the foundation for the Japanese attitude
toward life and the universe. To put it another way, the
cosmological orientation of the early Japanese took it for
granted that they were an integral part of the cosmos,
which to them was a gigantic organism permeated by the
kami (sacred) nature. Thus, the mode of human existence
must be consonant with the rhythm of nature which
manifests itself as the creative and rejuvenating activities
of *kami.* In such an orientation, " no tree could be marked
for felling, no bush tapped for lacquer juice, no oven built
for smelting or for pottery, and no forge fire lit without
appeal to the *Kami* residing in each." [3]

If the notion of *kami* provides an important clue to the
ancient Japanese cosmic orientation, the term " *uji* "
(clan) may be taken as the key to our understanding of

the principle of ancient Japanese social solidarity. Understandably, the various ethnic groups that had migrated to the Japanese islands during the prehistoric period brought with them different kinds of family, kinship, and social systems. Meanwhile, sometime toward the latter part of the prehistoric period, a tribe, most probably of Altaic origin, which had a patriarchal clan (*uji*) system, migrated to the Japanese islands and eventually dominated the earlier settlers. In the course of time, the clan (*uji*) system of the dominant group became accepted by other groups as the general mode of social cohesion, so that it is safe to say that Japanese society during the early historic period consisted of many independent clans. Each clan (*uji*) had clansmen (*uji-bito*), and professional groups of persons (*be*), who were not necessarily blood relations of the clansmen, and slaves (*nuhi*), all of whom were ruled by the clan chieftain (*uji-no-kami*).

Each clan was not only a social, economic, and political unit but also a unit of religious solidarity centering around the *kami* of the clan (*uji-gami*), who was usually attended to by the clan chieftain. Indeed, in early Japan sharing the same *kami* was taken more seriously than blood relationship as the basis of group solidarity. In the event that a certain clan should be subjugated by another, the clansmen of the former group were incorporated into the structure of the latter clan, whereas the *kami* of the former was venerated as an auxiliary *kami* of the latter clan. It might be mentioned, too, that the early Japanese acknowledged the existence of numerous other kinds of *kami* and spirits, and that there were men and women who had special skills or training in dealing with spiritual and mundane problems, e.g., diviners, shamans, healers, and sorcerers.

The Yamato Kingdom

In recent years there has been heated debate among scholars regarding the exact point of transition from prehistory to early history in Japan. Nevertheless, piecing together scattered references from Chinese and Korean sources with archaeological data which are now available in Japan, we are on safe ground in assuming that there were in western Japan a number of small principalities, which were in effect no more than autonomous clans, during the early centuries of the Christian era. Then, during the latter half of the fourth century, the rival clans in Japan were unified into a kingdom, which also established a small military base of its own on the southern tip of the Korean peninsula. This kingdom is referred to as the Yamato kingdom, because the ruling clan, presumably the descendant of the powerful Altaic tribe mentioned earlier, resided in the Yamato (present Nara prefecture) district. In reality, the so-called Yamato kingdom was nothing more than a confederation of powerful clans, held together by the religious, as much as military, authority of the ruling imperial (tenno) clan chieftain, who claimed the sovereignty by virtue of solar ancestry. This claim was the central thread of a body of myths that had been handed down in the imperial clan.

With the ascendancy of the imperial clan over other rival clans, its myths were accepted widely by others, and conversely, myths of other clans were transformed and incorporated into the general framework of myths of the dominant clan. The main theme of the early Japanese myths, thus developed, was the divine origin of the imperial clan, and from this perspective various myths came to be compiled as the foundations for the eighth-century historical writings entitled the *Records of Ancient Matters* (*Kojiki*) and the *Chronicles of Japan* (*Nihon-shoki* or *Nihon-gi*), respectively. While these myths, like their counterparts in other parts of the world, deal with cosmogony and theogony, they are greatly concerned with the nature of Japan as a unique divine national community, an earthly model of the heavenly community of *kami*.

Ancient Japanese myths accepted a three-dimensional universe, namely, the Plain of High Heaven where male and female *kami* dwell, the manifested or phenomenal world where human and other beings reside, and the nether world where unclean spirits dwell.[4] The lines of demarcation between these realms were not sharply drawn, however. We are told that there appeared in primordial time three self-created *kami*, who created a series of *kami*. From this line of *kami* came Izanagi ("Kami who invites") and Izanami ("Female kami who is invited"), who together were commissioned to create the land and give birth to a host of *kami*. It was Izanagi who commanded his daughter, Ama-terasu, usually referred to as Sun Goddess, to rule the Plain of High Heaven. In turn, Ama-terasu sent her grandson, Ninigi, to rule Japan. She also gave him the myriad curved beads, the mirror, and the "grass-mower" sword, which were to become the sacred regalia of the imperial authority. Ninigi, accompanied by attending *kami*, then descended to a sacred mountain in the island of Kyushu.

The myths concerning the activities of the heavenly *kami* are followed by accounts of legendary emperors, who are direct descendants of the Sun Goddess and Ninigi. The most prominent among them is Jimmu, the first legendary emperor, who is said to have led his troops from the island of Kyushu eastward to the district of Yamato where he established the court modeled after the heavenly court of the Sun Goddess. In a real sense, the accounts of the legendary emperors were the earthly extension of heavenly myths, and as such should not be taken as history. For instance, the sovereigns were portrayed as *kami*, confined, to be sure, to the manifest world. There was no line of demarcation between the sacred and the profane dimensions of life or between religious rituals (*matsuri*) and political administration (*matsuri-goto*), both of which were under the authority of the sovereign who was the chief priest as well as the political head of the kingdom. Also, every human activity, from marriage to the method of planting seeds and weaving, followed the mythical accounts of what had taken place in the heavenly domain. Moreover, no decision, major or minor, was made by the sovereign without consulting the will of heavenly *kami* by means of divination or otherwise. These notions, derived from myths, provided a basic framework for the political structure of the national community in Japan. Admittedly, the political reality of the Yamato kingdom was often at variance with the ideal of early Shinto tradition, because ambitious chieftains of powerful clans greatly restricted the political authority of the sovereign. But, the religious authority of the sovereign was rarely questioned throughout the history of early Japan. Indeed, Shinto, the way of *kami*, was also the way of the emperor in whom the role of the manifest *kami* as well as those of the chief priest and the sovereign were rolled into one.

FOREIGN INFLUENCES

Chinese Civilization

The historical situation from the fifth century A.D. onward brought Japan close to the Asiatic continent. Inevitably, Japan underwent a series of social, cultural, political, and religious changes under the impact of Chinese, or more strictly Sino-Korean, civilization. In the course of time, the Yamato kingdom, which earlier was a loosely knit confederation of autonomous clans held together by the religious and military power of the imperial clan, was transformed into a centralized nation, modeled after the Chinese empire, even though it retained its unique Japanese characteristics.

Evidently, the Yamato kingdom began to extend its influence in the Korean peninsula during the fifth century. It was through Korea that a sizable number of Chinese and Koreans migrated to Japan, and they were eagerly welcomed as instructors, interpreters, clerks, and technicians by the court and great clan chieftains in Japan. In this situation, Japan, which hitherto had no written language, adopted the Chinese script, which greatly enriched Japanese culture. Japanese society, which had been based on primitive communal rules and authorities, accepted Confucian ethics, political theory, legal and educational institutions. Thus, while the traditional paternalistic authoritarianism was retained, interpersonal relationships came to be regulated in terms of such Confucian concepts as filial piety, the veneration of ancestors, and reciprocal rights and obligations between superiors and inferiors. Even imperial edicts stressed such Confucian virtues as uprightness, sincerity, and honesty as the guiding moral principles for the nation. Also, the traditional indifference of the Japanese to metaphysical speculations gave way to acceptance of many Chinese philosophical concepts, especially those of Taoism and the Yin-Yang system. Numerous kinds of divination and witchcraft, palmistry and fortune-telling, too, were introduced from China, and the influence of astrologers and sorcerers was strongly felt, even in the imperial court.[5]

Meanwhile Japan, having lost its military base in Korea in A.D. 562, turned its attention more directly toward China. In this situation the establishment of the Chinese empire under the Sui dynasty in 589 gave strong impetus to Japan to develop a strong centralized state, following the Chinese model. The first significant effort in this direction was made by Prince Regent Shōtoku (574–622), who accepted the Chinese concept of the emperor as the "Son of Heaven," who was to rule the nation on the basis of rational principles, and not on the basis of the unpredictable divine oracles that had been the custom before his time. Thus, he attempted to transform the chieftains of powerful clans into government officials. Besides, he tried to train a class of educated bureaucrats by sending talented young men to China for study. Soon Japan came to be governed by a series of imperial rescripts prepared by the bureaucrats who were motivated to apply Confucian learning to practical affairs of the nation. Their efforts resulted in the promulgation of a series of general and criminal laws, as well as minute regulations covering religious matters. Furthermore, the educational system came to be completely obviated by Confucian ideas, and Chinese classics, including the areas of ethics, literature, mathematics, and medicine, constituted the entire curriculum. The Chinese influence was also strongly felt in the growth of historical consciousness in Japan, as evidenced by the compilation of the *Records of Ancient Matters* (*Kojiki*) and the *Chronicles of Japan* (*Nihon-shoki* or *Nihon-gi*) during the eighth century.

Buddhism

The sixth century A.D. also witnessed the introduction of Buddhism to Japan when one of the Korean kings presented to the Japanese court a Buddhist image, copies of Buddhist scriptures, and liturgical ornaments. By that time, Buddhism was no longer the simple religion of an Indian mendicant; it was the bearer of civilization, blending within it the spiritual wisdom and learning of India and China, with well-organized ecclesiastical institutions and highly developed arts and architecture. Understandably, the conservative elements within the Japanese court were reluctant to accept Buddhism. It was the chieftain of the powerful Soga clan who became the advocate of the doctrine of the Buddha, and after a short period of resistance others, too, began to follow the footsteps of the Soga. Thus, Buddhist temples were built, and priests and nuns were trained with the support of the various clan chieftains, who wanted benefits both in this world and in the life to come. In short, Buddhism was accepted as a " clan-centered " religion in the initial stage.

Soon, with the ascendancy of the prestige of the court, the patronage for Buddhism was taken over by the court. By far the most important figure in this connection was Prince Regent Shōtoku, whose name has been mentioned earlier. In the so-called Seventeen Articles, moral injunctions issued by Shōtoku, we read: " Revere the three treasures — Buddha, the Law [or Teaching of the Buddha], and the Buddhist Community — for these are . . . the supreme object of faith in all countries." Shōtoku, himself a lay Buddhist, built temples, supported monastic orders, and lectured on Buddhist scriptures. He was also aware of the political significance of Buddhism as a stabilizing and unifying force for the national community. With such active support from the court, Buddhism, which earlier was a " clan-centered " religion, quickly became a " state-centered " religion, side by side with the indigenous Shinto.[6]

During the eighth century Japan erected its first permanent capital at Nara, modeled after the Chinese capital. While both Shinto and Buddhism were regarded as important departments of the state, it was Buddhism that enjoyed the special favor of the court. There were six Buddhist schools, which were philosophical traditions rather than sects, transplanted from China by that time. The two Hinayanistic schools, the Kusha (Sarvastivadin) and the Jōjitsu (Sautrantika), were concerned with analysis of cosmological and psychological problems. The Sanson (Madhyamika) presented a thoroughgoing dialectical analysis of concepts in order to attain transcendental wisdom. The Kegon (Avatamsaka) was a form of cosmotheism, while the Hossō (Yogacara) offered a physical and psychological analysis of elements. The Ritsu (Vinaya) was a nondoctrinal study of monastic disciplines and ordination rites.[7] The prestige of Buddhism reached its peak when the colossal image of Lochana Buddha was dedicated at the national cathedral at Nara in 752 in the presence of Emperor Shōmu, who declared himself the humble slave of Buddha. It must be admitted, however, that while lofty Buddhist doctrines intrigued some studious monks, most lay Buddhists were undiscriminating in their attitudes toward Buddhism, Shinto, and Confucianism. In the rural areas unordained holy men, who combined the teachings and practices of folk Shinto, Buddhism, and Taoism, influenced the masses. Out of this tradition developed the order of Mountain Ascetics, which was destined to play an important role in the subsequent periods.[8]

Esoteric Buddhism

In the year A.D. 794, the court moved the capital from Nara to Kyoto, ostensibly to be freed from the political pressure of powerful Buddhist institutions. During the three centuries that followed, Japanese culture integrated Chinese elements and developed its own style. By this time, Japanese society became sharply divided into three layers, namely, the elite on the top, the ordinary folk in the middle, and the masses at the bottom. As might be expected, the elite monopolized elegant art and culture. The ecclesiastical hierarchy, too, both of Shinto and Buddhism. especially those of the six schools of Nara mentioned above, were closely identified with the elite and paid little attention to others. There were two new schools of Buddhism, however, which were transplanted from China and attempted to unify the populace crossing the social and cultural classes. They were the Tendai (T'ien-t'ai in Chinese) and the Shingon (Chen yen in Chinese) schools. Both were much more eclectic than their respective counterparts in China. The former was systematized by Saichō, better known by his posthumous name Dengyō-daishi (768–822). He studied the T'ien-t'ai doctrines in China, but attempted to incorporate not only Ch'an (Zen in Japanese), monastic disciplines, and some features of Esoteric Buddhism but also Shinto as well into his system. Shortly after his death, his successors stressed the Esoteric elements, whereby the Tendai school came to be known primarily as an Esoteric school. The Shingon school, which considered itself to be the true heir of the Esoteric tradition of India and China, was introduced and systematized by Kūkai, or Kōbō-daishi (773–835). Both the Tendai and the Shingon schools combined lofty philosophy and magical incantations, although the latter, through the cult of the deified Kūkai, enjoyed a greater amount of popularity among all strata of Japanese society.[9] The eclectic character of Esoteric Buddhism was such that the Mountain Ascetics, mentioned earlier, allied themselves with both the Tendai and the Shingon schools. Furthermore, these two schools were credited with popularizing the notion that the original nature of the Shinto *kami* was Buddha, and that the *kami* were Buddha's manifestations in Japan. Such beliefs made possible the practical synthesis of Buddhism and Shinto, known as the Ryōbu ("Two-sided") Shinto, which lasted until the middle of the nineteenth century.

It did not take long, however, before both the Tendai and the Shingon schools became as institutionalized as the old Buddhist schools of Nara, with the support of the court and the aristocratic families, especially the Fujiwara family, which ruled the nation from behind the throne. Endowed with lucrative manors, the monasteries of both schools even trained armed bands of priests for the protection of their worldly interests. Nevertheless, these monasteries continued to attract both pious and learned men. It was the Tendai monastic center at Mt. Hiei, situated near Kyoto, which fostered the embryonic movement of Amida pietism, stressing the faith in the mercy of Buddha Amitabha, which became an independent and influential school of Buddhism in the thirteenth century. As far as the people of the folk and the mass levels were concerned, they were not allowed to share the benefit of the great institutions of Buddhism and Shinto. But they found spiritual consolation in their own brands of piety which blended the traditions of folk Shinto, Mountain Ascetics, various cults of saints, holy men, and popular deities, Esoteric Buddhism, and the Yin-Yang School (Onmyō-dō in Japanese).

In retrospect, it becomes apparent that the Japanese from the fifth to the twelfth centuries accepted many features of Chinese civilization and Buddhism " simply, humbly, in sincere and almost childlike fashion, and then they have laid the stamp of their own transforming genius upon . . . [them]." [10]

" THE CHRYSANTHEMUM AND THE SWORD "

The Feudal Regime

The medieval period of Japan began in 1192 when the military family of Minamoto established a feudal regime at Kamakura, near the present Tokyo, while the imperial court remained in Kyoto. This marked the breakdown of the age-old ideal, which to be sure was not always followed, of the unity of religious and political authority. Consequently, there were two sets of powers that governed the nation. The new political order, however, implied in a sense a return to the past, because the solidarity of the warrior class which was in power was based on the traditional clan (*uji*) system, even though the vertical relationship of the vassal to his lord was defined more rigidly than in ancient times in terms of loyalty, fidelity, and honor. Thus, in spite of the impressive pyramid type of feudal regime which governed the nation, rank-and-file warriors and the general populace were more conscious of their relationship to smaller, immediate circles such as the family, class, and regional community than to the total nation. It was not accidental that, under the feudal regime of Kamakura, Shinto cults of clan and regional *kami* regained a measure of popularity.

The picture changed radically with the invasions of Mongol forces in 1274 and 1281. The national crisis created a new sense of national consciousness and unified various segments of Japanese society. The national crisis also precipitated the decline of the feudal regime at Kamakura. However, the failure of a short-lived restoration of the imperial rule, 1333–1336, resulted in the establishment of the second feudal regime, under the Ashikaga family, so that the nation continued to be ruled by two sets of authority, namely, the feudal regime and the imperial court.

The Spiritual Awakening

This is not the occasion to discuss the intricate relationship that existed between the imperial court and the feudal regime, except to mention that while the former maintained nominal authority of appointing the head of the feudal regime (*shōgun* in Japanese), the actual political power was in the hands of the latter. The advent of the feudal regime also meant the eclipse of the traditional elite class, the aristocrats and court nobles as well as the ecclesiastical hierarchy, who were the bearers of culture. The rise of the warriors as the new elite thus implied the coming of a new cultural and religious, as much as political and social, climate which to a great extent reflected the mood and aspirations of the middle and lower classes in the traditional social scale. The new climate gave fresh impetus to Shinto leaders to develop the Shinto apologetics in order to emancipate Shinto from excessive Buddhist influence. The Mountain Ascetics, too, revitalized their activities in all strata of Japanese society.

By far the most significant development, however, took place in Buddhism during the thirteenth century. By that time, the great monastic centers of the established schools of Buddhism lost much spiritual vitality, even though they managed to preserve wealth and political influence. To be sure, there was a small number of clergy who tried to reform their ecclesiastical institutions from within, but their efforts were not successful. On the other hand, the new religious climate nurtured the development of the new schools of Buddhism, such as the Pure Land School, True Pure Land School, and Nichiren School, as well as the Rinzai and Sōtō Zen schools. One of the important factors that greatly stimulated the formation of the new schools was the Buddhist eschatological notion called *mappō* (the period of the latter end of Buddha's Law or Doctrines), based on a legend that divides history into three periods: the first thousand years after the Buddha's death, the period of perfect law; the second thousand years, the period of copied law, in which true faith declines even though formal adherence may be preserved; and the last thousand, the period of *mappō*, in which the Buddha's teaching declines and the world is overwhelmed by vice and strife. In the age of *mappō*, so it was widely believed, man can be saved only by the mercy of Amida (Buddha Amitabha). And, as though to fulfill this scheme of history, thirteenth-century Japan was confronted by internal and external difficulties, characterized by a series of natural calamities at home and attempted invasions by the Mongol forces from abroad.

Another important factor in the development of new schools of Buddhism was the extraordinary character of the founders or systematizers of these schools, although each one of them was so different from others in personal traits. The significance of this factor must be seen in the historic context of the Japanese religious heritage which depended on the saintly and/or charismatic quality of religious leaders as more efficacious than correctness of doctrine for the salvation of man. To be sure, all the leaders of new schools, convinced as they were of the correctness of their interpretations of Buddhism, presented their teachings as the vehicles of salvation for the people. But in the eyes of their followers it was the leaders themselves who became the vehicles of salvation, and with this twist their words and deeds took on new soteriological significance.

Closely related to the extraordinary character of these leaders was their dependence on the faith principle rather than on intellectual and moral exercise or traditional mysteries. For example, Hōnen (1133–1212), founder of the Pure Land (Jōdo) School, was persuaded that sanctification and enlightenment by traditional paths was theoretically possible but practically impossible. Thus, he dared to " choose," with all the risks which this action involves, to depend on the promise of Amida (Amitabha), who in his compassion had vowed to save all beings. Such a faith in Amida is expressed in the practice of invoking Amida's name, with the conviction that by so doing one is able to acquire rebirth in the Pure Land of Amida.[11] One of Hōnen's disciples, Shinran (1173–1262), founder of the True Pure Land (Jōdo Shin) School, combined faith in Amida and faith in his teacher. To him, however, even one's faith in Amida is nothing but Amida's saving gift, so that invoking Amida's name is to be the act of homage and thanksgiving.[12] An equally thoroughgoing faith principle was advocated by Nichiren (1222–1282), founder of the school bearing his name, who put his trust in the teachings of the Lotus Scripture and advocated the practice of invoking its title. Because of his charismatic personality and dramatic career, especially his audacious criticisms of the feudal regime at the time of the Mongol invasions, Nichiren is often called the Buddhist prophet of Japan.[13]

The spiritual awakening during the thirteenth century also resulted in the development of two schools of Zen — the Rinzai (Lin-ch'i in Chinese), systematized by Eisai (1141–1215), and the Sōtō (Ts'ao-tung), systematized by Dōgen (1200–1253).[14] In the main, the former combined the use of paradoxical dialogues (kōan in Japanese) for spiritual awakening and the practice of meditation, while the latter stressed concentrated, disciplined meditation in the cross-legged posture (zazen in Japanese). Despite these differences, both schools took it for granted that faith in the Zen experience as the path to enlightenment (satori in Japanese) is the essential prerequisite for religious life. Zen also shared with the Pure Land, the True Pure Land, and the Nichiren schools the conviction that there are no essential differences between the sacred and secular domains of life, and that the realm of phenomenal existence is the very arena of salvation.

Zen and Neo-Confucianism

The second feudal regime under the Ashikaga family, 1338–1573, had to contend with the increasing power of the rising feudal lords (daimyō) in various districts. The fact that the Ashikaga regime acknowledged the rights of hereditary succession of the positions of the feudal lords as well as those of other officeholders, ostensibly to ensure political stability, eventually resulted in undercutting its own authority over them and caused disunity of the national community. Inevitably, a succession of bloody wars was fought by ambitious feudal lords and high officials of the regime, while disgruntled peasants and fanatic religious groups, such as the followers of the True Pure Land and the Nichiren sects, rose up in a series of armed uprisings. The decline of the political and social order also resulted in the disintegration of the traditional clan system which was replaced by a smaller social and economic unit — the family system. Despite all the confusion and turmoil thus created, Japan under the Ashikaga regime attained a highly sophisticated level of art and culture, especially in ink painting, literature, poetry, flower arrangement, the *nō* play, architecture, and landscaping. The Ashikaga rulers were also keen in the lucrative China trade, and through this channel the cultural influence of China, notably Neo-Confucianism, penetrated Japan.

Religiously, Japan during the Ashikaga period reacted against the thirteenth-century emphases on the faith principle and the uniqueness of the Japanese form of religious experience. Indeed, Shinto as well as the various schools of Buddhism failed to exert significant religious influence, the only notable exception being the Rinzai school of Zen Buddhism, which was recognized by the Ashikaga regime as the *de facto* state religion. It was Zen that inspired various forms of art and culture, and it was Zen priests who made great contributions to education, foreign trade, and foreign relations, as well. As men of culture and learning, many Zen priests were convinced of the essential unity of Zen and Neo-Confucianism, and they were instrumental in propogating Neo-Confucian learning in Japan.

Neo-Confucianism, a complex religious and philosophical system incorporating some of the features of Buddhism and Taoism, provided a coherent metaphysical system, filling the need of the Japanese intellectual world for a universal principle transcending cultural provincialism. The system of Chu Hsi (Shushi in Japanese), combining metaphysics, physics, psychology, and ethics, was destined to leave a strong imprint on Japanese intellectual tradition, as we will discuss later. Neo-Confucianism spread quickly among Japanese intellectuals through the eager cooperation of Zen priests. In fact, many Zen temples became for all intents and purposes schools of Neo-Confucian learning. The popularity of Neo-Confucianism may be well illustrated by the fact that the official academy of the Ashikaga regime, which offered the most advanced study of Neo-Confucianism, was staffed by Zen priests and attracted several thousand Zen student priests early in the fifteenth century.

Parenthetically, it might be added that the foreign trade also brought Europeans, including Catholic missionaries, to Japan during the sixteenth century. By that time, the political fabric of Japan was all but broken, whereby strong men gathered forces and built their own domains at will, ignoring the will of the imperial court as much as the authority of the feudal regime, which had become totally impotent.

NATIONAL SECLUSION

Reunification of Japan

The task of reunification of Japan, which was attempted by Oda Nobunaga (1534–1582) and Toyotomi Hideyoshi (1537–1598), was consummated by Tokugawa Iyeyasu (1542–1616). In 1603 the new feudal regime was inaugurated at Edo (present Tokyo) under the Tokugawa, and it lasted until 1867. The Tokugawa regime was a highly regimented organism under the supreme power of the Tokugawa *shōgun* (military dictator).[15] The existence of the imperial court in Kyoto was barely tolerated, but it no longer was permitted to exercise even the ceremonial authority it had enjoyed under the previous feudal regimes. It is to be noted that the architects of the regime were fully aware of the actual and symbolic importance of the family in the sense that, on the one hand, the total nation was conceived of as an extended family with the *shōgun* as its head, while on the other hand, the family as the solidarity unit of society was taken very seriously. In practice, neighborhood units composed of several households were formed, and all the families of each unit were held responsible for the welfare and behavior of each and every member of the families involved.

Each family consisted of the family head and his wife, the eldest son and his wife and children, and any number of unmarried children of the head. The second and succeeding male children had to leave the household eventually, either as " adopted sons " of other families that had no male children or to establish branch households. Marriage, divorce, remarriage, adoption of sons, and financial matters were decided not by individuals but by the family council. The head of the family exercised supreme authority over the members of his family, while the wife was in charge of domestic affairs. The eldest son was trained in the occupation of his father, since the Tokugawa regime had " frozen " occupations.

The general populace was divided into four social classes — warriors, farmers, artisans, and merchants, in that order. There were those who were outside this general scale, such as members of the imperial family, court nobles, and clergy, however. For the most part, it was wellnigh impossible for a person to climb the social ladder. In principle, the whole populace existed to support the warrior class, and the warriors served their masters, who in turn served the Tokugawa family, even though in actual practice rich farmers and merchants exercised a considerable amount of power over the warriors. The nation was divided into roughly 270 fiefs of feudal lords (*daimyō*), which were expected to contribute heavily to public undertakings sponsored by the Tokugawa regime. In a sense, the whole nation, the *daimyō*'s fief, and individual households were all defined in terms of paternalistic, patriarchal family principles, with the nation represented by the Tokugawa regime claiming the supreme loyalty of the people.

Religious Policy and National Seclusion

The religious policy of the Tokugawa regime was based on the notion that all religious institutions were in effect departments and instruments of the regime. Thus, the regime was assiduous in utilizing the religious institutions and leaders for its own cause, but did not tolerate any sign of insubordination on their part. As to Roman Catholicism, which boasted a membership of 150,000 toward the end of the sixteenth century, the initial attitude of the regime was rather tempered, partly no doubt due to the fact that the regime was interested in trade with Portugal and Spain from which many missionaries came. Soon, however, a series of incidents, real or imagined, gave the feudal rulers reason to suspect that the Catholic missionary work might be a vanguard of European colonial empire, with the result that stern measures were taken against missionaries as well as Japanese converts. The severest blow came to Catholicism in 1637, when thousands of men and women in one of the strongholds in the island of Kyushu rebelled against the Tokugawa regime. Following this uprising, strict edicts were issued against Catholicism. Although a small number of "hidden Catholics" maintained their faith in disguise until the modern period, the colorful page of medieval Catholicism in Japan thus abruptly came to an end.[16] Also, in the aftermath of the uprising, the Tokugawa regime adopted the extreme policy of "national seclusion," forbidding all contacts with foreign nations, with the exception of a very limited trade with the Netherlands and China. This policy of national seclusion, which was enforced for over two hundred years, however detrimental it was to the advancement of the nation in the global scene, provided Japan with a unique opportunity to consolidate its own style of culture and develop a sense of the unity of its national community.

Under the Tokugawa regime Buddhism played an important role not only as an arm of the government but also as an effective framework for family and social cohesion. Significantly, it was the feudal regime, and not Buddhism, which universalized the Buddhist "parochial system," whereby every Japanese household was compelled to accept nominal affiliation with a particular parish temple. With the prohibition of Catholicism, every Japanese was required by law to secure a certificate from his parish temple to prove that he was not an adherent of the forbidden religion. Understandably, every family and every community as well as numerous professional and devotional associations throughout the nation depended heavily on Buddhist temples which were in charge of registration regarding birth, marriage, and divorce, and also conducted funerals, memorial services, and various forms of communal festivities and celebrations. In turn, all schools and sects of Buddhism were organized hierarchically and were strictly controlled by the commissioners of religious affairs of the regime.

Despite the Tokugawa regime's heavy dependence on Buddhism, the official guiding principle for the regime was based on Confucianism, or more strictly the system of Chu Hsi (Shushi), mentioned earlier, of Neo-Confucianism.[17] The Tokugawa *shōgun* and many of the prominent feudal lords relied heavily on Confucian advisers to develop practical administrative policies. In addition to the system of Chu Hsi, two other Confucian traditions, namely, the school of the Old Learning or Antiquity, which stressed the teachings of the early Confucian sages, and the school of Wang Yang-ming (Ōyōmei in Japanese; 1472–1529) also found eager adherents among Japanese intellectuals. Ironically, it was the Confucian scholars who consciously or unconsciously prepared the ground for the revival of Shinto during the Tokugawa period.

Shinto Revival

In discussing the revival of Shinto,[18] which was greatly aided by Japanese Confucianism, we may recall that Neo-Confucianism was actively propagated by many Zen priests during the fifteenth and sixteenth centuries. Many of them were initially Zen Buddhists first and Confucian scholars second, but soon they accepted the principle of the unity of Zen and Neo-Confucianism. Gradually, some of them began to accept the superiority of Neo-Confucianism to Zen to the extent that by the beginning of the Tokugawa period many Confucian scholars began to reject Zen Buddhism altogether. Moreover, under the Tokugawa rule, Japanese Confucianists, who were expected to advise the regime, began to interpret " the way of the ancient Chinese sage-kings " so as to fit into the religious and political situation of Japan. Inevitably, Japanese Confucianists, who were trying to emancipate themselves from the Buddhist framework, leaned emotionally toward Shinto. For example, Hayashi Razan (1583–1657), the leading Confucian tutor to the Tokugawa *shōgun* stressed the importance of the Shinto communal cult as the basis of social cohesion. He even equated the *li* (reason or principle) of Chu Hsi with the " way of the *kami*."

By far the most extreme pro-Shintoist among the Confucian scholars was Yamazaki Ansai (d. 1682), who attempted to synthesize Confucian ethics with Shinto, and developed a system called Suiga (" descent of divine blessing ") Shinto. Yamazaki stressed the virtue of " reverence " as the common principle in Shinto and Neo-Confucianism. Thus combining Neo-Confucianism and Shinto, learning and faith, and justice and devotion, Suiga Shinto exerted a significant influence on both the intellectuals and men of practical affairs, promoting emotional nationalism and loyalty to the throne. Also, it was the Mito school of Confucian scholars, so named because they were supported by the influential lord of Mito, which aroused a historical consciousness among the Japanese and provided a powerful incentive to the royalist movement. The historical consciousness and the activistic temper were injected through the Confucian-Shinto alliance into the veins of Shinto, which soon became rejuvenated and began to be self-conscious about its own unique heritage.

The revival of Shinto in the eighteenth century was also stimulated by the growth of " national learning," initiated by a series of able scholars. Kamo Mabuchi (d. 1769), for example, rejected both the Buddhist- and Confucian-centered interpretations of Shinto, and sought to reconstruct its pre-Buddhist and pre-Confucian meaning. Kamo's disciple Motoori Norinaga (d. 1801) was persuaded that ancient Shinto was a full-fledged religion of the Japanese and published the famous *Commentary on the Record of Ancient Matters* (*Kojiki-den*), which has remained to this day the authoritative interpretation of the theoretical aspects of Shinto. The most passionate spokesman for the purification of Shinto from foreign influences was Hirata Atsutane (d. 1843), who dedicated his life to the cause of Shinto as the guiding principle for the nation. The Tokugawa regime silenced Hirata a few years prior to his death because of his excessive imperial court-centered nationalism, but his disciples carried on their master's mission. Indeed, it was the combination of the influence of the Shinto restoration school (the name given to the tradition of Motoori and Hirata) [19] and the influence of the nationalistic Neo-Confucianists which championed the cause of the restoration of imperial rule and the termination of the feudal regime in the mid-nineteenth century.

MODERN JAPANESE NATIONAL COMMUNITY

From Perry to MacArthur

During the first half of the nineteenth century, the decline of the power and prestige of the Tokugawa feudal regime resulted in the general breakdown of the social and political fabric of the nation. Externally, Japan sensed the threat of European colonial powers which were then encroaching upon various parts of Asia, including Japan's immediate neighbor, China. The significance of the arrival in 1853 of four American battleships led by Commodore Matthew C. Perry off the shore of Uraga, not far from the present Tokyo, must be seen in this historic setting. The bewildered officials of the Tokugawa regime, realizing there was no alternative, signed a treaty of commerce with the Government of the United States, which was followed by similar treaties with the Netherlands, Russia, Great Britain, and France a few years later. Thus ended the " national seclusion," which had lasted for over two hundred years.

The treaties with Western nations provided a convenient issue to unite the anti-Tokugawa forces in order to topple the feudal regime. Caught by both internal and external problems which he was unable to solve, the last *shōgun* of the Tokugawas surrendered his power in 1867 to Emperor Meiji, who then established the capital in Tokyo.[20] The dream of restoring the ancient ideal that had envisaged the unification of the whole nation under imperial authority was thus fulfilled. The new government was in essence an oligarchy consisting of fewer than one hundred men, mostly lower warriors and a few minor court nobles, who were united in their practical policies. These men, during Emperor Meiji's reign (1867–1912), made every effort to consolidate the national community by reshaping Japan into a modern nation-state with a strong defense system and industrial economy, without, however, losing the traditional religious and cultural foundation. In order to achieve this end, the Meiji regime welcomed the Western knowledge and technology needed for modernization, while at the same time it depended on Shinto and Confucianism to provide a foundation for national moral and cultural life.

Externally, the architects of the Meiji regime were determined to make Japan a leading imperialist power in Asia. This policy was followed by the leaders during the reigns of Emperor Taishō (1912–1926) and the present emperor, Hirohito (1926–   ) as well. Thus, from the Meiji era to the end of World War II in 1945, Japan competed with Western powers to obtain her share in exploiting Asia. Japan claimed sovereignty over Okinawa (1881), took possession of Taiwan following the Sino-Japanese War (1894–1895), joined the Western nations in combating the Boxer Rebellion in China (1900), occupied Port Arthur and Dairen following the Russo-Japanese War (1904–1905), annexed Korea (1910), and gained the former German island possessions in the Pacific after World War I as a mandate from the League of Nations. But Japan's audacious attempt to extend her power over Manchuria and China during the 1930's and to superimpose the so-called Greater East Asia Co-Prosperity Sphere on other Asian nations during World War II failed, and Japan was occupied by the Allied forces under General Douglas MacArthur. In 1952 military occupation by Allied forces ended, and Japan became once again a member of the family of nations.

State Shinto

Religious development in Japan during the modern period was decisively shaped by the initial religious policy of the Meiji regime, which reflected the aspirations of Shintoists and nationalistic Confucianists who had envisaged the restoration of the ancient Japanese ideal of the unity of religious cult and political administration (*saisei-itchi* in Japanese). Accordingly, the regime established the department of Shinto and issued the edict of separation of Shinto from Buddhism. Buddhist priests who had been connected with Shinto shrines were either returned to lay life or made Shinto priests, who were now *de facto* government officials. In such an atmosphere there developed a popular anti-Buddhist movement. This movement, which reached its climax in 1870–1871, destroyed many Buddhist temples and forced many Buddhist priests to return to lay life. But, it soon became apparent that Buddhism was too deeply imbedded in the fabric of Japanese life, and the government softened its extreme anti-Buddhist policy. Nevertheless, the government established in 1871 the Shinto Ministry, replacing the department of Shinto, and conducted a nationwide campaign to promote patriotism, reverence for Shinto *kami*, and the emperor cult. Such an active policy to uphold the supremacy of Shinto, however, encountered resistance and criticism from various quarters, and the government adopted more restrained religious policies.

Meanwhile, in 1873 the combined pressures of Western nations persuaded the Meiji regime to lift the edict, carried over from the Tokugawa period, banning Christianity, and religious freedom was guaranteed, at least officially, in the Constitution of 1889. With the lifting of the ban against Christianity, more especially after the promulgation of the Constitution, various branches of Christianity — the Russian Orthodox Church, the Roman Catholic Church, and Protestant denominations — initiated vigorous missionary, educational, and philanthropic activities. Although Christianity gained very little numerical strength, " the ethics and ideals of Christianity had a much more profound influence on Japanese thought and life than one might assume from the fact that less than 1 per cent of the population became professing Christians." [21]

The appearance of Christianity, which was accompanied by many features of Western culture and learning, brought Buddhists, Shintoists, Confucianists, and cultural traditionalists close together in their united effort in an all-out anti-Christian campaign. Meanwhile, the government, which grudgingly guaranteed freedom of religion, banned religious instruction in schools, on the other hand, even though according to the regulation " moral teaching, if applicable to all religions, could be given." Obviously, the government intended to give a special advantage to Shinto, by interpreting it not as a religion but as a patriotic cult, applicable to adherents of all religions. Furthermore, after the promulgation of the Imperial Rescript on Education in 1890, the government required a course on moral teaching in public schools and advocated obeisance at Shinto shrines by all Japanese subjects as a nonreligious patriotic duty.

The government also created a category of Sect Shinto for various kinds of popular messianic and healing cults in order to separate them from the state-sponsored Shinto. Between 1882 and 1908 the thirteen Sect Shinto denominations were recognized as " churches " (*kyōha* or *kyōkai*), which, like Buddhist and Christian denominations, were dependent on nongovernmental, private initiative for their support.[22] These Sect Shinto denominations were in a real sense the prototypes of the so-called " new religions," which have mushroomed since the end of World War II.

Following the severe depression in 1908, the government faced the discontent and unrest of the general populace. The government, partly to deal with this situation, sponsored in 1912 the " Conference of the Three Religions," involving representatives of Sect Shinto, Buddhism, and Christianity. From then onward until the end of World War II, all religious groups in Japan were compelled to cooperate with the will of the government. Indeed, all religions became, reluctantly or otherwise, shadowy appendages to State Shinto.

Divine Nation vs. Modern Nation-State

The disestablishment of State Shinto, effective immediately after World War II, had a far-reaching effect on the status of Shinto. Orders from the Supreme Commander for the Allied Powers to the Japanese government prohibited the sponsorship, support, perpetuation, control, and dissemination of Shinto by the Japanese national, prefectural, and local governments. or by public officials. Equally drastic was the abolition of the moral teaching from the school curriculum and the public denial of the emperor that he was divine. Assured of freedom of religious belief, practice, and propaganda, the Buddhist, Christian, and Sect Shinto denominations are now carrying on their activities. Shinto, too, now that it has recovered from the shock of the disestablishment, is showing signs of growing into a genuine religion of the people. Besides, taking advantage of the religious freedom, numerous " new religions " have emerged.[23]

The principle of religious liberty and that of separation of religion and state were clearly elucidated in the new Constitution, inspired undoubtedly by the Allied occupation forces and promulgated in 1946. There seems to be a rather widespread feeling among the populace, however, that they have lost the spiritual heritage of Japan. To them, religion is more than the complex of doctrines, cults, and ecclesiastical institutions. Rather, it is a way of life, a mode of apprehending human reality in this mysterious universe, securely grounded in the cosmological orientation of their ancestors. Moreover, it is inseparably related to the notion that Japan is not only their homeland but is a sacred land hallowed by the presence of *kami*. As such, to be a Japanese means more than to be a member of a nation-state; it means acceptance of prerogatives and duties for each member, regardless of his or her formal affiliation with a particular religious tradition such as Shinto, Buddhism, or what have you, to participate in the task of unfolding the underlying meaning of the national community which is their sacred trust.

Throughout the long history of Japan, from its prehistoric period to the end of World War II, the Japanese appropriated various forms of religious beliefs and practices. Nevertheless, they always accepted, implicitly at any rate, the notion that the meaning of their human existence was integrally related to the well-being of the divine land and the sacred national community. And the question that confronts all religions in Japan today is whether or not the kind of modern nation-state which Japan has become can also retain meaning and significance as a communal manifestation of the sacred, i.e., a hierophany.

Notes

◈ ◈

Chapter 1. INTRODUCTION: " ONE WORLD " AND RELIGIONS

1. *Webster's New International Dictionary,* Second Edition, Unabridged, 1952, p. 2105.

2. Smith, Wilfred Cantwell, " The Comparative Study of Religion," *Inaugural Lectures* (McGill University, Faculty of Divinity, 1950) , p. 43.

3. Adlai Stevenson's statement, *Chicago Sun-Times,* Sept. 14, 1953.

4. Woodard, William, " Japan's New Religions," *Japan Harvest,* V (Winter, 1957) , pp. 19–21.

5. Slater, Robert Lawson, *Paradox and Nirvana* (University of Chicago Press, 1951) , p. 17.

6. Marett, Robert R., *Head, Heart and Hands in Human Evolution* (Hutchinson & Co., Ltd., London, 1935) , p. 81.

7. See Buber, Martin, *I and Thou,* tr. by R. G. Smith (T. & T. Clark, Edinburgh, 1937) .

8. Van der Leeuw, G., *Religion in Essence and Manifestation,* tr. by J. E. Turner (George Allen & Unwin, Ltd., London, 1938) , p. 32.

9. Bleeker, C. J., " The Nature and Destiny of Man in the Light of the Phenomenology of Religion," *Anthropologie religieuse,* ed. by C. J. Bleeker (E. J. Brill, Leiden, 1955) , p. 183.

10. See Otto, Rudolf, *The Idea of the Holy,* tr. by John W. Harvey (Humphrey Milford: Oxford University Press, 1923) .

11. Macmurray, John, " The Celebration of Communion," *The Listener* (Dec. 20, 1956) , p. 1027.

12. Redfield, Robert, " The Folk Society," *American Journal of Sociology,* LII (Jan., 1947), p. 299.

13. Redfield, Robert, *The Primitive World and Its Transformations* (Cornell University Press, 1953), p. 12.

14. Eliade, Mircea, *The Myth of the Eternal Return,* tr. by W. R. Trask (Pantheon Books, Inc., 1954), p. 5.

15. See Niebuhr, H. Richard, *Christ and Culture* (Harper & Brothers, 1951).

16. Hocking, William Ernest, *The Coming World Civilization* (Harper & Brothers, 1956), p. 3. Quotations from this book are used by permission.

17. *Ibid.,* p. 4.

18. *Ibid.,* p. 6.

19. *Ibid.,* p. 27.

20. *Ibid.,* p. 47.

Chapter 2. CHINESE RELIGIONS AND THE FAMILY SYSTEM

The Middle Kingdom

1. Panikkar, K. M., *In Two Chinas* (George Allen & Unwin, Ltd., London, 1955), p. 48.

2. For example, communist historians hold that Chinese society at the time of Confucius was a slaveholding system and that Confucius accepted such a social order, whereas some Sinologists consider Confucius a pioneer and champion of democratic ideals and the rights of the underprivileged.

3. Buck, Pearl S., *The Good Earth* (Pocket Books, Inc., 1938), pp. 340–341.

4. Andersson, J. G., *Researches Into the Prehistory of the Chinese* (Bulletin of the Museum of Far Eastern Antiquities, No. 15, Stockholm, 1943), p. 297.

5. Bishop, Carl W., " The Beginning of Civilization in Eastern Asia," *Supplement to the J. A. O. S.* (No. 4, Dec., 1939), p. 52.

6. White, W. C., " Some Revelations of Recent Excavations," *China,* ed. by H. F. MacNair (University of California Press, 1946), p. 31.

7. Wittfogel, Karl A., " Chinese Society: An Historical Survey," *The Journal of Asian Studies* (XVI, 3, May, 1957), p. 344.

China's Religious Heritage

8. Hu Shih, " Religion and Philosophy in Chinese History," *Symposium on Chinese Culture,* ed. by S. H. Chen Zen (China Institute of Pacific Relations, Shanghai, 1931), p. 32.

9. Hodous, Lewis, " Folk Religion," *China,* p. 233.

10. Lin Yutang, *My Country and My People* (John Day Co., Inc., 1935), pp. 103–104.

11. Bodde, Derk, " Dominant Ideas," *China,* p. 20.

12. *Ibid.,* p. 22.

13. See *The Wisdom of Confucius,* ed. and tr. by Lin Yutang (Random House, Inc., 1938), p. 5.

14. Creel, H. G., *Confucius: The Man and the Myth* (John Day Co., Inc., 1949), p. 29.

15. Hu Shih, *loc. cit.,* p. 38.

16. Fung Yu-lan, " Confucianism and Taoism," *History of Philosophy Eastern and Western,* ed. by S. Radhakrishnan *et al.* (George Allen & Unwin, Ltd., London, 1952), I, p. 562.

17. *The Wisdom of China and India,* ed. by Lin Yutang (Random House, Inc., 1942), p. 580.

18. *Ibid.,* p. 583.

19. Waley, Arthur, *The Way and Its Power* (George Allen & Unwin, Ltd., London, 1934), p. 141.

20. *The Way of Life, Lao Tzu,* tr. by R. B. Blakney (Mentor Books, 1955), p. 53.

21. Fung Yu-lan, *A Short History of Chinese Philosophy,* ed. by Derk Bodde (The Macmillan Company, 1950), pp. 65–66.

22. Hu Shih, *loc. cit.,* pp. 39–40.

23. *Ibid.,* p. 41.

The Development of Chinese Religions

24. Granet, Marcel, *Chinese Civilization* (Barnes & Noble, Inc., 1951), p. 123.

25. Hu Shih, *loc. cit.,* p. 123.

26. Creel, H. G., *Chinese Thought from Confucius to Mao Tse-tung* (University of Chicago Press, 1953), p. 181.

27. Hu Shih, *loc. cit.,* p. 45.

28. Quoted in Fung Yu-lan, *A Short History of Chinese Philosophy,* p. 286.

29. Dubs, Homer H., " Taoism," *China,* p. 286.

30. Latourette, Kenneth S., *The Chinese, Their History and Culture* (The Macmillan Company, 1934) , p. 125.

31. Dubs, *loc. cit.,* p. 287.

32. See Teggart, Frederick J., *Rome and China* (University of California Press, 1939), p. viii. During the period from 58 B.C. to A.D. 107, " of the wars in the Roman East, eighteen followed wars in Chinese Turkestan, so that, of the forty occasions on which outbreaks took place in Europe, twenty-seven were traceable to the policy, or rather change of policy, of the Han government."

33. See Mullikin, Mary A., " China's Great Wall of Sculpture," *The National Geographic Magazine* (LXXIII, No. 3, March, 1938) , pp. 313–348.

34. Wright, Arthur F., " The Formation of Sui Ideology, 581–604," *Chinese Thought and Institutions,* ed. by J. K. Fairbank (University of Chicago Press, 1957) , p. 104.

35. Hu Shih, *loc. cit.,* p. 51.

36. Chan, Wing-tsit, " Transformation of Buddhism in China," *Philosophy East and West* (VII, Nos. 3–4, Oct., 1957– Jan., 1958) , p. 115.

37. Tsukamoto, Zenryu, " Buddhism in China and Korea," *The Path of the Buddha,* ed. by K. W. Morgan (The Ronald Press Company, 1956) , p. 220.

38. Hughes, E. R., and Hughes, K., *Religion in China* (Hutchinson House, London, 1950) , p. 75.

39. Eliot, Sir Charles, *Hinduism and Buddhism* (Barnes & Noble, Inc., 1954) , III, p. 271.

40. *Ibid.,* p. 270.

41. Creel, *Chinese Thought from Confucius to Mao Tsetung,* p. 195.

42. Chan, Wing-tsit, *loc. cit.,* p. 112.

43. Anesaki, Masaharu, *History of Japanese Religion* (Kegan Paul, Trench, Trubner & Co., London, 1930) , p. 209.

44. Fung Yu-lan, *A History of Chinese Philosophy,* tr. by Derk Bodde (Princeton University Press, 1953) , II, p. 424.

45. Ch'u Chai, " Neo-Confucianism of the Sung-Ming Periods," *Social Research* (XVIII, No. 3, Sept., 1951), pp. 370–371.

46. Fung Yu-lan, *A Short History of Chinese Philosophy*, p. 280.

47. Hu Shih, *loc. cit.*, p. 55.

48. Ch'u Chai, *loc. cit.*, p. 371.

49. Hu Shih, *loc. cit.*, p. 56.

50. Quoted in Fung Yu-lan, *A Short History of Chinese Philosophy*, p. 297.

51. Earthy, E. Dora, " The Religion of Genghis Khan," *Numen*, II, No. 3, Sept., 1955, p. 230.

52. Eliot, *op. cit.*, III, pp. 272–273.

53. Henke, Frederick G., *The Philosophy of Wang Yangming* (The Open Court Publishing Company, 1916), p. 13.

54. Quoted in Fung Yu-lan, *A Short History of Chinese Philosophy*, p. 315.

55. *Ibid.*, p. 254.

56. *China in the Sixteenth Century: The Journal of Matthew Ricci: 1583–1610*, tr. by Louis J. Gallagher (Random House, Inc., 1953), p. 93.

57. *Ibid.*, p. 95.

58. In China, an imperial edict was issued against Roman Catholicism in 1724. In turn, in 1742 the Vatican decided against the use of Chinese rites by the Constitution *Ex quo singulari* of Pope Benedict XIV.

59. Chan, Wing-tsit, " Confucianism," *Religion in the Twentieth Century*, ed. by V. Ferm (Philosophical Library, Inc., 1948), p. 99.

Triumph of the Confucian Tradition

60. " Chinese Terminology," *An Encyclopedia of Religion*, ed. by V. Ferm (Philosophical Library, Inc., 1945), p. 144.

61. Soothill, W. E., *The Three Religions of China* (Humphrey Milford: Oxford University Press, 1923), p. 15.

62. *Ibid.*, p. 13.

63. Hocking, William E., *Living Religions and a World Faith* (The Macmillan Company, 1940), p. 69.

64. Lin Yutang, *My Country and My People*, p. 117.

65. Stuart, J. Leighton, " Christianity and Confucianism," *The Christian Life and Message in Relation to Non-Christian Systems of Thought and Life* (International Missionary Council, 1928), p. 43.

66. " Chinese Terminology," *loc. cit.*, p. 150.

67. King, Winston L., *Introduction to Religion* (Harper & Brothers, 1954), pp. 207–208.

68. Fung Yu-lan, *A Short History of Chinese Philosophy*, p. 21.

69. Wei, F. C. M., *The Spirit of Chinese Culture* (Charles Scribner's Sons, 1947), p. 147.

70. Lowie, R. H., *Primitive Society* (Liveright Publishing Corp., 1920), p. 66.

71. Lin Yutang, *My Country and My People*, p. 175.

72. *Chinese Philosophy in Classical Times*, ed. and tr. by E. R. Hughes (J. M. Dent & Sons, Ltd., London, 1942), p. 25.

73. Creel, *Confucius: The Man and the Myth*, p. 150.

74. Hughes, *Chinese Philosophy in Classical Times*, p. 13.

75. *Ibid.*

76. *Ibid.*

77. Smythe, Lewis S. C., " The Composition of the Chinese Family," *Nanking Journal* (V, No. 2, Nov., 1936), p. 371.

78. Broom, Leonard, and Selznick, Philip, *Sociology* (Row, Peterson & Company, 2d ed., 1958), pp. 168–169.

79. Eberhard, W., " The Political Function of Astronomy and Astronomers in Han China," *Chinese Thought and Institutions*, p. 37.

80. Wittfogel, *op. cit.*, p. 356.

81. Wright, *op. cit.*, p. 88.

82. " Chinese Terminology," *loc. cit.*, pp. 143–144.

Crisis of " Family-ism "

83. Lin Yutang, *My Country and My People*, p. 178.

84. Bodde, *loc. cit.*, p. 23.

85. Lin Yutang, *My Country and My People*, p. 212.

86. Hu Shih, *loc. cit.*, p. 38.

87. Eckel, Paul E., *The Far East Since 1500* (Harcourt, Brace and Company, Inc., 1949), p. 53.

88. *Ibid.*, pp. 53–54.

89. Toynbee, Arnold, *The World and the West* (Oxford University Press, 1953), pp. 51–54.

90. Chan, Wing-tsit, *Religious Trends in Modern China* (Columbia University Press, 1953), p. 12.

91. *Ibid.*, p. 17.

92. *Ibid.*, p. 19.

93. Quoted in Berkov, Robert, *Strong Man of China* (Houghton Mifflin Company, 1938), p. 258.

94. Wright, Mary C., "From Revolution to Restoration: The Transformation of Kuomintang Ideology," *The Far Eastern Quarterly* (XIV, No. 4, Aug., 1955), p. 519.

95. *Ibid.*, p. 529.

96. Northrop, F. S. C., *The Taming of the Nations* (The Macmillan Company, 1952), p. 119.

97. Morgenthau, Hans J., *In Defense of the National Interest* (Alfred A. Knopf, Inc., 1951), p. 205.

98. Nivison, David S., "Communist Ethics and Chinese Tradition," *The Journal of Asian Studies* (XVI, No. 1, Nov., 1956), p. 74.

99. Ravenholt, Albert, "The Chinese Communes: Big Risks for Big Gains," *Foreign Affairs* (July, 1959), p. 581.

100. Panikkar, *op. cit.*, p. 179.

Chapter 3. HINDUISM AND THE CASTE SYSTEM

India

1. *India, A Reference Annual, 1953* (The Publication Division, Government of India, Delhi, 1953), pp. 4–6.

2. See Emeneau, Murray B., "Languages," *India, Pakistan, Ceylon,* ed. by W. Norman Brown (Cornell University Press, 1951), pp. 47–50.

3. Bowles, Chester, *Ambassador's Report* (Harper & Brothers, 1954), p. 82.

4. Roosevelt, Eleanor, *India and the Awakening East* (Harper & Brothers, 1953), pp. 111–112.

5. Nehru, Jawaharlal, *The Discovery of India* (John Day Co., Inc., 1946), p. 579.

6. Pigott, Stuart, *Prehistoric India* (Penguin Books, Inc., 1950), p. 249.

7. Mahabharata, Karnaparva, LXIX, 59.

Hinduism in History

8. See *A Source Book in Indian Philosophy,* ed. by Sarvepalli Radhakrishnan and Charles A. Moore (Princeton University Press, 1957), p. xviii.

9. Quoted in Finegan, Jack, *The Archeology of World Religions* (Princeton University Press, 1952), pp. 180–181.

10. Sarma, D. S., " The Nature and History of Hinduism," *The Religion of the Hindus,* ed. by Kenneth W. Morgan (The Ronald Press Company, 1953), p. 37.

11. Piet, John H., *A Logical Presentation of the Saiva Siddhanta Philosophy* (The Christian Literature Society for India, Madras, 1952), p. 1.

12. Binyon, Sir Lawrence, *Akbar* (Appleton-Century-Crofts, Inc., 1932), pp. 2–3.

13. Finegan, *op. cit.,* p. 539.

14. Archer, John Clark, *The Sikhs* (Princeton University Press, 1946), p. 1.

15. Macfie, J. M., *The Ramayan of Tulsidas* (T. & T. Clark, Edinburgh, 1930), pp. xv–xvi.

The Hindu Faith

16. Kraemer, H., *The Christian Message in a Non-Christian World* (The Edinburgh House, London, 1938), pp. 160–161.

17. Mahadevan, T. M. P., *Outlines of Hinduism* (Chetana, Ltd., Booksellers & Publishers, Bombay, 1956), p. 23.

18. Haas, William S., *The Destiny of the Mind: East and West* (Faber & Faber, Ltd., London, 1956), p. 134.

19. Radhakrishnan and Moore, *op. cit.,* pp. xxi–xxii.

20. Heimann, Betty, *Indian and Western Philosophy* (George Allen & Unwin, Ltd., London, 1937), pp. 29–62.

21. Gītā, ii, 17.

22. *The Great Scriptures,* ed. by T. M. P. Mahadevan (The G. S. Press, Madras, 1956), p. 29.

23. Gītā, iv, 39.

24. Svetasvatvara Upanishad, iv, 3.

25. Rambach, Pierre, and De Golish, Vitold, *The Golden Age of Indian Art, Vth–XIIIth Century* (Taraporevala, Bombay, 1955), p. 33.

26. Thomas, P., *Epics, Myths and Legends of India* (Taraporevala, Bombay, n.d.), p. 44.

27. Schweitzer, Albert, *Indian Thought and Its Development* (Henry Holt & Co., Inc., 1936), pp. 1–2.

28. Eliade, Mircea, *Yoga: Immortality and Freedom*, tr. by Willard R. Trask (Pantheon Books, Inc., 1958), p. 13.

29. Kraemer, H., *Religion and the Christian Faith* (The Westminster Press, 1957), p. 107.

Hinduism and Indian Society

30. McKenzie, John, *Two Religions: A Comparative Study of Some Distinctive Ideas and Ideals in Hinduism and Christianity* (Lutterworth Press, London, 1950), p. 33.

31. *India, A Reference Annual, 1953,* pp. 6–7.

32. Prabhu, Pandharinath H., *Hindu Social Organization* (Popular Book Depot, Bombay, 3d ed., 1958), p. 215.

33. "Family," *Encyclopaedia of Religion and Ethics*, ed. James Hastings, V, p. 739.

34. Prabhu, *op. cit.,* pp. 219–222.

35. *Ibid.,* p. 216.

36. *Village India: Studies in the Little Community,* ed. by McKim Marriott (University of Chicago Press; also published as Memoir No. 83, The American Anthropological Association, June, 1955).

37. Srinivas, M. N., "The Social System of a Mysore Village," *ibid.,* pp. 1–35.

38. Marriott, McKim, "Little Communities in an Indigenous Civilization," *ibid.,* pp. 171–218.

39. Hutton, J. H., *Caste in India* (Cambridge University Press, 1946), pp. 57–59.

40. "Caste," *Encyclopaedia of Religion and Ethics*, III, pp. 231–232.

41. Hutton, *op. cit.,* pp. 45–46.

42. *Ibid.,* pp. 59–61.

43. *Ibid.,* pp. 97–106.

44. Smith, Marian W., "Anthropology and Sociology," *India, Pakistan, Ceylon,* p. 46.

Modern Hinduism and the Caste System

45. Toynbee, Arnold, "Problems of Indian Partition," *Chicago Sun-Times,* Aug. 16, 1957.

46. *Christianity and the Asian Revolution,* ed. by Rajah R. Manikam (Diocesan Press, Madras, 1954), p. 120.

47. *Ramakrishna, Prophet of New India,* tr. by Swami Nikhilananda (Harper & Brothers, 1942), p. x.

48. See Farquhar, J. N., *The Crown of Hinduism* (Humphrey Milford: Oxford University Press, 1913), p. 41.

49. *A Tagore Testament,* tr. by Indra Dutt (Philosophical Library, Inc., 1954), p. 67.

50. *Ibid.,* p. 107.

51. Gandhi, M. K., *Hindu Dharma* (Navajivan, Ahmedabad, 1950), p. 262.

52. *Ibid.,* p. 319.

53. Prasad, Beni, "The Influence of Modern Thought in India," *The Annals of the American Academy of Political and Social Science* (Vol. 233, May, 1944), pp. 46–54.

54. *The Manchester Guardian* (Jan. 28, 1954).

55. *Chicago Sun-Times* (Feb. 8, 1957).

56. Quoted in *The Manchester Guardian* (Dec. 28, 1954).

57. Quoted in Fisher, Margaret W., and Bondurant, Joan V., *The Indian Experience with Democratic Elections* (Indian Press Digests, Monograph Series, No. 3, 1956), p. 55.

58. Ball, W. Macmahon, *Nationalism and Communism in East Asia* (Melbourne University Press, Melbourne, 1956), p. 55.

59. *India,* pp. 14–15.

60. *Ibid.,* p. 16.

61. See Tennyson, Hallam, *Saint on the March* (Victor Gollancz, London, 1956).

62. Quoted in *The Manchester Guardian* (Oct. 4, 1956).

63. Radhakrishnan and Moore, *op. cit.,* p. 610.

64. Quoted in *Saturday Review* (June 27, 1957), p. 38.

65. *The Philosophy of Sarvepalli Radhakrishnan,* ed. by P. A. Schilp (Tudor Publishing Company, 1952), p. 766.

66. *Ibid.*, p. 842.

67. Quoted in *ibid.*, p. 775.

68. Moraes, Frank, *Jawaharlal Nehru* (The Macmillan Company, 1956), p. 349.

69. Singer, Milton, "Cultural Values in India's Economic Development," *The Annals of the American Academy of Political and Social Science,* Vol. 305 (May, 1956), p. 86.

70. Quoted in Moraes, *op. cit.*, p. 488.

71. Quoted in Bourke-White, Margaret, *Halfway to Freedom* (Simon and Schuster, Inc., 1949), p. 224.

72. *The Manchester Guardian* (Feb. 18, 1954).

73. Marriott, in *Village India*, pp. 192–194.

74. Hutton, *op. cit.*, p. 164.

75. Hocking, William E., *The Coming World Civilization* (Harper & Brothers, 1956), p. 47.

76. *Ibid.*, p. 26.

77. Coomaraswamy, Ananda K., *Hinduism and Buddhism* (Philosophical Library, Inc., 1943), p. 27.

78. Tagore, R., *Gitanjali* (The Macmillan Company, London, 1938), p. 27.

Chapter 4. BUDDHISM AND THE SAMGHA

Buddha

1. Thomas, E. J., *The History of Buddhist Thought* (Barnes & Noble, Inc., 1933), p. 1.

2. Mookerji, Radha Kumud, *Hindu Civilization* (Bharatiya Vidya Bhavan, Bombay, 1957), II, p. 285.

3. Eliot, Sir Charles, *Hinduism and Buddhism* (Barnes & Noble, Inc., 1954), I, p. 132. Published in Great Britain by Routledge & Kegan Paul, Ltd., 1954. Quotations used by permission of the publishers.

4. *Ibid.*, I, p. 135.

5. *The Padhana-sutta from the Sutta-nipata,* tr. by Lord Chalmers in *Buddha's Teaching* (Harvard Oriental Series, XXXVII), p. 68.

6. Jennings, J. G., *The Vedantic Buddhism of Buddha* (Oxford University Press, London, 1948), pp. 63–64.

7. *Ibid.,* pp. 66 ff.

8. *Ibid.,* p. 483.

9. See Poussin, L. de la Vallée, *The Way to Nirvana* (Cambridge University Press, 1917), p. 110.

10. *The Middle Length Sayings,* tr. by I. B. Horner (Luzac & Company, Ltd., London, 1954), I, p. 218.

11. Poussin, *op. cit.,* p. 138.

12. This perspective is clearly brought out in Bahm, A. J., *Philosophy of the Buddha* (Harper & Brothers, 1958), Ch. 6, " The Middle Way."

13. Nyanatiloka, *Buddhist Dictionary* (Frewin & Co., Colombo, 1956), p. 11.

14. Coomaraswamy, Ananda K., *Buddha and the Gospel of Buddhism* (Asia Publishing House, Bombay, 1956), pp. 197–198.

15. Murti, T. R. V., *The Central Philosophy of Buddhism* (George Allen & Unwin, Ltd., London, 1955), p. 17.

16. Samyutta-nikaya, II, 3, 8.

17. Quoted in Eliade, Mircea, *Yoga: Immortality and Freedom,* tr. by Willard R. Trask (Pantheon Books, Inc., 1958), p. 164.

The Buddhist Community: The Samgha

18. Thomas, *op. cit.,* p. 14.

19. Warren, Henry Clark, *Buddhism in Translation* (Harvard University Press, 1947), p. 420.

20. Zimmer, Heinrich, *Philosophies of India,* ed. by Joseph Campbell (Pantheon Books, Inc., 1951), p. 155.

21. Kraemer, H., *The Christian Message in a Non-Christian World* (The Edinburgh House, London, 1938), pp. 173–174.

22. See Warren, *op. cit.,* p. 413.

23. Eliot, *op. cit.,* I, p. 262.

24. Thomas, *op. cit.,* pp. 16–21.

25. Pachow, W., *A Comparative Study of the Pratimoksa* (The Sino-Indian Cultural Society, Santiniketan, 1955), p. 61.

26. Anesaki, M., " Docetism (Buddhism) ," *Encyclopaedia of Religion and Ethics,* IV, p. 836.

27. Thomas, *op. cit.,* p. 133.

28. Zimmer, *op. cit.,* pp. 127–133. Also see Miyamoto, Shoson,

" Freedom, Independence and Peace in Buddhism," *Philosophy East and West,* I, 4 (Jan., 1952), p. 40.

The Development of the Samgha

29. Eliot, *op. cit.,* I, p. 265.

30. Sankalia, Hasmukh D., *The University of Nalanda* (B. G. Paul & Co., Madras, 1934), p. 32.

31. Stcherbatsky, Th., *The Conception of Buddhist Nirvana* (The Academy of Sciences of the U.S.S.R., Leningrad, 1927), p. 1.

32. Slater, Robert L., *Paradox and Nirvana* (University of Chicago Press, 1951), p. 3.

33. *Ibid.,* p. 118.

34. *Ibid.,* p. 74.

35. Stcherbatsky, *op. cit.,* p. 61.

36. Smith, F. Harold, *The Buddhist Way of Life* (Hutchinson University Library, London, 1951), p. 111.

37. Takakusu, Junjiro, *The Essentials of Buddhist Philosophy* (University of Hawaii, Honolulu, 1947), p. 107.

38. Smith, *op. cit.,* p. 113.

39. Takakusu, *op. cit.,* p. 193.

40. *Ibid.,* pp. 192–193.

41. Winternitz, Morris, *History of Indian Literature,* tr. by S. Ketkar (University of Calcutta, Calcutta, 1927–1933), II, p. 228.

42. Hamilton, Clarence H., " The Idea of Compassion in Mahayana Buddhism," *J. A. O. S.,* Vol. 70, No. 3 (July–Sept. 1950), p. 150.

43. Quoted in Steinilber-Oberlin, E., *The Buddhist Sects of Japan,* tr. by Marc Logé (George Allen & Unwin, Ltd., London, 1938), p. 104.

44. See Eliade, Mircea, *The Myth of the Eternal Return,* tr. by W. R. Trask (Pantheon Books, Inc., 1954), p. 159.

Buddhism Outside India

45. Pratt, J. B., *The Pilgrimage of Buddhism* (The Macmillan Company, 1928), p. 105.

46. Gard, Richard A., *Buddhist Influence on the Political*

Thought and Institutions of India and Japan (Society for Oriental Studies, 1949), p. 4.

47. Sircar, D. C., *Inscriptions of Asoka* (Government of India, The Publication Division, 1957), p. 53.

48. *Ibid.*, p. 54.

49. *Ibid.*

50. Nakamura, Hajime, " Maurya-O-cho-jidai ni okeru Bukkyo no Shakaiteki-kiban," *Indogaku Bukkyogaku-ronshu, Dedicated to S. Miyamoto* (Sanseido, Tokyo, 1954), pp. 195 ff.

51. Kasugai, Shinya, " Asoka-O-Shochokubun no Shakaiteki-haikei," *Indogaku Bukkyogaku-ronso, Dedicated to S. Yamaguchi* (Hozokan, Kyoto, 1955), pp. 96 ff.

52. Adikaram, E. W., *Early History of Buddhism in Ceylon* (D. S. Puswella, Migoda, Ceylon, 1946), p. 50.

53. Eliot, *op. cit.*, I, pp. xlix–l.

54. Pachow, W., " Ancient Cultural Relations Between Ceylon and China," *The University of Ceylon Review,* XII, 3 (July, 1954).

55. Eliot, *op. cit.*, III, p. 176.

56. *Atlantic,* Vol. 201, No. 3 (Feb., 1958), p. 118.

57. Eliot, *op. cit.*, III, p. 215.

58. Hu Shih, " Religion and Philosophy in Chinese History," *Symposium on Chinese Culture,* ed. by Sophia H. Chen Zen (China Institute of Pacific Relations, Shanghai, 1931), p. 49.

59. Latourette, K. S., *The Chinese, Their History and Culture* (The Macmillan Company, 1934), pp. 171–172.

60. Hocking, W. E., " Living Religions and a World Faith," *The Asian Legacy and American Life,* ed. by A. E. Christy (John Day Co., Inc., 1942), p. 206.

61. Tang Yung-Tung, " On ' Ko-Yi,' the Earliest Method by Which Indian Buddhism and Chinese Thought Were Synthesized," *Rādhākrishnan: Comparative Studies in Philosophy,* ed. by W. R. Inge, *et al.* (Harper & Brothers, 1951), pp. 276 ff.

62. Tsukamoto, Zenryu, " Buddhism in China and Korea," *The Path of the Buddha,* ed. by Kenneth W. Morgan (The Ronald Press Company, 1956), p. 184.

63. See *Chinese Thought and Institutions,* ed. by John K. Fairbank (University of Chicago Press, 1957), pp. 71 ff.

64. Chan, Wing-tsit, *Religious Trends in Modern China* (Columbia University Press, 1953), pp. 94–95.

65. Pratt, *op. cit.*, p. 457.

66. Warner, Langdon, *The Enduring Art of Japan* (Harvard University Press, 1952), p. 18.

67. Eliot, Sir Charles, *Japanese Buddhism* (Edward Arnold & Co., London, 1935), p. 179.

68. Eliot, *Hinduism and Buddhism*, III, p. 345.

The Modern World and the Samgha Universal

69. Snellgrove, D. L., *Buddhist Himalaya* (Philosophical Library, Inc., 1957), pp. 51–52.

70. Haas, William S., *The Destiny of the Mind: East and West* (Faber & Faber, Ltd., London, 1956), p. 37.

71. *Ibid.*, pp. 68–69.

72. *Ibid.*, p. 61.

73. Mead, Margaret, *Cultural Patterns and Technical Change* (Mentor Books, 1955), pp. 31–33.

74. Dean, Vera Micheles, *The Nature of the Non-Western World* (Mentor Books, 1957), pp. 141–144.

75. *Atlantic,* Vol. 201, No. 3 (Feb., 1958), p. 118.

76. *Ibid.*, pp. 119–120.

77. *The Interrelations of Demographic, Economic, and Social Problems in Selected Undeveloped Areas* (Milbank Memorial Fund, 1954), pp. 101–102.

78. *The Revolt in the Temple* (Sinha Publications, Colombo, 1953), p. 587.

79. Wijesekera, O. H. De, *Buddhism and Society* (The Bauddha Sahitya Sabha, Colombo, n.d.), p. 6.

80. *The Revolt in the Temple,* p. 586.

81. *Ibid.*, pp. 555–556.

82. Quoted in Charles, G. P., *Let God Speak* (Burma Christian Council Annual, 1953), pp. 27–28.

83. Hamilton, Clarence H., "Buddhism," *China,* ed. by H. F. MacNair (University of California Press, 1946), p. 297.

84. Malalasekera, G. P., *The Buddha and His Teachings* (The Lanka Bauddha Mandalaya, Ceylon, 1957), p. 69.

Chapter 5. Islam and the Ummah

The World of Islam

1. Toynbee, Arnold, *The World and the West* (Oxford University Press, 1953), p. 21.

2. *Ibid.*, p. 22.

3. Ghorbal, Shafik, "Ideas and Movements in Islamic History," *Islam — The Straight Path*, ed. by Kenneth W. Morgan (The Ronald Press Company, 1958), p. 84.

4. Gunther, John, *Inside Asia* (Harper & Brothers, 1939), p. 521.

5. Gibb, Sir Hamilton A. R., *Mohammedanism: An Historical Survey* (Oxford University Press, 1953). Quotations used by their permission. (Mentor Books, M136, 1955), p. 6. Page numbers are from the Mentor edition.

6. Finegan, Jack, *Light from the Ancient Past* (Princeton University Press, 1946), p. 191.

7. Young, T. Cuyler, "Near East Perspective: The Past and the Present," *Near Eastern Culture and Society*, ed. by T. C. Young (Princeton University Press, 1951), p. 5.

8. Della Vida, Giorgio Levi, "Pre-Islamic Arabia," *The Arab Heritage*, ed. by Nabin Amin Faris (Princeton University Press, 1946), p. 44. Quotations from this book are used by permission of the publisher.

9. *Ibid.*, p. 51.

10. Caskel, Werner, "The Bedouinization of Arabia," *Studies in Islamic Cultural History*, ed. by Gustave E. von Grunebaum (The American Anthropological Association Memoir No. 76, April, 1954), p. 36.

11. *Ibid.*, pp. 36–37.

12. Della Vida, *loc. cit.*, p. 50.

13. Caskel, *loc. cit.*, p. 38.

14. "Mecca," *Shorter Encyclopaedia of Islam*, ed. by H. A. R. Gibb and J. H. Kramers (E. J. Brill, Leiden, 1953), p. 368.

15. Della Vida, *loc. cit.*, p. 53.

16. "Allah," *Shorter Encyclopaedia of Islam*, p. 33.

17. Della Vida, *loc. cit.*, pp. 55–56.

18. *Ibid.*, p. 33.

The Prophet of God

19. Abbott, Nabia, *Aisha, The Beloved of Mohammed* (University of Chicago Press, 1942), p. vii.
20. Guillaume, Alfred, *Islam* (Penguin Books, Inc., 1954), p. 20.
21. *Ibid.*, p. 24.
22. Abbott, *op. cit.*, pp. vii-viii.
23. *The Koran*, tr. by J. M. Rodwell (J. M. Dent & Sons, Ltd., London, 1909), pp. 19–20.
24. *Ibid.*, pp. 21–22.
25. Gibb, *op. cit.*, p. 29.
26. *Ibid.*
27. *Ibid.*
28. Muir, Sir William, *The Life of Mohammed*, ed. by T. H. Weit (John Grant, Edinburgh, 2d ed., 1923), p. 118.
29. Gibb, *op. cit.*, p. 30.
30. Abbott, *op. cit.*, p. 6.
31. Hitti, Philip K., *The Arabs — A Short History* (Princeton University Press, 1949), p. 29.
32. Gibb, *op. cit.*, p. 31.
33. Hitti, *op. cit.*, p. 29.
34. Gibb, *op. cit.*, p. 32.
35. Von Grunebaum, Gustave E., *Medieval Islam* (copyright, 1946, by the University of Chicago Press), p. 79. Quotations from this book are used by permission of the publisher.
36. Abbott, *op. cit.*, p. viii.
37. *Ibid.*
38. Gibb, *op. cit.*, p. 35.

The Ummah, the Congregation of God

39. "Umma or Ummah," *Shorter Encyclopaedia of Islam,* pp. 603–604.
40. Levy, Reuben, *The Social Structure of Islam* (Cambridge University Press, 1957), p. 273. Quotations from this book are used by permission of the publisher.
41. *Ibid.*, p. 274.
42. *Ibid.*, p. 275.

43. Von Grunebaum, *Mediaeval Islam,* p. 79.

44. Hitti, *op. cit.,* p. 32.

45. Von Grunebaum, p. 72.

46. Gaudefroy-Demombyness, Maurice, *Muslim Institutions,* tr. by John P. MacGregor (George Allen & Unwin, Ltd., London, 1950) , p. 19.

47. Hilliard, F. H., *The Buddha, the Prophet and the Christ* (George Allen & Unwin, Ltd., London, 1956) , pp. 76–77.

48. Von Grunebaum, *Medieval Islam,* p. 94.

49. Overmann, Julian, "Islamic Origins: A Study in Background and Foundation," *The Arab Heritage,* p. 114.

50. *Ibid.,* p. 117.

51. Von Grunebaum, *Medieval Islam,* p. 85.

52. *Ibid.,* p. 96.

53. Kraemer, H., *The Christian Message in a Non-Christian World* (The Edinburgh House, London, 1938) , pp. 217–218.

54. Gibb, *op. cit.,* p. 62.

55. *Ibid.*

56. Guillaume, Alfred, *The Tradition of Islam* (The Clarendon Press, Oxford, 1924) , p. 15.

57. *Ibid.,* pp. 22–23.

58. *Ibid.,* p. 23.

59. Quoted in von Grunebaum, *Medieval Islam,* pp. 109–110.

60. Fyzee, A. A. A., *Outlines of Muhammadan Law* (Geoffrey Cumberlege: Oxford University Press, London, 1949) , p. 15.

61. *Ibid.,* pp. 15–17.

62. Levy, *op. cit.,* p. 150.

63. Gibb, *op. cit.,* p. 78.

64. *Ibid.*

65. Guillaume, *Islam,* p. 101.

66. Gibb, *op. cit.,* p. 82.

67. *Ibid.,* p. 83.

68. *Ibid.*

69. Guillaume, *Islam,* pp. 102–103.

70. Fyzee, *op. cit.,* pp. 31–32.

71. Levy, *op. cit.,* p. 155.

72. *Ibid.*, p. 187.

73. *Ibid.*, p. 159.

74. Quoted in *ibid.*, p. 160 (Sura 2:183).

75. Quoted in *ibid.*, p. 161 (Sura 3:90, cf. 22:27–30).

76. Hitti, *op. cit.*, p. 43.

77. Von Grunebaum, *Medieval Islam,* p. 9.

The Ummah in History

78. Levy, *op. cit.*, p. 58.

79. Guillaume, *Islam,* p. 82.

80. Hitti, *op. cit.*, p. 89.

81. Jurji, Edward J., " Islam," *The Great Religions of the Modern World,* ed. E. J. Jurji (Princeton University Press, 1947), p. 205.

82. Gibb, *op. cit.*, p. 93.

83. Smith, Margaret, *Studies in Early Mysticism in the Near and Middle East* (The Sheldon Press, London, 1931), p. 254.

84. " al-Hallaj," *Shorter Encyclopaedia of Islam,* pp. 127–128.

85. Smith, Margaret, *Al-Ghazālī: The Mystic* (Luzac & Co., Ltd., London, 1944), p. 227.

86. Macdonald, Duncan B., *Development of Muslim Theology, Jurisprudence and Constitutional Theory* (Charles Scribner's Sons, 1903), pp. 238–239.

87. Von Grunebaum, *Medieval Islam,* p. 5.

88. Lamonte, John L., " Crusade and Jihad," *The Arab Heritage,* pp. 160–161.

89. Cragg, Kenneth, *The Call of the Minaret* (Oxford University Press, 1956), p. 265.

90. *Ibid.*, p. 186.

91. Calverley, Edwin E., " Islamic Religion," *Near Eastern Culture and Society,* p. 103.

92. Hitti, *op. cit.*, p. 177.

93. Hitti, Philip K., *History of the Arabs* (St. Martin's Press, London, 5th ed., 1953), p. 671.

94. Miller, Barnette, *The Palace School of Muhammad the Conqueror* (Harvard University Press, 1941), p. 4.

95. Thomas, Lewis V., " The Nationalism and International Relations of Turkey," *Near Eastern Culture and Society,* p. 169.

The Ummah in the Modern World

96. Toynbee, *op. cit.*, p. 22.

97. Adnan-Adivar, Abdulhak, " Interaction of Islamic and Western Thought in Turkey," *Near Eastern Culture and Society,* p. 123.

98. Gibb, H. A. R., " Near Eastern Perspective: The Present and the Future," *ibid.,* p. 229.

99. Husaini, Ishak M., " Islamic Culture in Arab and African Countries," *Islam — The Straight Path,* p. 239.

100. Siddiqi, Mazheruddin, " Muslim Culture in Pakistan and India," *ibid.,* p. 321.

101. Quoted in Dewick, E. C., *The Christian Attitude to Other Religions* (Cambridge University Press, 1953), p. 16.

102. Gibb, in *Near Eastern Culture and Society,* p. 230.

103. Smith, Wilfred Cantwell, *Islam in Modern History* (Princeton University Press, 1957), p. 41.

104. Dewick, *op. cit.,* p. 16.

105. Quoted in Husaini, Ishak M., *The Moslem Brethren* (Khayat, Beirut, 1956), p. 7.

106. *Ibid.,* p. 24.

107. Gibb, H. A. R., *Modern Trends in Islam* (University of Chicago Press, 1945), p. 117.

108. *Ibid.,* pp. 27–28.

109. Zeine, Zeine N., *Arab-Turkish Relations and the Emergence of Arab Nationalism* (Khayat, Beirut, 1958), p. 119.

110. Dib, G. Moussa, *The Arab Bloc in the United Nations* (Djambatan, Amsterdam, 1956), p. 14.

111. Zeine, *op. cit.,* pp. 124–125.

112. *Ibid.,* p. 125.

113. *Ibid.,* p. 126.

114. *The Manchester Guardian* (July 18, 1957).

115. Toynbee, *op. cit.,* pp. 78–79.

116. Dib, *op. cit.,* p. 17.

117. Smith, W. C., *op. cit.,* p. 160.

118. Cantay, Hasan Basri, " Islamic Culture in Turkish Areas," *Islam — The Straight Path,* p. 282.

119. *Chicago Daily News* (Nov. 9, 1957), p. 2.

120. Cantay, *loc. cit.,* p. 294.

121. Ball, W. MacMahon, *Nationalism and Communism in East Asia* (Melbourne University Press, Melbourne, 1952), p. 1.

122. Azad, Maulana Abul Kalam, *India Wins Freedom* (Orient Longmans, Bombay, 1959), p. 227.

123. *Report of the Basic Principles Committee* (Karachi, 1952), p. 1.

124. These comments were made by Dr. Charles J. Adams at the Carus Memorial Symposium, held at Peru, Illinois, September, 1957.

125. Ball, *op. cit.*, p. 154.

126. Gibb, *Modern Trends in Islam*, p. 115.

Chapter 6. JAPANESE RELIGIONS AND THE NATIONAL COMMUNITY

Early Shinto

1. See Kitagawa, J. M., " The Prehistoric Background of Japanese Religion," *History of Religions,* II, No. 2 (Winter, 1963), pp. 292–329.

2. On this subject, see Holton, Daniel C., " The Meaning of Kami," *Monumenta Nipponica,* III, No. 1 (1940), pp. 1–27; III, No. 2 (1940), pp. 32–53; and IV, No. 2 (1941), pp. 25–68.

3. Warner, Langdon, *The Enduring Art of Japan,* p. 19.

4. See Kitagawa, J. M., " Shinto," *Encyclopaedia Britannica,* XX, pp. 390–393.

Foreign Influences

5. See Kitagawa, J. M., " Japan: Religion," *Encyclopaedia Britannica,* XII, pp. 899–904.

6. See Kitagawa, J. M., " The Buddhist Transformation in Japan," *History of Religions,* IV, No. 2 (Winter, 1965), pp. 319–336.

7. On these schools, see Takakusu, Junjiro, *The Essentials of Buddhist Philosophy.*

8. See Hori, Ichiro, *Folk Religion in Japan: Continuity and Change,* ed. by J. M. Kitagawa and Alan L. Miller (The University of Chicago Press, 1968).

9. See Kitagawa, J. M., " Master and Saviour," *Studies of*

Esoteric Buddhism and Tantrism (Koyasan University, Koyasan, Japan, 1965), pp. 1–26.

10. Pratt, James B., *op. cit.,* p. 47.

" The Chrysanthemum and the Sword "

11. See Coates, Harper H., and Ishizuka, Ryūgaku, *Hōnen the Buddhist Saint* (Chion-in, Kyoto, 1925).

12. See *The Tanni Shō: Notes Lamenting Differences,* tr. by Fujiwara, Ryōsetsu (Ryukoku Translation Center, Kyoto, 1962).

13. Anesaki, Masaharu, *Nichiren the Buddhist Prophet* (Harvard University Press, 1916).

14. Dumoulin, Heinrich, *A History of Zen Buddhism,* tr. by Paul Peachey (Pantheon Books, Inc., 1959), Chs. 9 and 10.

National Seclusion

15. Regarding the Tokugawa regime, see Sansom, George B., *Japan: A Short Cultural History* (Appleton-Century-Crofts, Inc., 1943), Ch. 21.

16. See Boxer, C. R., *The Christian Century in Japan, 1549–1650* (University of California Press, 1951).

17. See the section on " Neo-Confucianism " in Ch. 2 of this book.

18. On this subject, see Anesaki, Masaharu, *History of Japanese Religion,* pp. 307–309.

19. On Motoori and Hirata, see Muraoka, Tsunetsugu, *Studies in Shinto Thought,* tr. by Delmer M. Brown and James T. Araki (Japanese National Commission for UNESCO, Ministry of Education, Tokyo, 1964).

Modern Japanese National Community

20. See Sansom, George B., *The Western World and Japan* (Alfred A. Knopf, Inc., 1962).

21. Reischauer, Edwin O., *Japan Past and Present* (Alfred A. Knopf, Inc., 2d ed., 1952), p. 143.

22. See Holtom, Daniel C., *The National Faith of Japan* (E. P. Dutton & Company, Inc., 1938).

23. Regarding the religious situation in postwar Japan, see Kitagawa, J. M., *Religion in Japanese History* (Columbia University Press, 1966), Ch. 6.

Selected
Bibliography

◈ ◈

A. METHODOLOGICAL

Eliade, Mircea, *Patterns in Comparative Religion,* tr. by Rosemary Sheed. Sheed & Ward, Inc., 1958.
—— *The Sacred and the Profane,* tr. by Willard R. Trask. Harcourt, Brace & Company, Inc., 1959.
Eliade, Mircea, and Kitagawa, Joseph M. (eds.), *The History of Religions: Essays in Methodology.* The University of Chicago Press, 1959.
Kitagawa, Joseph M. (ed.), *The History of Religions: Essays on the Problem of Understanding.* The University of Chicago Press, 1967.
Pettazzoni, Raffaelle, *Essays on the History of Religions,* tr. by H. J. Rose. E. J. Brill, Leiden, 1954.
Van der Leeuw, G., *Religion in Essence and Manifestation,* tr. by J. E. Turner. George Allen & Unwin, Ltd., London, 1938.
Wach, Joachim, *Sociology of Religion.* The University of Chicago Press, 1944.
—— *Types of Religious Experience.* The University of Chicago Press, 1951.
—— *The Comparative Study of Religions,* ed. with an Introduction by Joseph M. Kitagawa. Columbia University Press, 1958.
Weber, Max, *The Sociology of Religion,* tr. by Ephraim Fischoff. Beacon Press, Inc., 1963.

B. GENERAL

Adams, Charles J. (ed.), *A Reader's Guide to the Great Religions*. The Free Press of Glencoe, Inc., 1965.

Chan, Wing-tsit; Faruqi, Isma'il R.; Kitagawa, Joseph M.; and Rajui, P. T., *The Great Eastern Religions: An Anthology*. The Macmillan Company, 1968.

Dye, James W., and Forthman, William H., *Religions of the World*. Appleton-Century-Crofts, Inc., 1967.

Eliade, Mircea, *From Primitives to Zen*. Harper & Row, Publishers, Inc., 1967.

Kitagawa, Joseph M. (ed.), *Modern Trends in World Religions*. The Open Court Publishing Company, 1959.

Kitagawa, Joseph M., and Long, Charles H. (eds.) *Myths and Symbols: Studies in Honor of Mircea Eliade*. The University of Chicago Press. To be published in 1969.

Moore, George Foot, *History of Religions*, 2 vols. Charles Scribner's Sons, 1948.

Nakamura, Hajime, *Ways of Thinking of Eastern Peoples*, ed. by Philip P. Wiener. East-West Center Press, 1964.

Ringgren, Helmer, and Ström, Ake V., *Religions of Mankind*, ed. by J. G. G. Greig, tr. by Niels L. Jensen. Fortress Press, 1967.

Zaehner, R. C. (ed.), *The Concise Encyclopedia of Living Faiths*. Hawthorn Books, Inc., 1959.

C. CHINESE RELIGIONS

Chan, Wing-tsit, *Religious Trends in Modern China*. Columbia University Press, 1953.

Creel, H. G., *Confucius: The Man and the Myth*. John Day Co., Inc., 1949.

Fairbank, John K. (ed.), *Chinese Thought and Institutions*. The University of Chicago Press, 1957.

Fung Yu-lan, *A Short History of Chinese Philosophy*, ed. by Derk Bodde. The Macmillan Company, 1950.

Hughes, E. R. (ed. and tr.), *Chinese Philosophy in Classical Times*. Everyman's Library, J. M. Dent & Sons, Ltd., London, 1942.

Latourette, Kenneth Scott, *The Chinese, Their History and*

Culture. The Macmillan Company, 1934.

Lin Yutang (ed. and tr.), *The Wisdom of Confucius*. Random House, Inc., 1938.

MacNair, Harley F. (ed.), *China*. University of California Press, 1946.

Wright, Arthur F. (ed.), *Studies in Chinese Thought*. The University of Chicago Press, 1953.

———— *Buddhism in Chinese History*. Stanford University Press, 1959.

D. HINDUISM

Brown, W. Norman (ed.), *India, Pakistan, Ceylon*. Cornell University Press, 1950.

Eliade, Mircea, *Yoga: Immortality and Freedom*, tr. by Willard R. Trask. Pantheon Books, Inc., 1958.

Heimann, Betty, *Indian and Western Philosophy*. George Allen & Unwin, Ltd., London, 1937.

Mahadevan, T. M. P., *Outlines of Hinduism*. Chetana, Ltd., Booksellers & Publishers, Bombay, 1956.

Marriott, McKim (ed.), *Village India: Studies in the Little Community*. The University of Chicago Press, 1955.

Morgan, Kenneth W. (ed.), *The Religion of the Hindus*. The Ronald Press Company, 1953.

Prabhu, Pandharinath H., *Hindu Social Organization*. Popular Book Depot, Bombay, 1940.

Radhakrishnan, Sarvepalli (Chairman of the Editorial Board), *History of Philosophy Eastern and Western*, 2 vols. George Allen & Unwin, Ltd., London, 1952–1953.

Radhakrishnan, Sarvepalli, and Moore, Charles A. (eds.), *A Source Book in Indian Philosophy*. Princeton University Press, 1957.

Zimmer, Heinrich, *Philosophies of India*, ed. by Joseph Campbell. Pantheon Books, Inc., 1951.

E. BUDDHISM

Bahm, A. J., *Philosophy of the Buddha*. Harper & Brothers, 1958.

Conze, Edward, *Buddhism, Its Essence and Development*. Philosophical Library, Inc., 1951.

Conze, Edward (ed.), in collaboration with I. B. Horner, D. Snellgrove, A. Waley, *Buddhist Texts Through the Ages*. Philosophical Library, Inc., 1953.

Coomaraswamy, Ananda, *Buddha and the Gospel of Buddhism*. Asia Publishing House, Bombay, 1956.

Eliot, Sir Charles, *Hinduism and Buddhism*, 3 vols. Barnes & Noble, Inc., 1954.

Morgan, Kenneth W. (ed.), *The Path of the Buddha*. The Ronald Press Company, 1956.

Murti, T. R. V., *The Central Philosophy of Buddhism*. George Allen & Unwin, Ltd., London, 1955.

Pratt, James B., *The Pilgrimage of Buddhism*. The Macmillan Company, 1928.

Slater, Robert L., *Paradox and Nirvana*. The University of Chicago Press, 1951.

Thomas, Edward J., *The History of Buddhist Thought*. Barnes & Noble, Inc., 1951.

F. ISLAM

Fyzee, Asaf A. A., *Outlines of Muhammadan Law*. Geoffrey Cumberlege: Oxford University Press, 1949.

Gibb, Sir Hamilton A. R., *Mohammedanism: An Historical Survey*. Geoffrey Cumberlege: Oxford University Press, London, rev. ed., 1953. (Also available as a Mentor Book, 1955.)

—— *Modern Trends in Islam*. The University of Chicago Press, 1945.

Von Grunebaum, Gustave E., *Medieval Islam*. The University of Chicago Press, 1946.

—— *Islam: Essays in the Nature and Growth of a Cultural Tradition*. The University of Chicago Press, 1955.

Guillaume, Alfred, *Islam*. Penguin Books, Inc., 2d ed., 1956.

Levy, Reuben, *The Social Structure of Islam*. Cambridge University Press, Cambridge, 1957.

Morgan, Kenneth W. (ed.), *Islam — the Straight Path*. The Ronald Press Company, 1958.

Pickthall, Mohammed Marmaduke (tr.), *The Meaning of the Glorious Koran*. Mentor Books, 1953.

Smith, Wilfred Cantwell, *Islam in Modern History*. Princeton University Press, 1957.

G. JAPANESE RELIGIONS

Anesaki, Masaharu, *History of Japanese Religion*. Kegan Paul, Trench, Trubner & Co., London, 1930.

Eliot, Charles, *Japanese Buddhism*. Edward Arnold & Co., London, 1935.

Hasegawa, Nyozekan, *The Japanese Character: A Cultural Profile*, tr. by John Bester. Kodansha, Tokyo, 1965.

Hori, Ichiro, *Folk Religion in Japan: Continuity and Change*, ed. by J. M. Kitagawa and Alan L. Miller. The University of Chicago Press, 1968.

Kishimoto, Hideo (ed.), *Japanese Religion in the Meiji Era*, tr. by John F. Howes. Ōbunsha, Tokyo, 1956.

Kitagawa, Joseph M., *Religion in Japanese History*. Columbia University Press, 1966.

Muraoka, Tsunetsugu, *Studies in Shinto Thought*, tr. by Delmer M. Brown and James T. Araki. Japanese National Commission for UNESCO, Tokyo, 1964.

Reischauer, Edwin O., *Japan Past and Present*. Alfred A. Knopf, Inc., 2d ed., 1952.

Sansom, George B., *Japan: A Short Cultural History*. Appleton-Century-Crofts, Inc., 1943.

Suzuki, Daisetz T., *Zen and Japanese Culture*. Bollingen Series LXIV, Pantheon Books, Inc., 1959.

Subject
Index

❖ ❖

337

Author
Index

❖ ❖